Politics and Judgment in Federal District Courts

C. K. Rowland
Robert A. Carp

University Press of Kansas

Published by the University Press of Kansas (Lawrence, Kansas 66049), which was organized by the Kansas Board of Regents and is operated and funded by Emporia State University, Fort Hays State University, Kansas State University, Pittsburg State University, the University of Kansas, and Wichita State University

Library of Congress Cataloging-in-Publication Data

Rowland, C. K., 1943–
Politics and judgment in federal district courts / C. K. Rowland, Robert A. Carp.
p. cm.
Includes bibliographical references and index.
ISBN 0-7006-0776-5 (alk. paper)
1. District courts—United States. 2. Political questions and judicial power—United States. 3. Judges—Selection and appointment—United States. I. Carp, Robert A., 1943– . II. Title.
KF8754.R69 1996
347.73′22—dc20
[347.3072] 95-46680

British Library Cataloguing in Publication Data is available.

Printed in the United States of America

10 9 8 7 6 5 4 3 2 1

The paper used in this publication meets the minimum requirements of the American National Standard for Permanence of Paper for Printed Library Materials Z39.48-1984.

To my Aunt Carole Pardee Muchow,
with much love and affection
—R. A. C.

To Norma and John.
Thanks for always being there.
—C. K. R.

Contents

Preface

For students of the federal trial courts two important intellectual revolutions occurred approximately forty years ago. First, with the publication of Pritchett's work on the behavior of U.S. Supreme Court justices in 1948, political scientists rejected the assumptions of mechanical, precedent-bound jurisprudence in favor of the heretical notion that justices' decisions could be characterized as "votes," and that these votes were motivated by their personal beliefs and policy preferences. In the interim since 1948 this notion has evolved into the behavioral paradigm and sophisticated attitudinal models that continue to dominate and define studies of appellate judicial behavior. Second, with the publication of Peltason's work a few years later, political scientists began to recognize that federal trial courts were highly politicized policy-making institutions and that trial judges, like their appellate counterparts, were influenced by their personal values and policy preferences.

By the 1980s the two revolutions had merged. We and other political scientists interested in the federal district courts were routinely asking not *if* federal district judges' personal values influenced their decisions but *which* values or policy preferences influenced which policy decisions. We had, in other words, accepted as axiomatic the assumption that district judges' policy decisions were motivated by their personal policy preferences.

Today, like the octogenarians who followed Mao in 1949, those of us who follow in the footsteps of Pritchett and Peltason continue to consider ourselves revolutionaries even though our "revolution" is into its third generation. We continue to castigate traditional and contemporary legal models of judicial behavior, characterizing constitutional preferences as "meaningless social choices" and interpretations of original intent as "unintelligible" (Segal and Spaeth 1993, 64). And we may indeed appear rather revolutionary if our point of comparison is traditional legal analysis. But the fact of the matter is that, at least in its application to the behavior of trial judges, our "revolutionary" approach has become as predictable, prosaic, and pedestrian as the legalistic approaches that preceded it.

Nowhere is the pedestrian predictability of contemporary scholarship more apparent than in our own research questions, methods, findings, and analysis (Carp and Rowland 1983). Does anyone doubt, for example, that the Clinton appointees to the district courts will be more supportive of civil rights claims and underdog claims in general than are their brethren appointed by Presidents Reagan and Bush? And does anyone doubt that these appointment-based differences will be consistent with policy preferences enunciated by the president as judicial selection criteria?

Of course, there is nothing wrong with predictable, even prosaic, scholarship per se; after all, predictability and longitudinal research programs are scholarly virtues. There *is* something wrong, however, with scholarship based on an uncritical commitment to the axioms and assumptions of a scholarly revolution that is no longer revolutionary. Such a commitment encourages mundane measurement and discourages innovative questions, methods, and theories that fall outside the revolution's methodological and theoretical comfort zones.

We believe that the time has come to supplant the questions, methods, and theories that have dominated our subfield for forty years with new avenues of inquiry, new methods, and new theories. And we believe that each of these innovations should help us understand not only judicial policy making but also judicial fact finding, which is after all what these triers of fact spend most of their time doing. But we also believe that these innovations should be introduced in a spirit that contributes incrementally to the growth of knowledge about preferences and policy making, while at the same time insisting on the introduction of questions, methods, and theoretical concepts that help us understand how district judges evaluate facts and evidence. Thus, our goal in this book is to have it both ways by building on previous work while contentiously arguing for the abandonment of old theoretical and empirical blinders. That goal is reflected in the book's organization.

We begin by offering an overview of relevant scholarship. Chapter 1, "U.S. Trial Judge Decision Making," summarizes the current literature on district court decision making and emphasizes the reasons for exploring this lower level of the federal judiciary. It looks at the progress that has been made in studying the trial courts, as well as the gaps in theoretical and empirical knowledge that still exist. We conclude with an overview of the quantitative data that are used for analysis in the subsequent chapters.

In the next two chapters we meet our commitment to expend incrementally knowledge about the political correlates of district judges' policy-making patterns and bring up to date the work presented in our earlier volume (*Policymaking and Politics in the Federal District Courts,* 1983) on the effects of environment and background factors on trial judge decision making. Chapter 2 focuses on the influences of political party affiliation and the appointing president on district judge voting behavior. Our database of forty-five thousand cases that occurred over a span of fifty-five years is almost twice as large as the one used in our 1983 text, which addresses in part these same phenomena. We examine the degree to which the evolving Burger Court conservative majority has been mirrored by the lower federal judiciary, explore the extent of partisan voting during the Burger Court years, and present twenty-four specific case types. Finally, we address the impact of appointing presidents—from Woodrow Wilson to George Bush—on the subsequent court decisions of their trial judge appointees. Chapter 3 looks at sectional and geographic variations in trial judges' voting patterns. We demonstrate how such patterns have varied over time, note their marked decrease in the last decade, and provide a tentative explanation for this phenomenon.

In chapters 4 and 5 we meet our commitment to answer new empirical questions whose answers fall outside the bounds of current conventional wisdom and delve into territory that only recently has been explored systematically by public law scholars. Chapter 4 examines the politics of recruitment in a number of specially selected states. We not only look at obvious structural differences among the states, such as whether they utilize judicial selection commissions, but also analyze less visible distinctions, such as the relative involvement of the legal and political subcultures in the selection process. Of particular interest is the extent to which the importance of partisan allegiance and policy preferences parallels presidential reliance on these political criteria. We examine in chapter 4 the extent to which the politics of home-state recruitment exacerbate or mitigate presidential effects on judicial outcomes. Another relatively new area in these two chapters is unpublished opinions, which in fact constitute the vast majority of district court judgments. Chapter 5, "Appointment Effects on Unpublished Decisions," is significant because a number of recent studies have correctly noted that the scope and content of unpublished opinions by no means mirror those of judicial rulings that are formally printed. Using selected case categories in both the criminal and civil arenas, we compare the content and directionality of published and unpublished decisions for several recent presidents and then provide theoretical speculation for the contrasts and similarities within them.

In the final two chapters, after paying due homage to the theoretical paradigm that has heretofore guided virtually all research on trial judges' decision making—and under which we ourselves have long labored—we suggest that the prevailing theoretical approach is deficient in many respects and offer a conceptual alternative to the behavioral paradigm. Chapter 6, "Critique of Behavioral Modes of Trial Judging," reviews and evaluates both the traditional mechanical jurisprudence approach and more modern organizational, behavioral, and psychometric models for understanding and explaining the judicial decision-making process. We argue that the major shortcoming of these models, inter alia, is the anomalous and unwarranted assumption that federal trial judges are motivated primarily by their personal policy preferences. Chapter 7 outlines a cognitive model of judicial judgment as an alternative approach to the study of U.S. trial courts. Adapted from cognitive psychology and social judgment theory, this model posits the notion that decision making is a two-stage process in which the decision, that is, a vote or choice, is preceded by "framing," or the mental transformation of ambiguous evidence and law into proximate decisional cues. It likewise assumes that all humans, including judges, have computational limitations that constrain the nature of judgment protocols; and it accepts the behavioral premise that judges' policy preferences influence their policy judgments. However, our cognitive model rejects the general assumption that human judgment is necessarily goal-oriented. Likewise, it rejects the assumption inherent in a psychometric model that judicial judgment is motivated by judges' personal policy preferences. Moreover, because our model accepts the premise that preferences influence judgment, but not that decision making is motivated by these preferences, a cognitive theory of judicial judgment addresses the process by which preferences influence judgment in the context of principal-agent relationships, that is, between federal trial judges and their appellate "principals." We conclude with a number of hypotheses that future researchers may test to ascertain the credibility of our theory.

Acknowledgments

During the course of our long collaboration we have benefited from the support and encouragement of so many people that any attempt to acknowledge all, or even most, of them would be futile. We would, however, like to thank several people and institutions without whom this effort would not have been possible.

Sheldon Goldman generously shared with us key background data on the district judges whose decisions were studied in this book.

Collection of the data on unpublished opinions would not have been possible without support from the National Science Foundation (SES8711857) and the help of Bridget Jeffrey Todd.

Limited grants in aid from the University of Houston and faculty research grants from the University of Kansas supported the collection and analysis of data on which this study was based.

Colleagues in the Department of Psychology at the University of Kansas were extremely encouraging and helpful in our quest to adapt the lessons of social cognition and jury behavior to the behavior of trial judges. Especially important were Larry Wrightsman, whose work on juries caused us to rethink our work on judges, and Rick Snyder, whose tutoring in the intellectual history of psychology helped us realize how many untapped theoretical opportunities existed in his field.

Collection of the data on judicial recruitment would not have been possible without C. K. Rowland's year as a visiting scholar at the Brookings Institution. Helpful critiques of the early stages of this effort came from Paul Peterson, Terry Moe, Lynn Mather, and Mark Hansen.

Several colleagues in the public law subfield have helped by commenting on early drafts or ideas. For this feedback we are grateful to Larry Baum, Lee Epstein, Elliot Slotnick, and Thomas Walker.

Finally, the manuscript would never have been completed without the patience and persistence of Fred Woodward and Melinda Wirkus at the University Press of Kansas and Virginia Postoak of the University of Kansas Department of Political Science.

CHAPTER 1

U.S. Trial Judge Decision Making

"The people of this district either get justice here with me or they don't get it at all. I've had a number of cases appealed over the years, but I've never been overruled. And I've never had a case go to the Supreme Court. . . . Here at the trial court—that's where the action is."[1] So said former Iowa federal district judge Henry N. Graven to one of us as he reflected on his more than two decades of service on the bench. While his experience vis-à-vis the appellate courts may not be typical for all U.S. trial judges, we think that his perception of the significance and inviolability of trial judge decision making is as true today as it was when it was shared with us almost a quarter of a century ago. The primary purposes of this chapter are to reiterate the importance of federal district courts in the United States and to account for their increasing policy-making activities in recent decades, to provide a brief but systematic review of the literature on district judge decision making, and to outline the parameters of the data we have collected to analyze district judge voting behavior.

A second purpose is to introduce the rather heretical notion that although the last thirty years have witnessed an exponential increase in scholarly exploration, much of this endeavor has been somewhat facile. We have studied published opinions not only because they codified significant decisions but also because they were readily available in law libraries and in computerized databases. We have focused on independent (predictor) variables, such as the appointing president, not only because they were easily operationalized but also because their simplicity contrasted sharply with the richly variegated but not so easily studied impact of local, home-state politics. We adapted appellate models of judicial behavior to the decision making of trial judges not only because they were consistent with aggregate patterns of published policy decisions but also because these models conveniently avoided tedious questions about the relationship between judicial fact-finding and judicial politics. These empirical and theoretical pursuits have resulted in an understanding of district courts and judges that is, despite its clarity, limited in scope and detail.

IMPORTANCE OF DISTRICT JUDGE DECISION MAKING

The news media remind us daily that the rulings of our district judges affect all of us in one way or another on a whole panoply of issues: integration of our schools; the availability of abortions; standards for defining obscenity; the quality of the air we breathe and the water we drink; requirements for affirmative action programs; and standards for the maintenance of our prisons, public hospitals, and mental institutions. It is clear that our lives are affected by what federal trial judges say about the U.S. Constitution, federal laws, and the actions of government officials. Judges' decisions affect directly the residents of their own respective districts and, often indirectly, Americans in general insofar as their rulings serve as precedents for jurists in other districts.

For example, for more than two decades the State of Texas has been under a variety of district court orders dealing with standards to be maintained in the state's jails and prisons so to avoid the strictures of the Eighth Amendment prohibition against cruel and unusual punishment. The cost to the state has been in the billions of dollars. What the *Texas Monthly* said of a single federal judge (William Wayne Justice) several years ago is even more true today because it could as easily apply to several such jurists in the Lone Star State: The judge "did more to shape the appropriations bill than any member of the [state legislative] budget committees." Commenting on his many far-reaching decisions on criminal justice, public education, and legislative redistricting, the magazine suggested that were the judge "in the legislature he would never be able to legislate as effectively as he does from the bench."

In the State of Missouri Judge Russell G. Clark issued a series of school integration orders during the late 1980s that had the effect of nearly doubling Kansas City's property tax in order to pay the costs of equalizing educational opportunity. Cost estimates for the judge's decisions ranged as high as $700 million!

In February 1991 Judge Robert E. Coyle of the Eastern District of California ruled that an undocumented worker has the right to pursue a discrimination suit again an employer—regardless of legal residency status. The decision held that undocumented aliens have the same right to invoke the employment discrimination statutes as do permanent residents and citizens. Conservative estimates indicate that the ruling could affect hundreds of thousands of immigrants in the United States—not to mention their employers and the employers' insurance companies.

The impact of U.S. district courts is very great for all Americans, touching on our pocketbooks, our liberties, and the overall quality of our lives. We are intrigued by queries such as these: Why do trial judges engage in so much policy making when they are theoretically supposed to be "finding the law—not making it"? How does one account for this ever-increasing reality? Is it the result of liberal, activist judicial appointees who have no sense of judicial restraint, or does it stem from factors independent of (or in addition to) the personal values of the jurists themselves? Will this great activism of our U.S. trial judges recede now that the new conservative era of judicial restraint is upon us, or are there realities afoot that will keep judges in an activist posture in spite of the Reagan-Bush judicial revolution? And perhaps most intriguing, how is it that judges whose primary role in the federal judiciary is that of "trier of fact" have come to exert such vast influence over public policy?

NATURE OF TRIAL JUDGE DECISION MAKING

At the most simplistic level, the function of U.S. trial judges is to enforce legal norms by resolving individual disputes. In many cases dispute resolution is largely administrative, as when trial judges facilitate out-of-court settlements. In others it approximates the traditional, mechanical model of judicial norm enforcement—that is, the trial judge "finds" the law, "fits" the law to the facts, and rules in favor of the litigant whose facts fit the law. But trial judges do more than merely enforce norms promulgated by Congress and the appellate courts. Trial courts are also policy-making institutions that allocate social values and privilege. When judges hear cases of first impression, they establish precedent, and in a common-law system this is the essence of policy formation. When opinions are codified and published, they become the rules of the litigation process. When trial judges apply general statutes to individual cases, they implement legislative policies. And when federal trial judges devise and supervise equitable remedies to correct or prevent legal harm, they often impose their own policy judgments on administrators and elected officials.

Judges make policy even when they are acting as "fact finders." When, for example, a district judge supervising mass-tort litigation finds that the "facts" of exposure justify the certification of a plaintiff class, he simultaneously initiates a sequence of value reallocations and establishes evidentiary criteria for analogous future cases. In fact, the policy-making power inherent in fact-finding maximizes district judges' influence over the authoritative allocation of values because it is virtually immune from appellate review. Although litigants may appeal procedural decisions that defined the quantity and quality of the evidence presented, when the evidence convinces our mass-tort judge that the class of people exposed to externalities from a hazardous waste dump extends to a three-mile radius around the dump, that "finding" is virtually immune from appellate oversight.

Thus, judicial policy making in the federal trial courts assumes many overlapping forms. Many traditional distinctions, such as the difference between policy formulation and policy implementation, are obviated when the trial judge formulates specific policies in the process of implementing general legislative, administrative, or constitutional policies. Policy making in the federal trial courts can, however, be divided analytically into two functions—legal interpretation and equitable remediation—that parallel closely the traditional distinction between "law courts" and "equity courts" and require federal trial jurists to involve themselves simultaneously in the formulation and implementation of public policy.

The overlap among factual anlaysis, legal interpretation, policy formulation, and policy implementation can be illustrated by reference to the model of judicial policy implementation developed by Charles Johnson and Bradley Canon. In the context of this model, federal district judges are part of the "interpreting population," that is, the trial court "responds to the policy decisions of a higher court . . . interprets the meaning of the policy and develops the rules for matters not addressed in the original decision. . . . Interpretations of lower courts are distinguished from the interpretations of [others in the interpreting population] since theirs are viewed as authoritative in a legal sense by others in the political system" (1984, 16).

As part of the interpreting population, district judges are key components in the implementation process. However, when judges evaluate evidence and interpret the law, they are also formulating policy. Indeed, absent clear legal guidelines, judges may actually create policy in the process of implementing vague legal guidelines and fitting the interpreted facts of an instant dispute to the interstices of extant law. When, for example, a federal judge rules in a case of first impression that obesity is not a handicap covered by federal antidiscrimination statutes, the jurist is at the same time formulating policy to guide other judges and, more important, potential litigants. Even when a judge is asked to resolve an intensely personal dispute—for example, whether an unemancipated minor is mature enough to have an abortion without notifying her parents—his or her judgment becomes part of the common law and defines maturity for potential litigants in that jurisdiction.

Thus, interpretations of facts and law are judicial policy formulations, which are important links in the chain of policy implementation. When trial judges interpret the facts and law to mean that a legal harm has occurred—that is, when they assign legal liability to one or more parties to a dispute—they may be required to devise a legal remedy for that harm. To do so, they must participate in the formulation and implementation of equitable remediation policies designed to correct the causes of that harm and prevent its recurrence. When, for example, a judge finds that a state's prisons are overcrowded and that fact violates prisoners' Eighth and Fourteenth Amendment rights, not only can the judge order state officials to correct the overcrowding, he or she can participate actively in the formulation and administration of policies designed to correct this legal harm and prevent its recurrence.

Because equitable remediation involves district judges in the supervision of elected officials, it involves jurists directly in the highly politicized, authoritative allocation of social values and privilege. When, for example, a judge orders busing to implement school integration, the judge is allocating social values just as surely as if he were a legislator or school board member. Thus, equity judgments have important implications not only for judicial policy making but for the intergovernmental policy process. As such they are important links between the states and the federal government and between the judiciary and other policy-making institutions.

Despite the useful legal distinction between interpretation and remediation, in their eyes and in those of their appellate brethren, it is extremely important to remember that federal district judges are primarily fact finders. Moreover, the fact-finding function transcends remediation and interpretation, often rendering the distinction between the two a distinction without a meaningful difference. The judge's evaluation of the "facts" determines which competing precedent takes priority or which remediation plan will be implemented. Therefore, all forms of judicial policy making give individual judges the discretion and power to exercise judicial judgment—"the act of determining, as in courts, what is comfortable to law and courts."[2] This responsibility is most apparent when judges interpret facts and law; however, it is equally characteristic of the formulation and implementation of remediation policies that require the judge to estimate the scope of legal perceived harm, whether local officials exercise "good faith" in the remediation process, and a host of other determinations about "what is comfortable to law and courts" in the context of the local legal, socioeconomic, and political cultures.

This relationship between judicial discretion, judicial judgment, judicial outcomes, and public policy was encapsulated nicely in district judge C. J. Wyzanski's decision to remain on the trial bench and reject an offer of "promotion" to the appellate bench from Massachusetts Senator Saltonstall in 1959: "The district court gives more scope to a judge's initiative and discretion. The district judge so often has the last word. Even where he does not, heed is given to his estimates of credibility, his determination of the facts, his discretion in framing or denying relief upon the facts he found" (Murphy and Pritchett 1979, 956–967).

Thus, to the extent facts and laws are ambiguous, federal trial judges' perceptions and interpretations are the product of judicial discretion, even when the judges are "simply" evaluating facts, law, and the fit between the two. This exercise of discretionary judgment is, after all, why we call them "judges" and why these jurists perceive themselves as important policy makers.

While our contention is that significant discretion and policy making are inherent in the work of trial judges, still we readily concede that some judges perceive more room for maneuver in their decision making than others. Role theorists have identified three types of decision makers at the trial court level. First, there are the "lawmakers" who take a broad view of the judicial role. These jurists, often referred to as "activists" or "innovators," contend that they can and must make law in their decisions, because the statutory law and appellate or Supreme Court guidelines are often ambiguous or do not cover all situations and because legislative intent is frequently impossible to determine. In Kitchin's study of federal district judges, only 14 percent were classified in this category (1978, 107).

At the other end of the continuum are the "law interpreters," who take a very narrow, traditional view of the judicial function. Sometimes called "strict constructionists," they don't believe that judges should substitute judicial wisdom for the rightful power of the elected branches of government to make policy. They tend to eschew making innovative decisions that may depart from the literal meaning of controlling precedents. In the Kitchin study, 52 percent of the U.S. trial judges were found to be "law interpreters" (1978, 107). Midway between the law interpreters and the lawmakers are judges known as "pragmatists" or "realists," who believe that on occasion they are indeed obliged to make law but that for most cases a decision can be made by consulting the controlling law or appellate court precedents. About a third of federal district judges assume this moderate role (1978, 107). Thus, although ambiguous evidence forces judges to exercise fact-finding discretion, judges may have to determine how much discretion they have and how they wish to exercise it. This is obviously a subjective process, and, as has been noted, "activist judges will find more discretion in a given fact situation than will their more restrained colleagues" (Carp and Rowland 1983, 14).

CONTEMPORARY DISTRICT COURT JURISPRUDENCE

Allowing for differences in judicial role perceptions, all district judges still exercise substantial discretion. But they do so within boundaries defined by formal and informal legal constraints. The quantity and quality of legal constraints on judicial judgment have varied over time in tandem with diachronic change in the parameters of American jurisprudence and, indirectly,

American politics.[3] Most recently, these constraints have been redefined by a shift in the balance between contractual and fiduciary definitions of legal rights and duties.[4] Under the contractual model, rights and duties were assigned contractually. The assigned rights or duties might be specified at the individual level, as in a warranty nonbusiness contract, or at the societal level, as in common-law legislation or the Constitution. If not specified in a legal document, the right or duty simply does not exist. According to this model an implicit constitutional right is no right at all, but the right to Social Security payments or other entitlements upon meeting specific qualifications is an example of a contractual right. Therefore, a judge should be able to "find" rights and fit relatively specific, explicit laws to individual disputes.

Under the fiduciary model, by contrast, rights are balanced by relatively amorphous fiduciary duties based on trust and confidence among the parties. Because they are established by vague standards of care and equally ill-defined standards of trust, rights and duties must be inferred from the fiduciary relationship between litigants or, more important, between the state and its citizens. As with the fiduciary duty of an executor to the beneficiary of an estate, the manufacturer of a product has a duty to produce for the buyer a product that is safe even when used in an unanticipated or risky manner; this duty is nowhere specified but it is implicit in the manufacturer-buyer relationship. At the societal level, the government has a duty to recognize and enforce the individual's constitutional right to privacy, even though that right is nowhere specified in the Constitution.

Fiduciary jurisprudence has been characterized by legislation (for example, that establishing the Occupational Safety and Health Administration) that assigns a standard of care rather than creating specific obligations, and by judicial policies (such as constitutional standing) that create an ill-defined, fiduciary balance between rights and obligations, rather than specifying this balance contractually. It has also been characterized by the delegation of substantial authority to federal trial judges to devise and supervise remedies for legal harms (for example, prison overcrowding) when public officials do not meet their fiduciary obligations.

A cause and a consequence of this shift toward fiduciary jurisprudence has been a dramatic increase in the discretion of judges who preside over disputes engendered by fiduciary ambiguity. Examples of the judicial discretion inherent in fiduciary jurisprudence on federal trial courts could be drawn from cases having to do with the environment (Wenner 1982), prison reform (Taggart 1989), abortion policy (Rubin 1987), and a variety of other policy arenas. But whatever the policy arena, the effect of fiduciary jurisprudence on interpretation and equitable remediation is the same. Because it responds to ill-defined rights and obligations that cannot be fit mechanically to individual disputes or narrow dispute categories, fiduciary jurisprudence inevitably assigns federal triers of fact tremendous discretion to infer the contractual specificity omitted by the Constitution, Congress, administrative agencies, and the appellate courts. Thus, as a parallel to the evolution of fiduciary rights and duties, there exists in the federal courts an analogous change in the responsibility of federal judges to specify the authoritative allocation of values and privilege. Moreover, because it derives from a jurisprudence that embraces ambiguity, it is a responsibility that envelops the "law interpreter" as well as the "lawmaker."

Nowhere have the causes and consequences of fiduciary jurisprudence been more apparent than in the federal trial courts. Its effects are perhaps most obvious in the quantity of litigation.[5] In 1960, 79,200 cases were filed in the federal district courts; in 1987, 282,274 cases were filed. The increase in 27 years was more than 350 percent; moreover, the increase of 203,000 cases was about three times the increase recorded for the previous 175 years! However, changes in the quality of litigation have been even more dramatic. For example, of the new filings in 1960, only 306 were classified by the Federal Judicial Center as civil rights cases, By 1987, 19,785 civil rights cases were filed, an increase of almost 6,500 percent! More recently, the combination of speedy-trial legislation and tougher criminal statutes has engendered a dramatic increase in both the number of criminal filings and the percentage of federal court time devoted to criminal matters.

Changes in the quantity and quality of civil and criminal litigation parallel an increase in the district courts' policy-making responsibilities. Only the trier of fact can establish the factual foundations of a search-and-seizure claim or a race discrimination claim. But what about appellate review? Given their position at the bottom of the federal judicial hierarchy, one might argue that, even when their policy-making *responsibilities* are maximized, the policy-making *powers* of federal trial judges are constrained by the authority of appellate courts to reverse their judgments. To some degree this is true. Certainly the legal judgments of appellate courts and the prospect of appellate review constrain the interpretative and remedial discretion of trial judges. However, these institutional constraints are mitigated by several factors.

First, only about 20 percent of all district court cases are appealed in any given year.[6] Second, most appeals are unsuccessful, and, as anticipated by the expanded fact freedom inherent in the evolution of fiduciary jurisprudence, the reversal rate is declining. For example, the reversal rate in 1960 was almost 25 percent; by 1990 it had declined to 16 percent. In combination, the low rates of appeal and reversal ensure that only a very small number of the district courts' judgments will be reversed on appeal—about 3 percent ($.20 \times .16 = .032$). Finally, even when the appeals courts do reverse trial judges' decisions, these reversals impose no sanctions on the district judge. Indeed, it is common knowledge among judicial scholars that for some trial judges controversial reversals may become badges of distinction.

It should be noted that rates of appeal and reversal are higher for some litigation categories than for others. Remedial decrees, for example, are routinely appealed (Cooper 1988). And rates of appeal and reversal vary substantially among circuits and among dispute categories within circuits (Howard 1981). Nevertheless, the surprising low rates of appeal and reversal should confirm the fact-finding discretion of trial judges and remind us that the relative independence inherent in fiduciary jurisprudence is hardly vitiated by the threat of appellate review. This reminder is reinforced by the response of a noted federal trial judge to a question put to her about the susceptibility of district judges' factual judgments to appellate review: "The power [of the trial judge] is maximized when the outcome hinges on questions of fact. The judge can rely on those facts that persuade him and explain his decision in light of those facts. Legal truth, like beauty, is in the eye of the beholder. If there is an evidentiary basis for the judge's interpretation of the facts, this interpretation, unlike interpretations of law, is virtually immune from appellate review."[7]

To point out that fiduciary jurisprudence makes the federal district courts important policy-making institutions and increases the policy-making discretion of individual district judges is not to argue that these courts are necessarily the most *appropriate* policy-making institutions or that district judges are always competent policy makers. Indeed, many sociolegal scholars argue that contemporary jurisprudence has "politicized" the federal courts, that the scope of policy making by trial judges far exceeds the judicial role envisioned by the Constitution (Glazer 1978; Feeley 1989), and that courts often lack the capacity, and judges the competence, to fulfill the obligations inherent in fiduciary jurisprudence.[8]

Normative criticisms of political jurisprudence have important implications for all levels of the federal judiciary and for the larger political system. However, although the debates over activism and competence are fueled by empirical *evidence* of judicial policy making, we would argue that such criticisms are largely irrelevant for the political *study* of policy making in the district courts. Although their individual and aggregate decisions may encourage some claimants and discourage others, district judges do not initiate cases of first impression. They do not travel their districts looking for overcrowded prisons. They do not write the ambiguous statutes they must interpret. Rather, as federal judicial officials in a local setting they are *required* to respond to cases and controversies in their jurisdictions and to resolve controversial disputes between local majoritarian values and national, constitutional values. Thus, for those who study the federal trial courts as highly politicized policy-making institutions, the immediate task is not to decide whether federal trial judges should do what they are doing but to understand the politicization of policy making within the legal parameters defined by fiduciary jurisprudence. Fortunately, political scientists and others interested in understanding public policy have devoted substantial attention to these courts as policy-making institutions and to the influence of extralegal elements on the political subculture on district judges' fiduciary policy judgments.

EXTRALEGAL CORRELATES OF FEDERAL TRIAL JUDGES' POLICY JUDGMENTS

We next turn to a review of the literature that has sought to expose those extralegal factors that affect and circumvent the policy judgments of our U.S. trial judges. The seminal study of federal trial courts as political institutions was Jack W. Peltason's *Federal Courts in the Political Process*. Working from the pluralist perspective that dominated political studies at the time, Peltason rejected the legal fiction that federal judges, including district judges, simply enforce norms promulgated from above. His observation that trial judges, like other political actors, "had to choose between conflicting interests" (1955, 15) attracted political scientists and other sociolegal scholars to the study of federal trial courts as political, policy-making institutions. The resultant scholarship has tended to focus on the relative and interactive influence of the legal and political subcultures on trial judges.[9]

Although this scholarship spans more than thirty years, its focus has remained the desire to understand the unique influence of the political subculture on federal judicial institutions presided over by judges who are the political products of that subculture. A complete review of this work is beyond the scope of a single chapter; however, its flavor can be gleaned from a brief survey of two sets of exemplar studies. The first focuses primarily on the effects of the local and national political environments on judicial selection and judges' subsequent evaluations of ambiguous facts and laws. The second focuses on a nascent research program concerned primarily with the interactive effects of local legal and political environments and judges' formulation and administration of equitable remediation.

Environmental Effects on Judicial Evaluation

Much of the early work on environmental effects focused on relatively specific policy questions evoked by unique local environments. An important example is Kenneth M. Dolbeare's finding in 1969 that variation in the judicial agendas of urban federal trial courts was positively correlated with variation in local political environments and the agendas of local political institutions.

More typical were studies of the nexus of local subcultures with judicial interpretation and implementation of desegregation and other civil rights policies (Peltason 1961; Vines 1964; Giles and Walker 1975). These studies found that desegregation was correlated with local environments and the ties of presiding judges to those environments. For example, Michael W. Giles and Thomas Walker found that desegregation in southern school districts was correlated with the size of the district, the size of the district's black population, whether the district court was located within the school district's boundaries, and whether the judge presiding over the desegregation effort had been educated outside of the South. During the Vietnam War era, scholarly attention shifted to the influence of spatial and temporal environments on the conviction and sentencing of draft resisters. Researchers found significant correlations between temporal and spatial variation in public support for the war and the severity of sentences imposed upon resisters (Cook 1973; Kritzer 1978).

Most recently, work on environmental effects has been extended to topical policy categories and to legal environments defined explicitly by political jurisdiction. This effort is best exemplified by Lettie M. Wenner and Lee E. Dutter's study (1988) of differences among circuits in federal district judges' support for environmental regulation. They found, as anticipated by previous work, that support for environmental regulation varied significantly among circuits and that the level of judicial support coincided with the level of legislative support by members of Congress from states in that circuit. This led them to conclude that district judges, like legislators, were responsive to the political context of environmental disputes.

The Politics of Judicial Appointments

A second research path focuses on the relative influence of legal and political subcultures in the selection of district judges and the link between politicized selection criteria and policy making in the U.S. district courts. Studies of judicial selection are unanimous in their assumption that, despite the role of home-state senators in identifying candidates for judicial vacancies and the role of the Senate Judiciary Committee in screening nominees, the appointment of district judges is primarily a presidential prerogative. Therefore, virtually all such studies are organized by presidential administration.

One approach to the study of judicial selection is qualitative and somewhat historical. As exemplified by Neil McFeeley's study of the Johnson administration (1987), this approach uses interviews with participants and original sources available in presidential libraries to delineate the procedures and selection criteria that define a president's appointment strategy. This qualitative methodology enables researchers to describe in detail the criteria and strategies, such as negotiations with home-state senators, surrounding individual appointments.

Other scholars have focused their efforts on judicial recruitment by sitting presidents and supplemented qualitative descriptions of recruitment strategies with quantified descriptions of the judicial and political backgrounds of those presidents' judicial recruits. This work is best exemplified by the ongoing endeavors of Sheldon Goldman (1989). Goldman's work on judicial recruitment during the Reagan administration is valuable, among other reasons, because it documents the unprecedented success of former Attorney General Edwin Meese and the Justice Department's Office of Legal Policy in reconstructing the partisan and ideological balance on the lower federal courts.

An important recent addition to the study of judicial recruitment is Elliot E. Slotnick's review of research in this area. In addition to summarizing his own work on the Carter administration, Slotnick has synthesized recent work, including Goldman's, and placed it in a perspective that helps us understand the historical relationship between jurisprudence and the politics of recruitment. Slotnick's compilation reinforces the conclusions of others that, with few exceptions, presidents appoint judges who share the president's party affiliation, judicial philosophy, and basic policy predilections. Moreover, his perspective makes it clear that the importance of these extralegal appointment criteria is increasing in tandem with the evolution of fiduciary jurisprudence: "Presidents Carter and Reagan have enjoyed unique opportunities to re-make the lower federal bench. . . . Both presidents treated their lower court judicial selection responsibilities as primary domestic policy making opportunities, and both presidents generated public controversy over the clear ideological bent in their appointments" (1988).

The obvious question implicit in these findings is whether presidents' partisan, ideological appointment criteria are reflected in their appointees' subsequent policy judgments. A predictable proliferation of research has examined this link by comparing the published opinions of cohorts appointed under the same president.

Appointment Effects in Legal Interpretation

Using as their data source published opinions, which are assumed to be policy formulations that explain and defend the exercise of judicial discretion, many researchers have found a strong, aggregate link between local environments, politicized presidential appointment criteria, and appointment cohorts' subsequent policy judgments.[10] For example, in a work published a decade ago we looked at more than twenty-five thousand opinions published by district judges between 1933 and 1977. We found that judgment differences among presidential appointment cohorts were relatively small and insignificant before 1968 but that their growth after the inauguration of President Nixon and the appointment of Chief Justice Burger was dramatic. Johnson and Kennedy appointees were much more supportive of economic regulation, civil rights, civil liberties, and the rights of criminal defendants than were Nixon appointees (Carp and Rowland 1983). Moreover, the Johnson cohort was much more supportive of civil rights than was the Kennedy cohort, a difference that reflects the inordinate influence of Senator Eastland, the segregationist chairman of the Senate Judiciary Committee, over Kennedy's trial court appointments in the South (Navasky 1971).

Given the continued growth of fiduciary jurisprudence and the increased politicization of judicial appointment during the Carter and Reagan administrations, it is hardly surprising that the polarization of policy judgments between these two appointment cohorts appears to be significantly greater than the differences among previous presidential appointment cohorts. Although those appointment cohorts have not been examined as thoroughly or systematically as have their predecessors, separate studies found Carter appointees twice as likely as Reagan judges to support the claims of criminal defendants (Rowland, Carp, and Songer 1985) or civil rights claims (Stidham and Carp 1987). Moreover, as with the Kennedy and Johnson cohorts, these differences are much more pronounced in the South than in the North.

The importance of appointing presidents and executive appointment criteria is buttressed by evidence of consistency across ethnic, gender, and other subgroups within appointment cohorts. For example, President Carter's black and female appointees were not significantly more supportive of civil rights claims than were his white male appointees (Walker and Barrow 1985). And the judgments of Carter appointees recruited by selection commissions were indistinguishable from the judgments of his more traditional recruits (Todd 1985). In sum, twenty years of scholarship depict a consistent link among sociolegal environments, highly politicized presidential appointments, and aggregate patterns of political jurisprudence. It is, however, a picture painted with broad strokes. As such, it leaves unanswered many interstitial questions about the interactive influence of the legal and political subcultures on district judges' interpretations of laws and facts. Contemporary research that expands and refines this picture continues to focus primarily on the causes and consequences of politicized recruitment.

Current Research on Appointment Effects

Some ongoing research is concentrating on comparisons between the Carter and Reagan appointees' policy judgments but refines our understanding of these differences by using the new computerized legal information sources (such as Westlaw, Lexis) to go beyond the broad policy categories (such as civil rights) looked at by previous research and instead focus on relatively specific, highly politicized dispute categories (such as abortion). Although this work builds on earlier findings, it also expands previous efforts in two important ways. First, it is much more attentive to legal constraints and the qualitative interaction between legal and extralegal influences. Second, several of these studies pay careful attention not only to political links but to nonpolitical background characteristics, such as religion, that are theoretically linked to relatively specific dispute categories.

Steve Alumbaugh and C. K. Rowland (1990) compared the effects of appointing president and religion on district judges' support for abortion rights. They found, as anticipated by the 1980 Republican platform's criticism of *Roe v. Wade*, that the Carter appointment cohort was more supportive of abortion rights than was the Reagan cohort; in fact, Carter appointees ruled in favor of abortion rights 88 percent of the time while Reagan jurists did so only 23 percent of the time. However, they also found that Carter's Catholic appointees were substantially less supportive of these rights than were his Protestant judges.

Robert Dudley (1989) isolated district judges' obscenity decisions and examined the relative effects of appointing president and religion on these judgments. He found, among other things, that Johnson appointees were much less likely than Nixon judges to place allegedly obscene materials outside the protection of the First Amendment, but that Catholics in both appointment cohorts were less supportive of this form of expression than were Protestants.

Exceptions to Appointment Effects on Legal Interpretation

Although most work on appointment effects depicts a highly politicized jurisprudence, an interesting subset of studies has identified three important exceptions to this pattern. First, when attention shifts from aggregate patterns of case outcomes to individual, case-specific decisions, the effects of political influences are less apparent. Indeed, when appropriate legal variables are included in models of legal interpretation, they sometimes displace political predictors. An important example of this exception is Charles Johnson's examination (1987) of the congruence between Supreme Court policy formation and the implementation of these policies by the lower federal courts. To measure this congruence Johnson combined legal (such as specificity of Supreme Court guidelines) and political (such as trial judge's political party) variables in a statistical model of trial (and appellate) judges' responsiveness to Supreme Court precedent. He found that judges at both levels are more responsive to legal than political cues; however, the explanatory power of cues from the political subculture is substantially greater for district courts than for courts of appeals.

The second exception to the pattern of politicized policy judgments is limited to policy categories in which the formality of settled law and/or the norms of deference to other branches minimize the discretion of judges to invoke political preferences. Specific examples of this exception include Ronald Stidham and Robert Carp's study (1987) of labor and economic regulation judgments and the exploration of voting rights judgments by Rowland, Carp, and Todd.[11] Both studies found that for these relatively settled, unambiguous policy categories, in which key facts are often stipulated, differences between Reagan and Carter appointees are trivial and statistically insignificant. But the most interesting exception to the pattern of appointment effects was identified by Craig R. Ducat and Robert L. Dudley (1989). They found that the "two presidencies" thesis extended to appointment effects on district judges—that is, although federal trial judges are much more supportive of *domestic* policy initiatives from their appointing president than from other presidents, these appointment-based disparities do not extend to *foreign* or *military* policy initiatives. Thus, district judges, like members of Congress and Supreme Court justices, are much more deferential to presidential prerogatives when the president is acting as chief of state or commander in chief.

Deficiencies in Explanatory Theory

Despite the encouraging expansion of inquiry into the politics of the federal district courts since the publication of Peltason's groundbreaking work, there remain significant empirical and theoretical gaps in knowledge about these institutions and in their link to the larger political system. Each of these lacunae raises important questions that are addressed in the chapters that follow.

The most obvious empirical lacuna stems from the need to update and expand previous systematic analysis of the voting patterns of U.S. district judges. More than a decade has passed since the publication of *Politics and Policymaking in the Federal District Courts*, which relied on data from 1932 through 1977. The interim has been marked by the continued evolution of fiduciary jurisprudence and the addition to the district courts of two highly politicized appointment cohorts. Also, we know from the literature reviewed earlier that appointment effects have been exacerbated for specific case types (such as abortion and criminal rights) by the Reagan and Carter cohorts. Moreover, we have not systematically replicated our previous research that enables us to map the evolution of the effects of geography, political party, and appointing president since 1977, nor have we yet compared the

Carter and Reagan cohorts with their predecessors under controls for changing court environments. In sum, there is a need to update many questions examined in previous works by ourselves and by others, with special attention to the Carter and Reagan judicial cohorts.

A second empirical lacuna derives from the tendency of scholars—including ourselves—to rely exclusively on *published* opinions to estimate the link between politics and jurisprudence. As we argue later, disproportionate reliance on published opinions may be justified because published decisions tend to be policy judgments with greater political consequences than their unpublished counterparts. Indeed, federal judges are not encouraged to seek publication for routine decisions that have no precedential value. Still, it must be acknowledged that less than 5 percent of all district court opinions ever appear in print, and this reduces to some degree our capacity to generalize about the full scope of environmental and appointment effects. In other words, in order for us to have greater confidence in our conclusions about district judge behavior, we need to have at least some data about the nature and content of unpublished judicial opinions.

A final missing empirical link derives from our failure to recognize and account for the role of home-state senators in the recruitment of federal district judges. As we know, judicial selection is not in reality an exclusively presidential prerogative. It is common knowledge that home-state senators, particularly those of the president's political party, exert tremendous influence over the recruitment of candidates for federal judicial vacancies in their states. Moreover, anecdotal evidence suggests that these senators, like presidents, often rely on politicized, ideological selection criteria (Rowland 1991). Yet the effort to delineate the links between selection politics and political judgments has focused almost entirely on partisan and presidential effects on this linkage, while little attention has been paid to the recruitment of prospective judges or to the effects of the recruitment politics on the candidates' subsequent judicial behavior.

Underlying the empirical lacunae outlined here are some *theoretical* lacunae that inhibit our understanding of the judgment process that connects politics and jurisprudence. The limitations of extant models of decision making have become quite apparent to us since the 1983 publication of *Policymaking and Politics in the Federal District Courts*. In that book and in subsequent works the basic question underlying our approach was this: What theory of individual judicial decision making best explains the patterns of politicized judicial outcomes in which appointment effects grow over time but vary significantly from one case type to another? To answer this question we borrowed heavily from the behavioral paradigm and the attitudinal models of appellate judge behavior.[12] As adapted to trial settings, this theoretical approach accepted the basic, axiomatic assumption of attitudinal models that judges were motivated primarily by the personal political values that secured their appointments and that they manifested these values in their decisions when the factual and legal ambiguity of a dispute afforded them the opportunity to do so.

At first blush our adaptation of the behavioral perspective seemed to provide an acceptable level of explanation for our empirical findings. Certainly a value-based model of individual behavior was consistent with aggregate differences among presidential cohorts appointed on the basis of different values and policy preferences. In retrospect, however, there are several troubling aspects of the behavioral framework as it attempts to account for extralegal influences on judicial behavior. First of all, the assumption that all federal trial judges are motivated by extralegal, personal preferences is contrary to what studies of judicial role models have concluded, and it also gives offense to judges themselves, who consistently deny such an assertion. This approach has often had the effect of isolating researchers from the subjects of their inquiry, alienating judges from social science researchers, and bifurcating legal and social scientific inquiry.

Second, the axiomatic interpretation of aggregate outcomes as the product of extralegal policy preferences assumes away important questions about the cognitive process by which legalistic procedures produce politicized outcomes because we assume that these effects are the products of extralegal motives rather than unmotivated individual differences in the evaluation of legal and factual information. Particularly problematic is the failure of appellate adaptations to accommodate variance in evidence evaluation among judges sworn to neutrality by their judicial oath of office.

Finally, by clinging to behavioral models, we are ignoring important new developments in judgment psychology coming from the field of social psychology. It is not without reason that in the field of social psychology these new cognitive models have almost completely displaced the traditional "attitudes-cause-behavior" models of individual choice. Perhaps by adapting work on social cognition to judicial settings we can obviate concerns about unvalidated motives and focus instead on human differences in perception, attribution, and inferential judgments that precede decision making. If so, perhaps new models can accommodate evidence of aggregate extralegal effects on the special case of judicial judgment without assuming "illegitimate" political motives of individual judges.

EXPLANATION OF THE DATA SOURCE

The next two chapters examine the voting behavior of federal district judges from a variety of perspectives, such as comparing decisions rendered by Democratic versus Republican jurists, by the appointees of the most recent presidents, by judges holding court in different geographic locations, and so on. To perform all of these analyses it is necessary to examine in the aggregate the individual outputs of these jurists, that is, the decisions themselves. To do this we have turned to the *Federal Supplement*, the primary outlet for the publication of U.S. trial court opinions.

The source of our quantitative data, then, are 45,826 federal district court opinions issued by over fifteen hundred judges during fifty-four years (1933 through early 1987). Only those cases were used that fit easily into one of twenty-six case types which appeared to contain a clear underlying liberal-conservative dimension. They included such cases as state and federal habeas corpus pleas, labor-management disputes, questions involving the right to privacy, environmental protection cases, and so on; excluded were cases involving patents, admiralty disputes, and land condemnation hearings. The number of cases not selected was about the same as those included.

For each case, data were also collected on the date of the opinion and on the city, state, district, and circuit wherein the decision was rendered. Not included in the data set were decisions by appellate court judges acting as trial jurists, cases decided by judges outside the districts they regularly served, decisions handed down by special three-judge courts, and cases decided by judges in the "senior judge" status. Information was also gathered on the political party affiliation, the appointing president, and the year of the appointment of the fifteen hundred judges. The primary sources of this background data were the *Congressional Quarterly Almanac*, *The Federal Judicial Almanac*, *Who's Who in America*, and several of our professional colleagues, mentioned in the acknowledgments.

The *Federal Supplement* as a Data Source

In regard to the policy of West Publishing Company in its publication of the *Federal Supplement*, Allan Vestal tells us, "The attitude of the West Publishing Company . . . seems to be that it will publish any writing which a sitting federal district judge sends into the company. The initiative is with the writing judge. If he does not send in the material, it is not published" (Vestal 1966a). Such an observation finds support in an independent analysis of the subject performed by Kenneth Dolbeare and also in a more recent study conducted by the Federal Judicial Center (Dolbeare 1969, 377–378; Flanders 1977). Interviews with personnel at the Judicial Center and with several district judges indicate that occasionally the law clerks, rather than the judges, take the initiative for sending in to West the opinions that they think worthy of publication. Nevertheless, the central point remains that West routinely publishes all district court opinions that are sent in to them.

The evidence is overwhelming that most judges, lawyers, and public law scholars regard the *Federal Supplement* as preeminent in the field of publishing district court opinions. (West nurtures this exclusiveness by refusing even to acknowledge in its publications the existence of other series of reports.) As the author of numerous studies of the status and contents of the *Supplement*, Vestal comments, "When the average practitioner considers the actions taken by the federal district courts he thinks of the West publications—first the *Federal Supplement*, and then on a moment's reflection he will probably recall the *Federal Rules Decisions*. These two series are considered generally as the means by which the opinions of the district courts are made available to the legal profession" (1966b, 74).

The *Supplement* takes on added importance because the federal judiciary's publication guidelines discourage judges from publishing decisions that do not explain unique factual evaluations and/or legal interpretations. Thus, almost by definition West publishes only those decisions which the judges themselves (or their clerks) regard as inherently significant and worthy. As Dolbeare says in speaking of the *Supplement*, "At the very least, it would appear that the resultant body of cases would include most of the *major* policy decisions made by federal district judges" (1969, 378). In sum, the best evidence suggests that, although not all discretionary policy decisions are codified and published, the vast majority of published opinions are explications of discretionary policy decisions that directly or indirectly allocate value beyond the litigants of record.

Limitations of Reliance on the *Federal Supplement*

There are at least two main arguments against relying (at least exclusively) on the *Supplement* as the primary source of data for an empirical study of the behavior of federal district judges. One is that the final published opinions of a court tell only a small part of the real story of the case. Because it fails to take into consideration all the nuances of the case and how the judge ruled on the various motions made throughout the trial, a published opinion may be thought to be misleading. The argument is not without merit, but we would respond to it in precisely the same way as did Dolbeare, who relied on *Supplement* opinions in his analysis of federal trial courts and urban public policy:

> For what it may be worth in exculpatory terms, we may note that there appears to be no more rigorous way [other than relying on the *Supplement*] to gather data on the outcome of cases, short of a review of transcripts in each court's files—a task whose dimensions foreclose the prospect on more than case study or sampling, rather than comparative, terms. The body of cases actually devel-

> oped and employed in this inquiry must, therefore be viewed as an expedient and implications drawn from the following analysis taken as no more than tentative interpretations. (1969, 378)

Since our sample of cases is more than 150 times larger than Dolbeare's, we are somewhat more bold in support of our subsequent findings, although we are still quite prepared to concede that the published opinion does not tell "the whole story" of the judicial decision making that went into the case. There is a second qualification on our reliance on the *Federal Supplement*—only a small percentage of district court decisions are ever formally published. The vast majority are either not justified in written form at all or appear merely as slip opinions or memoranda that accompany a case on appeal. We know very little about the contents or impact of these many unreported opinions, although scholars at the Federal Judicial Center believe that "findings of fact and conclusions of law are probably the tasks represented most poorly. They are prepared in some form in all nonjury cases, though in some courts the judge may deliver findings and conclusions orally. Judges may differ more widely in their publications habits regarding findings and conclusions than in other types of work" (Flanders 1977, 153).

During the past decade several scholars have compared published with unpublished opinions in several diverse areas of the law and have concluded that there are real and substantive differences between the two types of cases.[13] For example, Peter Siegelman and John Donohue recently performed a study in which they compared published employment discrimination cases with those that did not find their way into print. Among other things, they concluded that "the occupational distribution of the plaintiffs, the kinds of discrimination being complained about, the laws allegedly being violated, and the outcome of litigation all differ significantly between published and unpublished cases" (1990, 1165). A broader examination of the differences between published and unpublished opinions involving criminal justice, labor, and antitrust cases was conducted by Donald Songer. He learned in part that "there are a substantial number of *unpublished* [emphasis added] district court decisions which cannot be assumed to be trivial or consensual cases. A substantial number of such unpublished decisions appear to have presented the district judges with potential law making opportunities in which their values could shape the outcomes" (1988, 213).

How, then, are we to justify our reliance (at least in the next two chapters) on opinions published in the *Supplement* when there is evidence to suggest that this source is by no means a random sample of all district court decision making and that there are many important trial court judgments that do not appear in print? First, we do not argue that the *Supplement* cases constitute a random sample of all district court decisions. Rather, we contend that they primarily reflect the key policy-making, precedent-setting judgments of trial court judges. As Dolbeare noted about his study based on a much smaller sample of cases from the *Supplement*, "We have noted a source of probable bias toward the major cases, and I think it is fair to argue that the cases employed, while not representative of the workload, are at least *indicative* of the major policy actions of the District Courts and that they are therefore serviceable for cautious outlining of the primary features of the policy product and impact of these courts" (1969, 378).

Second, while we do not quarrel with the findings of Songer and others that there may well be many inherently important unpublished district court decisions, still the extant studies have never challenged the key propositions about the impact of party identification and appointing president on trial judges behavior. For example, Bridget Todd, who has been studying in part the importance of judges' party identification and appointing president on judges' voting behavior, has generally found that differences between published and unpublished opinions in this realm were negligible.[14] This finding was echoed by Songer himself when he reported that partisan variations among judges were largely the same whether the researcher examined published or unpublished court decisions:

> Only in labor cases were the differences between the votes of Democratic and Republican judges statistically insignificant. And even in labor cases, the observed differences were in the direction which would be predicted if the judges perceived a sufficient choice situation to enable them to vote their policy preferences (i.e., Democrats were more pro-labor). On appeals from both the criminal and antitrust decisions of district judges which were not accompanied by a published opinion, the voting tendencies of Democratic and Republican appeals court judges were divergent to a significant degree. In both categories of cases the Democratic judges more frequently supported the liberal position (i.e., pro-defendant in criminal cases and pro-plaintiff in antitrust cases). . . . These data suggest that in a significant number of the district cases without published opinions the judges faced a choice situation which permitted them discretion to make decisions consistent with their personal values and policy preferences. (1988, 212–213)

Thus, while some unpublished decisions may evoke appointment effects, the cases that evoke these extralegal effects tend to resemble closely the published outcomes on which the next two chapters are based.

Finally, in chapters 4 and 5 of this book we shall seek to make up for this possible deficiency by examining appointment effects on a wide variety of unpublished decisions, including rulings on interim motions that would not be included in opined case outcomes.

Table 1-1. Liberal Decisions by Category of Case, 1933–1987

	1933–53	1954–68	1969–87	All Years
	% (*n*)	% (*n*)	% (*n*)	% (*n*)
Criminal justice	24 (1,353)	44 (4,014)	30 (9,309)	32 (14,676)
Government and the economy	50 (2,780)	23 (2,100)	17 (5,366)	22 (10,246)
Support for labor	5 (306)	12 (1,124)	13 (4,075)	12 (5,505)
Class discrimination	17 (933)	17 (1,552)	32 (10,044)	27 (12,529)
First Amendment cases	4 (239)	5 (418)	7 (2,213)	6 (2,870)
Total	100 (5,611)	101 (9,208)	99 (31,007)	99 (45,826)

The Basic Contours of the Data Base

We have developed five general categories and twenty-six subcategories of case content from the *Supplement* decisions we have coded. (See Appendix A for a more detailed discussion of each of these.) The first general category is that of criminal justice, and from it we developed four more precise sets of cases: U.S. habeas corpus petitions; state habeas corpus pleas; motions made immediately before, during, or after a criminal trial; and conviction for a criminal offense. Decisions favoring the petitioner or the defendant were classified as liberal. As indicated by Table 1-1, our data set contains 14,676 criminal justice cases, the most numerous of which involved criminal court motions made immediately before, during, or after trial. Additional analysis indicates that the amount of space in the *Federal Supplement* devoted to criminal justice issues has fluctuated greatly over time. Between 1933 and 1953 only 24 percent of our data set represented criminal justice matters; this jumped to 44 percent between 1954 and 1968 but has fallen back to 30 percent in the period between 1969 and 1987. In fact, deeper analysis of the data (not included in Table 1-1) reveals that the trend in the most recent decade is for fewer cases on criminal justice topics to appear in print: between 1969 and 1977, about 40 percent of our sample of cases involved criminal justice cases, while in the 1977 to 1987 period this dropped to a low of only 23 percent.

A second general category, government regulation of the economy, includes six subgroups of cases: federal commercial regulation; environmental protection, pure food and drug, and consumer protection; economic regulation by state and local governments; rent control, excessive profit, and price control; Fair Labor Standards Act; and government regulation of labor union activity. Judicial victories for the regulator were classified as liberal. This general category comprised 10,246 opinions, and the data show that the percentage of such cases has taken up a smaller and smaller portion of cases in the *Supplement*. Between 1933 and 1953, half of all our sample were government economic regulation cases; this dropped sharply to 23 percent in the 1954 though 1968 period; and for the next nineteen-year period the amount eased back to 17 percent.

The third category is support for labor, which included 5,505 cases in three subcategories: union versus company; union members versus union; and employees versus employer. Decisions coded as liberal were those in favor of labor (and decisions favoring workers in disputes with the labor union hierarchy). Labor cases constituted 5 percent of the total of our sample prior to 1954 and jumped to 12 percent in the 1954 through 1968 period; between 1969 through 1987 they leveled off at some 13 percent.

The fourth category deals with class discrimination and more specifically with ten subgroups of cases: alien petitions; Indian rights and law; voting rights cases; racial minority discrimination; reverse discrimination for race; Fourteenth Amendment and U.S. Civil Rights Act cases; women's rights; reverse discrimination for gender; rights of handicapped persons; and age discrimination suits. Court decisions favoring aliens, Indians, would-be voters, racial minority groups, those seeking to vindicate their Fourteenth Amendment rights, affirmative action programs for race and/or gender, victims of sex and of handicap discrimination, and older petitioners were defined as liberal. Some 12,529 cases on these topics are included in our sample: 17 percent of the total between 1933 and 1953 and also between 1954 and 1968; but in the period from 1969 through 1987 this almost doubled to 32 percent.

A final category pertains to First Amendment freedoms (freedom of expression and freedom of religion) and also the right to privacy. If the court supported a broadening of freedom of expression, found that the government had created an unconstitutional establishment of religion, favored the free exercise of religion, or supported the right to privacy, the cases were coded as liberal. A total of 2,870 cases are in these several categories. Between 1933 and 1953, only 4 percent of our sample contained cases on these topics, increasing to 5 percent for the 1954 through 1968 time frame. From 1969 through 1987, the percentage climbed to 7 percent. The most recent trend, however, (not detailed in Table 1-1) is downward, just as it has been with criminal justice cases. From 1969 though 1977, 8 percent of the total constituted First Amendment or privacy rights cases, while in the most recent ten-year period this dropped to 6 percent.

Using this database we shall now explore and test some general propositions about extrajudicial influences on the output of the district courts. We shall seek to determine the degree to which trial judge decision making is correlated with the judge's party affiliation, appointing president, and geographic location. We shall also examine how such correlations have varied over time and look at the degree to which district judge activity corresponds to similar decision-making trends on the U.S. Supreme Court.

CHAPTER 2

The Influence of the Appointing President and Political Party Affiliation on District Judge Voting Behavior

PARTISANSHIP AND THE DISTRICT COURTS: THE PAST HALF CENTURY

This chapter examines the overall extent of partisanship on U.S. trial judge decision making between 1933 and 1988. Has it made a difference that a Democrat rather than a Republican sat on the bench? Table 2-1 suggests an affirmative answer to this broad question.

Speaking in very general terms for all cases, 48 percent of the decisions rendered by Democrats for more than the past five decades have been in a liberal direction whereas this has been true of only 39 percent of the rulings by jurists from Republican ranks. Or, using the odds ratio as our guide, one may say that Democratic judges are 1.42 times more likely to render a liberal decision than are judges of Republican backgrounds.[1] This phenomenon is seen more profoundly over the years in cases involving civil rights and liberties. For Bill of Rights and Fourteenth Amendment cases, Democrats on the bench were 1.73 times more likely to uphold the civil rights or liberties of a petitioner than were their GOP colleagues.

Historically, partisan differences have been lowest for criminal justice matters. Here Democrats favored the criminal defendant 30 percent of the time, while Republicans did so in a quarter of the cases, with an odds ratio of 1.33. Between the two extremes are cases dealing with labor and economic regulation. For these issues Democrats favored the economic "underdog" or the regulator 61 percent of the time, while judges from the GOP did so in 52 percent of the cases. The odds ratio here is 1.40.

The preceding represents "the big picture" in fairly gross terms. We shall now replace the wide-angle lens with one that permits a more precise examination of the data and one that allows us to understand their meaning in terms of contemporary political jurisprudence. Our first detailed inquiry explores the degree to which the ever-increasing conservative orientation of the Burger Court impacted the decision making of federal district judges.

Table 2-1. Liberal and Conservative Decisions by Democratic and Republican Judges for All Cases, Civil Rights and Liberties, Criminal Justice, and Labor and Economic Regulation

	Democrats		Republicans	
	%	*n*	%	*n*
All cases				
Liberal	48	11,950	39	7,466
Conservative	52	13,101	61	11,588
Total	100	25,051	100	19,054
Odds ratio	1.42			
Civil rights and liberties				
Liberal	52	4,411	38	2,451
Conservative	48	4,109	62	3,962
Total	100	8,520	100	6,413
Odds ratio	1.73			
Criminal justice				
Liberal	30	2,497	25	1,436
Conservative	70	5,712	75	4,379
Total	100	8,209	100	5,815
Odds ratio	1.33			
Labor and economic regulation				
Liberal	61	5,041	52	3.577
Conservative	39	3,278	48	3,245
Total	100	8,319	100	6,822
Odds ratio	1.40			

LIBERAL-CONSERVATIVE VOTING PATTERNS DURING THE BURGER COURT ERA

It is no secret that the Supreme Court has grown more and more conservative since the end of the Warren Court era in 1969. The most obvious cause for this was that conservative, Republican presidents were able during this time period to make all six Supreme Court appointments. By 1975 alone, Presidents Nixon and Ford had appointed a majority on the high court, and that majority grew by one after Reagan's selection of Sandra O'Connor in 1981. Perhaps more than in any other period in recent memory, there was a dogged, systematic effort on the part of these administrations to select jurists who mirrored their own conservative values and attitudes. When Richard Nixon was elected to the presidency in 1968, he vowed to appoint "strict constructionist" (i. e., conservative) justices to the high court, law-and-order jurists who would eschew the liberal, activist doctrines of the Warren Court. Both Presidents Nixon and Reagan were determined that a more restrained and conservative federal judiciary would be part of their respective legacies to the American people. Both leaders took great pains to ensure that there would be no "liberal surprises" in their appointments to the nation's highest tribunal (such as Eisenhower's unhappy surprise in selecting the liberal Justices Warren and Brennan).

To what degree were these Republican presidents successful in securing a Supreme Court that reflected their right-of-center political philosophies? The answer to this important question seems to be that while Nixon, Ford, and Reagan were indeed able to shift the Court's center of gravity to the right, this shift was certainly not one of revolutionary proportions. What the renowned Court observer Alpheus Thomas Mason said of the Court in 1974 still seemed apt when Burger left the bench in 1986: "The three major pillars of the Warren Court's constitutional edifice—Race Relations, Reapportionment, and Rules of Criminal Procedure—though somewhat eroded, are still virtually intact" (1974, 35).[2] At the present time most judicial scholars would probably agree with the perceptive analysis of the Burger Court made recently by Charles M. Lamb and Stephen C. Halpern:

> All in all, it is difficult to label the Burger Court because of its mixed behavior regarding various issues. Still, several generalizations seem warranted. The Warren Court's liberalism in some areas of constitutional law was moderated by the Burger Court, but it was not expunged and replaced by an overarching conservative constitutional jurisprudence. While the Burger Court did decide a much smaller percentage of cases in favor of civil liberties claims, particularly in the 1980s, and did whittle at Warren Court reforms in some areas, it did not reverse the landmark civil liberties decisions for which the Warren Court is best known. Sometimes the Burger Court assumed a middle ground, serving up something to everyone (depending on the issue and the case). At other times it broke new liberal ground. (1991, 436–437)

Let us be more specific. In some areas, such as criminal procedure[3] and obscenity,[4] the Burger Court's conservative bent clearly manifested itself. For instance, the Warren Court's landmark decision of *Miranda v. Arizona*, 284 U.S. 436 (1966) was never overruled by the Burger Court, but it is fair to say that it was often significantly eroded. In 1977, for example, the Burger Court ruled that prosecutors may use at trial incriminating statements made by a witness in front of a grand jury even though the witness was never told that he was liable to be indicted; thus, tainted testimony before a grand jury can be used at trial even though the accused had not been advised of his *Miranda* rights.[5] As for the matter of obscenity, it, too, felt the effect of the Burger Court's chisel. Whereas the Warren Court had ruled in 1966 that the state could not outlaw sexually explicit material unless it was "*utterly* without redeeming social value" (*Memoirs v. Massachusetts*, 383 U.S. 413), the

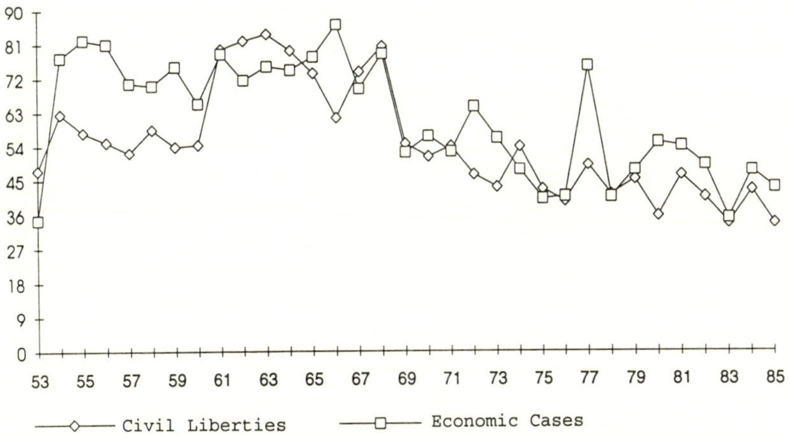

Figure 2-1. Percent liberal of Warren and Burger Courts' decisions, by term.

Burger Court made the prosecutor's task much easier. It ruled in 1973 that questionable material could be suppressed if it merely lacked "serious literary, artistic, political, or scientific value" (*Miller v. California*, 413 U.S. 15).

But to the delight (and perhaps surprise) of liberals, many of the Burger Court decisions expanded some of the Warren Court doctrines, and in some cases it carved out some new areas of liberal activism in realms that the Warren Court had ignored, such as abortion, sex discrimination, affirmative action, and busing.[6] Indeed, a major goal of President Reagan's judicial appointment strategy was the reversal of abortion rights spawned by the Burger Court in *Roe v. Wade* (1972), the 1970s most controversial decision.

Empirical Evidence for Liberal-Conservative Trends on the Burger Court

Using material taken from the U.S. Supreme Court Judicial Data Base, Jeffrey A. Segal and Harold J. Spaeth have sought to measure liberal-conservative trends on the Court in terms of the broad dimensions of civil liberties and economic cases (1989, 103–107). Table 2-2 presents the percentage of liberal decisions rendered in civil liberties and economic cases from 1953 through 1985—the last full year of the Burger Court. (The data in Table 2-2 are portrayed more vividly in Figure 2-1.) Further analysis of this data reveals that on civil liberties issues the liberal position prevailed on the Warren Court 65.9 percent of the time; for the Burger Court, the liberal win record dropped to 44.2 percent. For economic cases on the Warren Court

Table 2-2. Warren and Burger Courts' Liberal Decisions, by Term

			Civil Liberties			Economic Cases	
	Term		% Liberal	*n*		% Liberal	*n*
Warren Court	53		47.5	40		34.6	52
	54		62.5	40		77.4	31
	55		57.6	33		82.0	50
	56		55.0	60		80.9	47
	57		52.2	69		70.6	51
	58		58.3	48		70.0	60
	59		53.8	39		75.0	44
	60		54.3	70		65.2	46
	61		79.6	49		78.3	46
	62		81.8	55		71.4	56
	63		83.6	61		75.0	40
	64		79.2	48		74.1	27
	65		73.2	56		77.5	40
	66		61.4	70		86.1	68
	67		73.6	72		69.1	68
	68		80.3	76		78.3	23
Burger Court	69	$\bar{x}=50.4$	54.5	66	$\bar{x}=54.8$	52.2	23
	70		51.1	94		56.5	23
	71		53.8	104		52.4	42
	72		46.3	108		64.3	42
	73		43.0	100		55.9	34
	74		53.7	82		47.6	42
	75	$\bar{x}=42.1$	42.5	106	$\bar{x}=49.7$	40.0	35
	76		39.4	109		40.6	32
	77		48.8	82		75.0	48
	78		41.1	95		40.5	37
	79		45.1	91		47.5	40
	80		35.6	73		54.8	42
	81	$\bar{x}=39.3$	46.2	91	$\bar{x}=45.6$	53.8	39
	82		40.5	84		48.9	47
	83		33.7	104		35.0	40
	84		42.3	97		47.4	38
	85		33.7	101		42.9	21

the liberal position carried the day on the average of 72.8 percent, while for the Burger Court years this fell to 50.3 percent.

Looking at the trend over the Burger Court years, we can mark the ever-increasing conservative tide. Grouping the Burger Court into roughly three equal segments (1969–1974, 1975–1980, and 1981–1985), the percentage of liberal victories for civil liberties cases goes from 50.4 to 42.1 to 39.3. For economic cases the percentage of liberal triumphs drops from 54.8 to 49.7 to 45.6. As Segal and Spaeth note, the most persuasive explanation for this phenomenon was the appointment during this time frame of justices with clearly conservative judicial ideologies (1989, 103–107).

Empirical Evidence for Liberal-Conservative Trends on the District Courts During the Burger Court Years

To what extent was the momentum toward more conservative decisions mirrored at the trial court level during the Burger Court era? Despite the fact that district court jurists do not march in lockstep to the Supreme Court drummer, there is evidence that sooner or later ideological changes on the high court are reflected in trial court decision making.[7]

Table 2-3 reveals the percentage of liberal trial judge decisions by year for civil liberties issues and for labor and economic cases during the Burger Court era. More specifically, we look at the percentage of liberal victories for the years 1969 thruugh 1974, 1975 through 1980, and 1981 through 1985. While our categories are not precisely identical with those used in the Segal and Spaeth study, they are close enough for at least some initial, general comparisons in the trend in liberal-conservative voting for the same three intervals examined in Table 2-2.

Clearly, the conservative trend for civil liberties on the Supreme Court during the Burger years is reflected in the behavior of judges on the trial court bench. Between 1969 and 1975, 52 percent of district court decisions were in a liberal direction; this dropped to 48 percent during the next six-year interval and then declined modestly to 46 percent for the remainder of the Burger Court era.

The trend is roughly the same for cases involving economic and labor issues. Some 61 percent of these cases were liberal during the first six years of the Burger Court, whereas this figure dropped to 56 percent for the final eleven years of the Burger Court.[8]

Thus, in terms of a broad, macroanalysis of liberal-conservative judicial trends, the data suggest that the gradual shift to the right that characterized the Burger Court between 1969 and 1985 was also mirrored to a substantial degree by decision making on the trial court bench. For insight into why the shift was

Table 2-3. Percentage of Liberal Decisions Rendered by District Judges for the Categories of Civil Rights and Liberties and for Labor and Economic Regulation Under the Burger Court, 1969–1986

	Civil Rights and Liberties	Labor and Economic Regulation
1969–1974	52 (3,547)	61 (2,045)
1975–1980	48 (3,540)	56 (2,829)
1981–1986	46 (3,670)	56 (3,216)

less pronounced on the district courts than on the Supreme Court, we turn next to an examination of partisan effects on district court outcomes during this era.

Empirical Evidence for Liberal-Conservative Trends According to Judges' Party Affiliation

Just as the conservative trend on the Supreme Court between 1969 and 1986 was affected by the appointment of new justices,[9] so, too, is this likely to be the case on the trial court bench. But while the addition of conservative justices placed on the high court by ideologically conscious Republican presidents went unabated during this era, such was not the case at the district court level. Although President Carter had no opportunity to make any Supreme Court appointments during his four years in office, he did have the chance to pack about half the trial bench with staunchly liberal jurists.[10] With this fact in mind we pose this question: Was the movement to the right among trial judges between 1969 and 1986 primarily the product of more conservative decision making by Republican judges, or did Democrats on the bench begin to march to the same drummer? Did the liberal Johnson-Carter jurists fight a stiff rear-guard action during this time frame, or were they, too, forced more and more to swim with the ever-increasing conservative tide? Again we look to our empirical data for suggestions of an answer.

Table 2-4 strongly suggests that while Democratic judges are significantly more liberal than their GOP counterparts, they still moved with the overall ideological flow of the judiciary. For the three time frames of the Burger Court era, Republicans on civil rights and liberties cases decreased their percentage of support of the liberal position from 44 to 41 to 35. Their Democratic colleagues followed suit, as their liberal percentages dropped from 58 to 55 to 53 on this issue area. As for economic and labor issues, Republican jurists went from a 56 percent level of support to 50 for the re-

Table 2-4. Percentage of Liberal Decisions Rendered by Republican and by Democratic District Judges for the Categories of Civil Rights and Liberties and for Labor and Economic Regulation Under the Burger Court, 1969–1986

	Civil Rights and Liberties		Labor and Economic Regulation	
	Republicans	Democrats	Republicans	Democrats
1969–1974	44 (1,276)	58 (2,190) α=1.87	56 (855)	66 (1,153) α=1.71
1975–1980	41 (1,678)	55 (1,799) α=1.75	50 (1,404)	61 (1,377) α=1.60
1981–1986	35 (1,495)	53 (2,109) α=2.11	50 (1,370)	61 (1,782) α=1.65

maining eleven-year interval of the Burger Court. Democrats on the bench followed this pattern as their liberal percentage fell from 66 to 61 for both the 1975–1980 period and the following five-year interval.[11]

These data would suggest that the drift to right-of-center decision making by the Supreme Court during the Burger years had its impact on all judges regardless of their ideological orientations. While Democrats continued to opt for the liberal position when there was a sufficient amount of discretion in the cases to permit them to do so, still they were not oblivious to the new conservative judicial order as it slowly began to be articulated from the nation's highest tribunal. Nevertheless, the Democrats' most conservative eras for these two case categories were still more liberal than the Republicans' most liberal periods. Also, the decline in Republican liberalism was almost twice as great as the Democratic pullback.

LEVELS OF PARTISANSHIP DURING THE BURGER COURT ERA

In our earlier work on the subject of partisan voting by district court judges we observed the following: until fairly recent years the level of partisanship on the trial courts was minimal (Carp and Rowland 1983, chap. 2). Between 1933 and 1953 the difference between Democrats and Republicans on the bench was only 4 percentage points, that is, the liberalism score for Democrats was only 4 points higher than for judges with GOP backgrounds; the odds ratio was only 1.19. From 1953 through 1968, differences between the two groups became even smaller and almost random. Democrats outscored Republican judges on the liberalism index in ten of those sixteen years (the scores being identical in two of the years), but the average difference between the two sets of jurists was a mere 1 percent.[12] (The Democratic and Republican liberalism indices were, respectively, 41 and 40 percent, and the odds ratio was only 1.04.) It is little wonder that studies of U.S. trial court behavior conducted during the 1950s and 1960s concluded that there was very little correlation between political party affiliation and decision patterns, and, indeed, that the phenomenon was not worth further examination.

Beginning in 1969, however, a most interesting development began to appear: the tiny gap between Democrats and Republicans widened into a sizable chasm—some 17 percentage points by 1972 and a full 20 percent in 1984. Not only did Democrats score higher than Republicans for each year between 1969 and 1988, but the average difference was a more impressive 12 percent, whereas the disparity had been only 1 percent for the preceding sixteen years. (The odds ratio between 1969 and 1988 jumped to 1.61.)

What was to account for this abrupt and sustained surge of partisan voting that appeared in the late 1960s? At the time of our previous research we offered two general propositions to explain this phenomenon. First, "with the advent of the Burger Court, the trial court jurists could no longer count on the Supreme Court for as clear and unambiguous legal guidelines as they received from the Warren Court's more stable [albeit narrow] majority. With the decline of the fact-law congruence after 1968 the trial court judges became more free to take their decision-making cues from personal-partisan values rather than from guidelines set forth by the High Court" (1983, 37). Second, we hypothesized that the widening partisan gap (which was due mainly to a liberal surge among Democrats) was due to the impact of Lyndon Johnson's appointees to the federal bench. Johnson was a chief executive who, "unlike his predecessors, possessed both the desire *and* the political clout to put committed liberals on the district court bench, and it was in the late 1960s that the Johnson appointees began to make their impact felt among the lower federal judiciary" (1983, 37).

From the current vantage point, what reason is there to believe that the trend that began in 1969 continued throughout the entire era of the Burger Court (and beyond)? First, the evidence is fairly persuasive that between 1969 and 1988 the Burger Court was indeed sending off quite a mixed barrage of inconclusive, conflicting, and ambiguous ideological signals. As we have previously argued, this lack of clear, precise guidelines from the high court permits trial court judges much more discretion and leeway in their decision making than if the district judges were held to more exacting standards. As outlined earlier in this chapter, for some decisions the Burger Court seemed to move toward more conservative decision making while at other times and in other cases it appeared to move somewhat left of center. Moreover, there is more quantitative evidence that in recent decades the Court seems to have spoken with manifold and imprecise voices. This is manifested in the increasing number of five-to-four majorities, plurality decisions, and in the mounting number of concurring opinions. Putting this in historical perspective, scholar David M. O'Brien has noted,

> Whereas between 1801 and 1900 the average number of cases per term decided by a bare majority was one, between 1900 and 1937 it was four, between 1937 and 1955 about fourteen. During most of the Warren Court (1956–1969), sixteen cases a year were based on a five-to-four vote. The first three years of Burger's chief justiceship brought an average of more than eighteen five-to-four decisions, then the number of such decisions escalated dramatically, and continues to remain high: in 1979–1981, the average was twenty-seven per term; in 1983, twenty-six (17 percent) of the cases had the support of only a bare majority, and in Burger's last year on the Court (1985–1986) that number rose to forty-five (or 28 percent of all cases decided by written opinions). (1990, 312)

In terms of the number of plurality opinions, there were only ten of these all throughout the nineteenth century on the Supreme Court. Between 1901 and Chief Justice Warren's last year on the Court in 1969, there were only 51 opinions decided by less than an absolute majority. By contrast, between 1969 and 1986, when Warren Burger presided over the Supreme Court, there were some 116 plurality opinions—more than had been rendered by the high court in its past two-century history (O'Brien 1990, 313). This same trend is manifested in the increasing number of concurring opinions on the Supreme Court. Such opinions were uncommon for most of the nineteenth century and the early part of this century, but in recent decades their number has grown. In fact, the increase in concurring opinions has been the subject of much scholarly attention in recent years.[13]

In sum, the decline in consensual norms has devolved into a quagmire of doctrinal dissension. Looking at this entire phenomenon, noted Supreme Court observer David O'Brien has concluded, "Less agreement and more numerous and longer opinions invite uncertainty and confusion about the Court's rulings, interpretation of law, and policy-making" (1990, 322). Such an observation has even been made by a key member of the "offending" cohort, Justice William Rehnquist. In a moment of regretful candor he made the following statement while penning a dissent in the 1981 case of *Metromedia, Inc. v. San Diego:* "It is a genuine misfortune to have the Court's treatment of the subject be a virtual Tower of Babel, from which no definitive principles can be clearly drawn; and . . . I regret even more keenly my contribution to this judicial clangor, but find that none of the views expressed in the other opinions written in the case come close enough to mine to warrant the necessary compromise to obtain a Court opinion."[14]

In addition to confirming the mixed and uncertain ideological signals that characterized the Burger Court, a review of judicial appointment criteria during this same era indicates clearly that since the time of the Johnson administration there has been a pronounced tendency for district court appointees to be screened for their ideological purity. That is to say, the vast majority of district judges who sat during the Burger Court years were carefully selected for their commitments to fairly clear-cut policy preferences, attitudes, and values that mirrored those of the appointing president. While previous research has shown that Presidents Truman, Eisenhower, and Kennedy either did not choose (or lacked the political clout) to make ideologically based appointments, such was not the case with Presidents Johnson, Nixon, Carter, and Reagan,[15] whose judicial cohorts were chosen with a keen eye toward the ideological direction of their subsequent voting behavior.[16]

Finally, a third contributor to the increase of partisan effects has become apparent since this increase reemerged in the late 1960s: the evolution of fiduciary jurisprudence has engendered an unprecedented increase in factual ambiguity and a commensurate increase in the responsibility of judicial fact finders to resolve these ambiguities. For example, let us say that a minority employee is fired from her job. The employee claims that the real reason was gender and racial discrimination, while the employer asserts that the employee wasn't doing her job properly and had poor relations with her fellow employees. The judge in such a case would have to determine the facts by weighing such diverse matters as performance reports, eyewitness accounts of employee altercations, safety records, employment profiles of males who had been terminated, and so on. To the extent that such factual judgments are influenced by the judge's own personal background, experiences, and values, one would expect appointment-based differences to be reflected in partisan effects on these U.S. jurists—the primary fact-finders in the federal judiciary.

Given this combination of imprecise Supreme Court guidelines, ideologically based selection criteria, and increasing fact-finding discretion during the Burger Court years, there is every reason to believe that the increased partisan voting among district court judges that began after 1969 flourished throughout the entire era. Do the empirical data back up this hypothesis?

Table 2–5 reveals that the surge of partisan voting patterns that was unleashed after 1969 flourished throughout the entire Burger Court era. (Figure 2-2 illustrates the phenomenon more vividly.) During the first six years

Table 2-5. Level of Partisan Difference for all Cases Under the Burger Court, 1969–1986

	Democrats	Republicans	% Difference	Average[a]
1969	45 (467)	38 (146)	7	12
1970	44 (491)	35 (155)	9	α=1.59
1971	48 (515)	38 (234)	10	
1972	56 (510)	39 (265)	17	
1973	51 (437)	38 (252)	13	
1974	50 (412)	34 (241)	16	
1975	49 (404)	34 (243)	15	10
1976	48 (379)	39 (317)	9	α=1.54
1977	50 (321)	40 (308)	10	
1978	51 (429)	42 (377)	9	
1979	54 (362)	44 (277)	10	
1980	54 (400)	46 (196)	8	
1981	53 (329)	44 (145)	9	13
1982	51 (667)	37 (295)	14	α=1.74
1983	51 (683)	36 (356)	15	
1984	54 (356)	34 (201)	20	
1985	50 (526)	41 (413)	9	

[a] Overall average = 12%; overall odds ratio = 1.61.

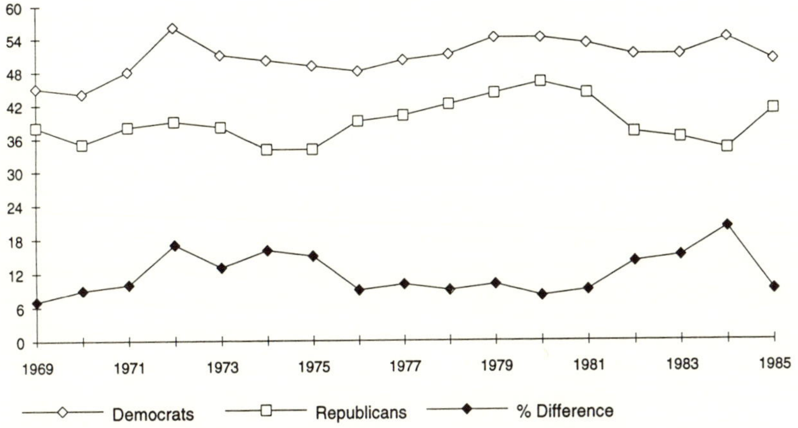

Figure 2-2. Level of partisan difference for all cases under the Burger Court, 1969–1986

of the Burger Court, 12 percentage points separated Democrats from Republicans on the bench. This figure pulled back slightly to 10 percent for the next six-year period but then jumped again to some 13 percent in the final segment of the Burger years. In fact, by 1984 the Democrats were some 20 percentage points more liberal than their GOP counterparts—the highest figure for which we have data. During the period 1981 through 1985, the odds ratio indicates that Democratic judges were 1.74 times more likely to vote for the liberal position than were judges from Republican backgrounds.

From 1969 through 1985 the coefficient of variation (which measures the relative entropy or homogeneity of aggregates that have different means) was a mere 0.32.[17] This indicates a great degree of stability in partisan voting patterns during these years; that is, Democrats were consistently more liberal in their decisional patterns than were Republicans.[18] (Between 1953 and 1969 the coefficient of variation had been 3.55, which indicated a great deal of fluctuation during this period; that is, in some years Republican judges were more liberal than Democrats while in other years the reverse was true.)

Is there any prospect that the solidifying of the Rehnquist Court's conservative majority after 1985 has served to decrease partisan voting among the district judges? That is, has the Court's more unified voice in recent years (coupled with Reagan judge majorities on most appellate court panels) reduced the ambiguity and freedom of maneuver that had permitted the high degree of partisan voting during the Burger Court years? Because our complete data set ends with the year 1986, we can only hint at what the answers to these questions might be. For the year 1986, the first year of the more unified and conservative Rehnquist Court, partisan voting differences among trial court judges fell to only 7 percentage points—the lowest since 1969. Although this reduction is consistent with ideological change at all levels of the federal judiciary, it would obviously be premature to declare this change an aberration or the beginning of a new trend. We can, however, clarify the patterns of partisan effects during the Burger era by looking more closely at the qualitative details of these effects.

While we have up to this moment explored partisan differences in terms of all cases decided, it is also instructive to examine this phenomenon in terms of more specific issue categories. Thus in Table 2-6 we present data for civil rights and liberties issues, for labor and economic regulation matters, and for criminal justice cases.

Looking at the first of these issue dimensions, civil rights and liberties, partisan voting differences have been substantial. Whereas the average difference for "all cases" was 12 percent, it is clear that this mean was surpassed for almost all years on issues pertaining to the Bill of Rights. In fact, during the last five years of the Burger Court the partisan difference was some 18 percent, and the odds ratio indicates that Democrats were 2.11 times more likely to take the liberal position on matters of civil rights and liberties than were their GOP colleagues. This is hardly surprising considering the "hottest" political-judicial issues of the past couple decades have been in areas such as abortion, busing, the right to privacy, prayer in the public schools, gender discrimination, and so on. In fact, partisan differences seem to have increased during the latter years of our sample for civil rights and liberties issues. That is all the more significant because, as we shall see momentarily, the partisan gap *decreased* markedly for the other issue dimensions we are about to examine.

As for labor and economic regulation cases, partisan differences were substantial but fairly stable during the Burger years. Some 10 percentage points separated the more liberal Democrats from their Republican colleagues during the first six years of the Burger Court, increasing modestly to 11 percent during all the remainder of the Burger years.

For criminal justice cases, 11 percentage points separated the Democrats from the Republicans during the first six years of the Burger Court. That is, Democrats were 1.68 times more likely to favor the position of the criminal defendant than were jurists coming from Republican ranks. This difference was cut almost in half during the next six-year interval (6 percent) and then increased a bit to 8 percent for the remainder of the Burger years. Interestingly, however, it was during the first full year of the Rehnquist Court that partisan differences were nipped in the bud. For the year 1986 Democrats were more liberal than Republican judges by only 1 percentage

Table 2-6. Level of Partisan Difference for the Issue Dimensions of Civil Rights and Liberties, Labor and Economic Regulation, and Criminal Justice Under the Burger Court, 1969–1986

	Civil Rights and Liberties		Labor and Economic Regulation		Criminal Justice	
	Democrats	Republicans	Democrats	Republicans	Democrats	Republicans
1969	61 (311)	47 (95)	62 (172)	64 (87)	31 (561)	22 (203)
1970	57 (420)	49 (136)	70 (172)	62 (68)	24 (532)	20 (236)
1971	56 (360)	45 (227)	65 (228)	59 (137)	34 (489)	20 (253)
1972	65 (389)	46 (249)	66 (197)	49 (198)	39 (329)	23 (240)
1973	56 (371)	43 (264)	65 (191)	51 (177)	35 (299)	22 (215)
1974	52 (339)	32 (305)	69 (143)	48 (188)	35 (294)	24 (218)
1975	53 (317)	33 (296)	61 (211)	49 (174)	35 (305)	23 (256)
1976	53 (313)	39 (330)	64 (207)	50 (230)	30 (268)	29 (256)
1977	56 (277)	40 (288)	54 (182)	50 (272)	38 (184)	27 (213)
1978	52 (327)	44 (367)	60 (293)	49 (313)	36 (228)	30 (220)
1979	59 (284)	43 (252)	64 (202)	52 (241)	36 (183)	31 (140)
1980	54 (281)	48 (145)	64 (282)	48 (174)	39 (175)	40 (107)
1981	55 (243)	43 (132)	59 (230)	55 (109)	39 (150)	32 (89)
1982	50 (548)	35 (325)	66 (451)	49 (294)	32 (302)	21 (170)
1983	52 (575)	33 (404)	62 (493)	49 (339)	31 (265)	27 (260)
1984	53 (300)	30 (241)	63 (237)	44 (227)	39 (123)	23 (120)
1985	53 (443)	34 (393)	56 (371)	53 (401)	35 (242)	31 (214)

	Democrats	Republicans	% Difference	Odds Ratio
	Summary: Civil Rights and Liberties			
1969–1974	58	44	14	1.88
1975–1908	55	41	14	1.75
1981–1986	53	35	18	2.11
	Summary: Labor and Economic Regulation			
1969–1974	66	56	10	1.15
1975–1980	61	50	11	1.60
1981–1986	61	50	11	1.83
	Summary: Criminal Justice			
1969–1974	33	22	11	1.68
1975–1980	36	30	6	1.36
1981–1986	35	27	8	1.41

point: for that year Democrats supported the criminal defendant 31 percent of the time but their GOP counterparts did so in 30 percent of the cases.

These findings would suggest that partisan effects are concentrated primarily in the realm of civil rights and liberties, and that partisan polarization in this realm is increasing. However, because each of these several broad categories includes relatively disparate subcategories (e.g., the right to privacy and freedom of the press within the general category of civil rights and liberties), the quality of these effects cannot be delineated accurately without narrowing the focus of our examination.

PARTISAN VOTING LEVELS IN RECENT YEARS

At this point we wish to examine partisan voting trends on specific issues for the most recent ten-year interval for which we have complete data: 1977 through 1986. In our previous major work in this realm we provided data ranking the level of partisanship on nineteen separate case types for the period 1933 through 1976. (A summary of that information is found in Appendix B.) For that forty-four-year period we concluded the following:

> Differences between judges from the two parties was greatest for cases involving state and local government efforts to regulate the economic lives of their citizens, race relations issues, disputes involving interpretation of the Fourteenth Amendment (excluding racial matters), and cases involving conviction for criminal offenses. Partisan differences were almost totally absent in cases involving the interpretation of Indian laws and treaties, suits brought by the secretary of labor (or the National Labor Relations Board, NLRB) under the Fair Labor Standards Act, disputes involving rent control and excessive profits, and, finally, cases dealing with reapportionment and the right to vote. (Carp and Rowland 1983, 37)

In the middle were eleven case categories that clustered around the themes of criminal justice, class discrimination, First Amendment freedoms, labor-management, and environmental protection issues.

With the exception of the category of local economic regulation, which we argued was a multidimensional "special case" (1983, 40–41), nine of the next ten items that invoked the greatest partisanship among the district judges dealt with themes of civil rights and liberties and of criminal justice. Such a finding, we argued, was consistent with our overall knowledge of judicial behavior, for with the decline of substantive due process after 1937 (at least at the national level), the federal courts have tended to be rather deferential toward the elected branches of government and to the various regulatory and administrative agencies regarding economic matters in general. Furthermore, since the 1930s Congress has legislated with relative precision in the realm of labor and economic relations, and this further limited the discretion of judges in these areas.

As for the issues of civil rights and liberties and of criminal justice, they seem to have evoked among trial court judges the same level of partisanship and divisiveness as they had among Supreme Court justices since the late

1930s. The "great" and controversial decisions of the Stone, Vinson, Warren, and Burger Courts focused mainly on Bill of Rights issues, and it is precisely those same issues that evoked the greatest partisan schisms among the justices. We concluded that federal district judges, like their high court counterparts, seemed to have split along "political" lines more often on criminal justice and on civil rights matters than they did with other types of cases.

Writing in 1983, we noted (as we might today) that

> fostering this propensity of the trial judges to vote along more partisan lines on Bill of Rights and Fourteenth Amendment issues is the fact that the state of the law seems to be less precise there than on issues for which there is a greater abundance of clear, unambiguous Supreme Court decisions and/or precise statutory guidelines, for example, labor and economic matters. The ambiguity (or perhaps the constant flux) of the law on matters such as the rights of criminal defendants, freedom of expression, equal protection of the law, and so on, reduces fact-law congruence and gives the district judges greater opportunity to respond to their personal (partisan) orientations in deciding cases than they have with other matters where their freedom of action was more circumscribed. (1983, 39)

With benefit of hindsight, we would add to the preceding conclusion that these case types inherently contain an inordinant amount of new, ambiguous fact situations. Nowhere, for example, is evidence less "factual" than in a complex search-and-seizure case. And it is difficult to imagine a more discretionary "factual" judgment than deciding whether an unemancipated minor is mature (the ultimate fiduciary standard) enough to circumvent parental notification laws.

Although the factual and legal ambiguity that encouraged partisanship from 1969 to 1973 does not appear to have diminished, our first major study of this overall topic ended in 1976, some eight years into the Burger Court era. What about the next decade? Table 2-7 brings the data set into more recent times. Table 2-7 presents, in order of magnitude, partisan voting levels of federal district judges on some 17,821 cases decided between 1977 and 1986. To explore what this table tells us, we shall pose and suggest answers to several general questions. First, what are the characteristics of those cases that rank high on this list—particularly as contrasted with those found at the bottom? That is, why should partisanship manifest itself profoundly in certain types of judicial questions and hardly at all in others?

The six issue categories that provoked the largest differences between Republicans and Democrats on the district courts appear to contain one or more of the following three characteristics. They provide the judge with an inordinate amount of fact-finding discretion and, concomitantly, relatively

Table 2-7. Liberal Decisions in Order of Magnitude of Partisan Voting Differences for Twenty-five Types of Cases, 1977–1987

	Overall (%)	Democrats (%)	Republicans (%)	Partisan Difference (%)	Odds Ratio
1. Race discrimination	46	58	30	28	3.19
2. Local economic regulation	68	80	57	23	3.01
3. Freedom of religion	50	60	36	24	2.71
4. Freedom of expression	59	67	51	16	1.98
5. Age discrimination	44	53	38	15	1.85
6. Criminal conviction	36	43	30	13	1.81
7. Excessive profits	57	64	50	14	1.77
8. Right to privacy	58	65	52	13	1.77
9. Fourteenth Amendment	39	45	32	13	1.77
10. U.S. commercial regulation	71	77	65	12	1.77
11. Rights of the handicapped	53	60	47	13	1.66
12. Women's rights	50	56	44	12	1.62
13. Union vs. company	52	58	46	12	1.62
14. Employee vs. employer	38	44	33	11	1.59
15. Alien petitions	45	49	39	10	1.52
16. Voting rights cases	48	54	44	10	1.47
17. Criminal court motions	34	38	30	8	1.44
18. Environmental protection	61	64	57	7	1.38
19. Indian rights and law	49	52	44	8	1.34
20. U.S. habeas corpus pleas	32	35	30	5	1.23
21. NLRB vs. union	64	65	61	4	1.20
22. Union member vs. union	38	39	37	2	1.08
23. State habeas corpus pleas	29	30	28	2	1.08
24. NLRB vs. employer (Fair Labor Standards Act)	68	67	68	–1	.95

little fear of being overruled by an appellate court; they consist of issues that in recent years have been at the center of heated partisan debate either in the judicial arena or in the larger body politic; or (relatedly) they figure prominently in the president's judicial appointment criteria.

The issues of race discrimination, freedom of religion (free exercise and establishment), and freedom of expression have all evoked strong divisions between Republicans and Democrats—not only on the Supreme Court but also among presidential and congressional candidates. Topics such as busing, quotas and affirmative action, church-state relations, governmental aid to private and parochial schools, flag burning, First Amendment rights of high school students, and so on have caused significant discord among members of the Supreme Court and between Americans of liberal and conservative persuasions. Moreover, cases like these typically present a unique set of facts to be fed to an ambiguous legal standard. Was busing, for example, the least disruptive remedy for de jure segregation? It is not surprising then that these same issues should provoke high levels of partisanship among U.S. trial judges.

Several of these partisanship-evoking case categories share a second characteristic: many involve primarily factual determinations that are seldom overturned by courts of appeals. This is particularly true for the lion's share of race discrimination cases, questions of local economic regulation, age discrimination, and conviction for a criminal offense. In our data sample a huge portion of the cases dealing with racial and age discrimination deal with situations where someone was not hired (or promoted) to a particular job or was fired from a position in which the litigant claimed the reason was the employer's discriminatory intent. Conversely, the employer argued that there were legitimate, nondiscriminatory reasons for the employment decision that clearly overrode the appearance of bias.

For the most part such cases boil down to the basic question of whom the judge is to believe. (If the evidence were overwhelming one way or the other, it would probably have been settled out of court.) The trial judge is called on to seek out the truth and make a factual determination depending largely on who appears to be the more credible. Very, very seldom are such determinations overruled by an appellate court. Likewise, the decision to convict someone for a criminal offense is largely a factual determination that judges make with little fear of being overruled unless there happens to be some unusual, overriding legal determination that he or she was obliged to make at trial (not a common phenomenon). To reiterate what noted U.S. trial judge Constance Motley once observed: "The power [of the trial judge] is maximized when the outcome hinges on questions of fact. The judge can rely on those facts that persuade him and explain his decision in light of those facts. . . . If there is an evidentiary basis for the judge's interpretation of the facts, this interpretation, unlike interpretations of the law, is virtually immune from appellate review."[19]

These observations are consistent with the thrust of our book *Policymaking and Politics*, namely, that when judges perceive that they have a great deal of uncensored discretion in deciding a given case, they will be more likely to give vent to their own personal set of attitudes. Judges who know from experience that their discretion is not likely to be challenged by an appellate body are more likely to act on the bench as Republicans and Democrats than are jurists whose decision making is bridled by clear-cut legal guidelines monitored by vigilant appeals courts.

What about cases involving local economic regulation, the category that involves primarily the attempt of a state or local governmental body to regulate the economic freedom of businesses and individuals? The appearance of this variable near the top of our partisanship list should appear as an anomaly for at least two reasons. First, because we have previously argued in this chapter that the main zone of judicial combat (at least since the late 1930s) has been with Bill of Rights and criminal justice matters and not in the economic realm. Second, local regulation of the economy has certainly not been an issue that has significantly entered into the national political debate, nor have there been many recent significant Supreme Court decisions that have evoked partisan schisms in this policy realm. Why, then, do U.S. trial judges show their true partisan colors so vividly on matters of local economic regulation? The answer to this query takes some effort to articulate; an administrative law text by Robinson and Gellhorn provides the first clue:

> Although . . . the Supreme Court has now withdrawn from its erstwhile scrutiny of federal and state regulatory schemes . . . it would be a mistake to suppose that that is an end to the issue of constitutionality. Constitutional bird-watchers who have concentrated their gaze upon the United States Constitution, and upon the federal courts have frequently overlooked the path of state constitutional law, and the state courts which apply it. Sparrows they may be—and, to a crowd of eagle observers, drab and dull—state courts nevertheless can and do, exercise a significant and distinctive constitutional role in the area of economic legislation. . . . In the economic arena, the withdrawal of the United States Supreme Court from the field has left the way open for state courts to impose, under state constitutions, restrictions beyond what is mandated by federal law and Supreme Court doctrine. (1974, 624)

Thus the doctrine of substantive due process is still alive and well at the state level in many parts of the country, and it is still a battleground of some importance for economic conservatives and liberals. But what does this have to do with *federal* judges? We think the linkage comes in part from the 1938 Supreme Court decision of *Erie v. Tompkins* (304 U.S. 64). In their casebook *American Constitutional Law*, Mason and Beaney note:

> In matters of purely local importance the federal courts are supposed to follow decisions of state courts, but as a practical matter they are bound by the rule chiefly in cases dealing with rights in real property. . . . The Judicial Code now provides that "the laws of the several states . . . shall be regarded as rules of decision in trials at common law in the courts of the United States." Equity, admiralty, and criminal cases are excluded from the operation of this clause, and its scope was further limited by construing the word "laws" to mean only state statutes. However, since the judicial interpretation of a statute is an integral part of

that statute, federal courts follow the decisions of the highest court of the state in construing a state statute. (1978, 7–8)

Given this reality and the fact that virtually all U.S. trial judges practice law in the state where they hold court and have other powerful links with the local culture, it is perhaps not surprising that local economic regulation is second from the top in terms of generating partisan decision making (Richardson and Vines 1970, chap. 4). A district judge may not feel free to give way to partisan values when it comes to determining the validity of an NLRB order for a union to end a secondary boycott. The same judge, however, may sense a much greater discretion when it comes to determining whether a local government's regulation of a business constitutes a "taking of property" in violation of the due process clause. Finally, there is evidence that when no substantial federal issue is at stake, there is a strong tendency for the appeals courts to defer to the judgment of the "local specialist," that is, the federal district judge who has been called on to interpret his or her own state's law.[20] Again we reiterate our thesis that in areas where district judges perceive that they have ample discretion, free from very strict appellate court scrutiny, their voting patterns are more likely to reflect their partisan political values and orientations. It is for these reasons that local economic regulation is an area of fairly active partisan decision making.

As a rebuttal to the preceding analysis, one might argue thus: While it is true that the judiciary and the nation have been divided in recent years on issues of race and First Amendment matters, so, too, have they been divided on topics such as the right to privacy, discrimination against women, and environmental protection. Why do these issues not rank higher on the list than eighth, twelfth, and eighteenth, respectively?

We do not presume to answer fully this interesting but formidable question, but we would point in the direction of a credible response. First of all, public opinion polls and samples over the years have demonstrated clearly that Americans who are most committed to the right to privacy, to gender equality, and to protection of the environment are for the most part well-educated, upper-middle-class, white Americans. Such a profile mirrors very accurately not only the constituency of the Republican Party but also of federal district judges in general.[21] Despite the fact that official Republican rhetoric on these issues tends to be conservative, GOP leaders are well aware that much of their more elite constituency holds attitudes and values on these topics that are more akin to the positions of the Democratic Party.

Furthermore, there is no reason to assume a priori that Democratic judges as a group would automatically be substantially more liberal on the issues of privacy, gender discrimination, and environmental protection. Neither Presidents Kennedy, Johnson, nor Carter emphasized any of these issues in their judicial appointment criteria (with the possible exception of Carter on the matter of sex discrimination). Furthermore, as for environmental protection, many of the Democratic judges were sponsored by home-state senators who were under pressure not to pursue the environmentalist cause. For example, it is common knowledge that labor unions representing Detroit auto workers and Pennsylvania coal miners have strongly urged their states' senators to softpedal environmental legislation that might endanger their jobs. Such senators would have been unlikely to sponsor candidates for judicial office who were at the forefront of the environmentalist cause.[22] Because of all these factors it is perhaps not terribly surprising that Republican trial judges are only modestly more conservative than their Democratic colleagues on these issues.

So much for the primary and secondary partisan battlegrounds. What characterizes those issue dimensions where partisanship is almost void, and do our earlier explanatory propositions shed any light on cases that do not reveal partisan cleavages? There are three types of cases that manifested virtually no partisan voting patterns: union members versus the union, state habeas corpus pleas, and suits brought by the NLRB or the secretary of labor against an employer (usually under the Fair Labor Standards Act).

The category of "union member versus the union" was initially chosen to be part of our data set in the belief that Democrats would more likely favor the "underdog" in a dispute in which a union member was at loggerheads with his union. Republicans, on the other hand, were hypothesized to be somewhat more deferential to the established power structure, in this case to the union leadership. Indeed, this is what our data set reveals, along with a previous study that covered the years 1933 to 1977. (Four percentage points differentiated Republicans from Democrats during that period, and the odds ratio was 1.14 [Carp and Rowland 1983, 38].) But the partisan differences are terribly modest, as intuition suggests they would be. While Democrats (liberals) often do sympathize with the "underdog," they are going to be under enormous cross pressure when such underdogs confront a traditional racehorse of economic liberalism—organized labor unions. Likewise, traditional Republican deference toward organized authority may pale to almost nothingness when confronted with an intraunion dispute for which the instinctive response might well be: "A plague on both your houses."

State habeas corpus pleas likewise engender very little in the way of partisan differences. This may come as something of a surprise, since the partisan effects on other types of criminal justice cases create an expectation of partisan differences for this category, and indeed for the study that covered the years 1933 through 1977 this issue category did evoke a modest cleavage between Republicans and Democrats on the bench. (There was a 5 percent difference for those years, with an odds ratio of 1.32 [Carp and Rowland 1983, 38].) The reason partisan differences have diminished over the past decade and a half is that the Supreme Court has significantly restricted access to the federal courts on matters involving state court criminal proceedings.[23] In doing so the Court has significantly narrowed the discretion of federal district judges to involve themselves with state habeas corpus pleas. Thus, while the judges' partisan spirit may have been willing, the opportunities to manifest partisan values and attitudes simply eluded them.

As for the matters of suits by the NLRB or the secretary of labor against an employer (largely Fair Labor Standard Act cases), this, too, in theory should have rung the partisan chimes of the judges, but in fact it did not. Indeed, on this single variable Republican jurists were in fact 1 percent more liberal than their Democratic colleagues. Why the anomaly? We suggest this explanation.

For most of the years covered by this analysis the secretary of labor and/or a majority of the NLRB were Republicans. These GOP regulators, who were often enforcing the policies of the judge's appointing president, were in litigation against entities that have historically been part of the Republican mainstream—businessmen and manufacturers. It is reasonable to hypothesize that the district judges were unable to perceive a keen liberal-conservative dimension in suits between such parties. Just as in litigation that pitted union members against their union, which blurred the liberal-conservative distinction, likewise we suggest that U.S. district judges were under equal cross pressures here.

In past decades when secretaries of labor under liberal, Democratic presidents have gone against conservative businessmen for allegedly violating the rights of their employees, district judges had little problem separating the sheep from the goats. But when regulators are conservative Republicans, such distinctions are by no means clear—either to public law theorists or, apparently, to the judges themselves, and partisan voting patterns melt away.[24] Finally, one might add here that since the passage of the Fair Labor Standards Act in 1937, the definition of what are and are not "unfair labor practices" has become highly precise and refined. Thus, there may well be increasingly less room for maneuver and judicial discretion in this arena even if the judges were inclined instinctively to favor one party over another.

THE PARTISAN IMPACT OF THE APPOINTING PRESIDENT

While stressing that Democrats often behave differently as judges than do Republicans, we should not lose sight of the fact that how and why the judges got to the bench are equally important factors in the political equation. Potential jurists are sifted and weighed on political scales by home-state senators and their staffs, by the Justice Department, and by the president and his staff. Moreover, as noted in our analysis of partisan effects, presidents from the same party often nominated judges on the basis of different policy preferences. For example, opposition to abortion rights, which was a centerpiece of Reagan's appointment criteria, was nowhere to be found among the law-and-order values that dominated Nixon's criteria. Thus, to explore fully the effect of partisanship on trial court outcomes, we must at the very least also examine the impact of the chief executive, who has the legal mandate to nominate candidates to the district courts.

We will use the resources of our database here to achieve several objectives, all of which parallel the preceding analysis of partisan effects: to update our overview of the impact of the appointing president from the days of Woodrow Wilson to those of George Bush; and then to examine the presidential appointment effects of four recent presidents (Nixon, Ford, Carter, and Reagan) on the issue dimensions of criminal justice, civil rights and liberties, and labor and economic regulation. We shall then explore in greater detail the appointment effects of Presidents Carter and Reagan on twenty-three specific issue categories. Finally, we shall offer some tentative assessment of the impact that President Bush will have on the ideological orientation of the federal judiciary.

Presidential Appointment Effects on the U.S. Trial Courts for the Past Eighty Years

Table 2-8 brings up to date our continuing research that has sought to map the effect of appointing presidents on the output of the district judges they appoint. We will not discuss here the separate liberalism scores of each individual presidential cohort because we have already done that elsewhere.[25] Rather, we would reiterate our thesis, now bolstered with more recent data, that across time the raw numbers continue to tell us something meaningful about the centers of gravity of the two principal political parties. For example, we compare the liberalism scores of Presidents Wilson, Johnson, and Carter (51, 52, and 53, respectively) with those of Presidents Eisenhower, Nixon, and Reagan (38, 39, and 36, respectively), and we see at once that the values of the nominator can and do make a difference in the way decisions are subsequently made on the trial bench. The appointees of Democratic presidents are clearly more liberal in their decision making than are judges chosen by Republican chief executives.[26]

There are, of course, methodological problems in placing too much emphasis on these precise liberalism numbers. For example, the case mixture

Table 2-8. Liberal Decisions for All Cases for the Appointees of Presidents Wilson Through Bush

Appointing President	%	*n*
Woodrow Wilson	51	95
Warren Harding	42	538
Calvin Coolidge	43	693
Herbert Hoover	42	1,068
Franklin Roosevelt	47	3,076
Harry Truman	40	4,341
Dwight Eisenhower	38	4,457
John Kennedy	41	5,156
Lyndon Johnson	52	7,975
Richard Nixon	39	7,944
Gerald Ford	44	1,724
Jimmy Carter	53	6,015
Ronald Reagan	36	2,628
George Bush	33	177

has varied greatly over time (Baum 1988). As noted in chapter 1, prior to the 1940s most federal court cases dealt with economic and labor matters, and few civil rights and liberties cases found their way to the U.S. trial courts; but during the past several decades these courts have focused more and more on Bill of Rights and Fourteenth Amendment issues. Also, definitions of "liberalism" and "conservatism" have varied to some degree over the years. For instance, prior to about 1952 liberals were much more supportive of states' rights and of the police power of the states than they have been in more recent decades. Likewise, a judge who was liberal when confronted with flagrant de jure segregation in the 1960s might, without changing her own values, appear conservative when confronted with busing as a remedy for that segregation ten years later. Or one might note that at one time it was Democratic dogma to support government regulation of the economy, but at least since the presidency of Jimmy Carter this traditional distinction has been blurred. Still, we think the indices do provide some genuine insight into differences in the impact of the appointing president across time.[27]

The Appointment Effects of Presidents Nixon, Ford, Carter, and Reagan

We shall now examine the effect of four recent presidents on the general issue dimensions of criminal justice, civil rights and liberties, and labor and economic regulation. Table 2-9 illustrates vividly that to a very large degree modern presidents have obtained the kind of judiciaries they have sought after, or at least that their district judges mirror to an impressive degree the values and attitudes of the appointing president. Richard Nixon's law-and-

Table 2-9. Liberal Decisions for Three Categories of Cases for the Appointees of Presidents Nixon Through Reagan

Appointing President	Criminal Justice %	Criminal Justice *n*	Civil Rights and Liberties %	Civil Rights and Liberties *n*	Labor and Economic Regulation %	Labor and Economic Regulation *n*
Richard Nixon	27	2,298	40	3,180	49	2,466
Gerald Ford	37	385	40	673	52	666
Jimmy Carter	39	1,361	53	2,544	61	2,110
Ronald Reagan	28	534	31	1,096	47	998
George Bush	33	40	24	67	43	70

order theme in the 1968 election has been manifested in the conservative voting patterns of his district court appointees on the issue of the rights of criminal defendants; his cohort opts for the liberal side of this issue dimension only 27 percent of the time. Gerald Ford was much less associated with the "get tough on crime" theme, and his appointees have a liberalism score that is not far from that of Carter appointees (37 and 39 percent, respectively.) The law-and-order cry was taken up again by Ronald Reagan in the 1980 campaign, and his judicial cohorts decide for the criminal defendants only 28 percent of the time.

The issue dimension of civil rights and liberties likewise reveals much in our contrast of presidential ideologies. The Nixon and Ford judges take the liberal position in this area 41 percent of the time, but this increases to 53 percent with the Carter cohort. Then, not unexpectedly, the Reagan jurists move clearly to the right of center with a liberalism score of only 31 percent.

Finally, the dimension of labor and economic regulation offers less evidence for independent presidential appointment effects. Nixon's team supports the regulator and/or the worker in 49 percent of the reported cases, and the Ford jurists do so 52 percent of the time. Then, true to form, there is a dramatic jump in the liberalism index with the judges chosen by Jimmy Carter; his cohorts take the liberal position in 61 percent of the cases. The conservative reaction with the Reagan judges is, by contrast, similar to the reactions of other Republican cohorts, as his cohort votes in a liberal direction only 47 percent of the time.

We now compare the voting patterns of the Carter and Reagan cohorts on twenty-three specific issue types. The data in Table 2-10 provide the most vivid impression yet of how the appointees of two different presidents may manifest quite divergent styles in their authoritative allocation of values. There is no question about whose judicial cohort is more liberal when one compares the decisional patterns of the Carter and Reagan teams. On each of twenty-three separate types of cases the Carter jurists are to the left of the Reagan cohort. The overall odds ratio tells us that for any given case

Table 2-10. Liberal Decisions in Order of Magnitude of Differences Between Carter and Reagan Appointees for Twenty-three Case Types

	Carter % Liberal	Reagan % Liberal	Difference (%)	Odds Ratio[a]
1. Race discrimination	78	18	60	6.73
2. Right to privacy	78	45	33	4.39
3. Local economic regulation	81	58	23	3.05
4. Freedom of expression	59	39	20	2.32
5. Criminal conviction	46	25	21	2.55
6. Voting rights cases	58	36	22	2.44
7. Fourteenth Amendment	45	26	19	2.37
8. Freedom of religion	59	39	20	2.32
9. Alien petitions	53	33	20	2.28
10. Women's rights	56	36	20	2.27
11. Union vs. company	61	43	18	2.08
12. Union member vs. union	43	28	15	2.00
13. Indian rights and law	56	40	16	1.91
14. U.S. commercial regulation	77	65	12	1.84
15. U.S. habeas corpus pleas	37	25	12	1.76
16. Criminal court motions	44	31	13	1.73
17. Employee vs. employer	45	33	12	1.67
18. Rights of the handicapped	58	46	12	1.62
19. Age discrimination	50	40	10	1.52
20. State habeas corpus pleas	31	24	7	1.45
21. NLRB vs. employer (Fair Labor Standards Act)	68	63	5	1.26
22. Environmental protection	65	61	4	1.20
23. NLRB vs. union	63	60	3	1.13

[a] Overall odds ratio = 1.96

a Carter judge is almost twice as likely to opt for the liberal position than is a colleague chosen by Ronald Reagan.

For cases dealing with racial minority discrimination the difference between the behavior of the two presidential cohorts is astonishing. The solid support that black voters gave to Jimmy Carter in his bids for the presidency were not without consequence in the way the Carter team responded to the judicial pleas of minority litigants. Carter jurists upheld the minority position in an overwhelming 78 percent of the reported cases, while Reagan judges did so only 18 percent of the time. Thus the odds that a Carter judge would opt for the minority position were some 6.73 times higher than for someone nominated by Ronald Reagan.

The right to privacy also differentiates the two presidential cohorts. A Carter jurist is some 4.39 times more likely to find a violation of one's right to privacy as a Reagan colleague. (Recall that in Table 2-7 the right to privacy ranked a more distant eighth place when all Republicans were compared with all Democrats on the bench.) Also noteworthy is the fact that at the state and local level Carter judges were much more likely to vote in favor of the regulator than were Reagan jurists—81 percent versus 58 percent. Here, however, the Carter and Reagan cohorts behave about the same as their other Democratic and Republican colleagues. (Table 2-7 reveals that after race discrimination cases, local economic regulation manifested the second most significant differentiation between Democratic and GOP judges.) Finally, we note that on the issue of age discrimination the Carter and Reagan jurists are *more similar* in their voting behavior than are Democrats and Republicans generally. This issue category ranked fifth in terms of partisan intensity when all judges were compared, but in a contest between the Carter and Reagan cohorts the category assumed only nineteenth out of twenty-three places.

For some issues the sparring between the two presidential cohorts was less dramatic. In general the categories that ranked lowest in terms of partisan conflict when all judges were compared (Table 2-7) were about the same when the Carter cohort was contrasted with the Reagan team. Suits between the NLRB and an employer (often involving the Fair Labor Standards Act), environmental protection cases, and disputes between the NLRB and a labor union invoked only modest differences between the two presidential cohorts.

The one surprise here, we think, is the paucity of difference with cases involving protection of the environment. Carter's 65 percent liberalism score is about in keeping with the overall score of 64 for Democrats. However, the Reagan cohort index of 61 is somewhat higher than the overall GOP support score for environmental protection—57 percent. The direction and magnitude of this finding are consistent with a recently published study of differences in appellate judges' voting patterns on environmental issues. In an analysis of several hundred Clean Air Act and Clean Water Act cases, William Kovacic concluded that appellate "judges appointed by President Reagan are more inclined than those judges appointed by President Carter to adopt positions that either narrow the application of existing pollution abatement requirements or discourage the recognition of new abatement obligations" (1991b, 672). However, Kovacic also noted that while the Reagan judges voted more conservatively on environmental issues than did Carter jurists, the difference was "not by the dramatic margin often predicted in evaluations of the Reagan administration's judicial selection process" (1991b, 680).

Do these findings cast doubt on our arguments for presidential appointment effects? We suggest that one possible answer for this supposed anomaly can be found in the public opinion literature suggesting that support for environmental protection is not a clear-cut partisan issue. In fact, many studies reveal that persons most supportive of the environment are upper-middle-class, college-educated whites—the very heart of the Republican constituency. Furthermore, while citizens who consider themselves "strong" liberals and conservatives disagree on many issues, disagreement tends to be rather modest when it comes to supporting increased federal government efforts to improve the environment.[28] Finally, we would note that while Carter and Reagan judicial candidates were screened for their ideological purity, the screening tended to focus on issues of civil rights and liberties—not the candidates' views on the environment. Add to these extralegal reasons the fact that many of these environmental cases were filed by the Reagan administration's Justice Department, and it is not too surprising that the differences are very modest between the Carter and Reagan judicial cohorts. This is in keeping with the ideological centers of gravity of the two political parties in the recent past and also consistent with our knowledge of the criteria by which the Carter and Reagan judicial candidates were screened.[29] It also reflects the fact that for many cases Reagan jurists were responding to environmental claims as defined and presented by the Reagan administration.

An Assessment of President Bush's Impact on the Federal Judiciary

Because the size of our sample of Bush appointees is not large, we approach our conclusions here with some caution.[30] Still it is noteworthy that with a liberalism index of 33 percent, the Bush judicial team is the most conservative of all the presidential cohorts for which we have data.[31] Is such a finding surprising, given our knowledge of presidential effect on the behavior of their judicial cohorts? To explore this phenomenon we would restate our four-part model for predicting the impact of the appointing president on the subsequent output of his trial court judges.[32]

For a president to have a significant impact on the orientation of the district courts, he first of all must possess a firm commitment to make ideologically based appointments. Without a strong and consistent policy of nominating judges who mirror his ideological values, there will obviously be no reflection of these values in the subsequent behavior of his trial judge nominees. It is meaningful to make this observation because not all presidents have ranked ideology terribly high in their judicial selection criteria. For instance, President Truman's primary concern when appointing judges was to select persons who had remained loyal to him in the 1948 campaign. In that election Truman was deserted on the right by the Dixiecrats who jumped on Strom Thurmond's bandwagon and by the Progressive Party on the left, formed by Democrats who left Truman for Henry Wallace. As president, when Truman had a judicial vacancy to fill, he was much more concerned with the nominee's past loyalty to him than he was with any divinations about the candidate's ideological behavior on the bench. Thus, the Truman cohort became quite a mixed bag of liberals and conservatives who for whatever reasons had hitched their wagons to his winning star. Likewise, there is the example of President Eisenhower, who was an almost apolitical man for whom ideological purity counted little. For him "experience" and "solid common sense" were ranked high in making judicial appointments, and as a consequence, his judicial cohort, like Truman's, lacked a clear-cut ideological bent (as is now common knowledge). What about George Bush?

President Bush moved very slowly in making appointments to the federal judiciary, and in fact some court watchers referred to his appointment process as a "paralysis." University of Massachusetts political scientist Sheldon Goldman noted that those who ran the Justice Department under Bush suffered from a "lack of focus" and that they were "torn between different imperatives. The Reagan administration knew what it wanted and went out and got it."[33] Simple raw data support this analysis: the Senate confirmed only fifteen Bush appointments to the federal bench in 1989, compared with forty-two in 1988, the last full year of Ronald Reagan's presidency. After that, the lag between the number of vacancies on the federal bench and the number Bush bothered to fill continued to grow. At the end of his presidency there were ninety unfilled vacancies on the district court bench—almost a fifth of the total number of authorized judgeships!

Putting aside the low priority President Bush gave to his lower court vacancies, what can one say about the ideological and personal profile of the Bush cohort? In his summary of the Bush judges Sheldon Goldman observed:

> The Bush administration, building upon the Reagan legacy, particularly with Supreme Court and appeals court appointments, but also to some extent with district court appointments, sought to transform the federal judiciary. Liberal activists in the tradition of Earl Warren, William Brennan, and Thurgood Marshall were not welcome. . . . [T]here is a body of literature that suggests that the Reagan judges on the whole have had a decisional impact that has made the federal bench far more conservative than when Reagan took office. It is reasonable to expect that on the whole . . . the Bush appointees will have a similar effect. (1993, 296)

What Goldman said about Bush's first two-year cohort was largely true of the entire judicial team: the "overwhelming proportion of appointees . . . [are] middle-aged, well-to-do white male Republicans" (1991, 294–306). Both empirical and anecdotal evidence reveals that the Bush team consists largely of conservative, upper-income white males who have worked with the larger law firms and who hold conservative social and political values. Not atypical is the following newspaper report about a Bush appointment to the district court bench in Texas in the summer of 1989. Replacing a liberal, black female appointed by President Carter (Gabrielle McDonald) is John D. Rainey, a conservative, white male with long-standing right-of-center credentials. The report quoted the state's Republican senator who "helped" Bush with the selection as saying that Rainey "is a conservative and a believer in strict construction of the Constitution."[34]

In appointing unabashed conservatives to the bench, President Bush kept the promise made to the nation during his first presidential campaign. In a subtle attack on judicial liberalism (code-named "activism"), Bush told the American Judicature Society, "I am firmly committed to appointing judges who are dedicated to interpreting the law as it exists, rather than legislating from the bench" (1988, 77).

Returning to our original question about Bush's willingness to make strong ideologically based judicial appointments, the evidence seems to be that he did possess such a commitment. Although he was somewhat lackadaisical in filling the lower court vacancies that became available to him, the empirical evidence indicates that the Bush cohort continues to march to the conservative drumbeat first sounded by his predecessor, Ronald Reagan.

Besides a commitment to make ideologically based appointments, our model suggests that before a president can have any measured success in this regard he must have the opportunity to make a significant number of such appointments. For example, Gerald Ford's short tenure in the White House deprived him of the opportunity to make his mark on the judiciary, and President Carter's lack of an opportunity to make a Supreme Court appointment handicapped his effectiveness in this regard. On the other hand, when Presidents Kennedy and Carter were first elected, friendly Democratic Congresses created 71 and 152 new district judgeships, respectively, thus giving these presidents ample potential to make their ideological mark in the filling of these vacancies.

How did George Bush fare in this regard? In 1990 Congress passed a "Judgeships Act," which gave the president seventy-four new federal district court positions (and eleven for the courts of appeals) to fill. That is not an overwhelming number, but it represents better than a 12 percent increase in the number of existing judgeships. And as Sheldon Goldman has noted, "George Bush, in just one term, has left a judicial legacy that will last well into the next century. . . . To the federal courts of general jurisdiction Bush made 187 lifetime appointments (two Supreme Court justices, 37 appeals court judges, and 148 district court judges)" (1993, 296). Thus the president possessed both the desire and the capacity to make a very real impact on the federal judiciary.

A third criteria for presidential capacity to make an imprint on the judiciary is whether he possesses the political clout (primarily vis-à-vis the Senate and its Judiciary Committee) to obtain confirmation for his ideologically based appointments. We recall that President Kennedy's liberal bent was often thwarted by the powerful chair of the Senate Judiciary Committee, Senator James Eastland of Mississippi. With the support of other conservative senators, Eastland often blocked outright some of Kennedy's potential nominees thought to be too liberal for the senator's taste, or he was able to force Kennedy into a sort of judicial horse trade whereby Kennedy was able to appoint a liberal to the bench only in return for a presidential promise to appoint a countervailing conservative-segregationist.[35] Likewise, President Hoover's choice for a position on the Supreme Court, John J. Parker, was defeated in the Senate by a mere two-vote margin. Many observers feel that had not the depression taken Hoover's popularity by the throat, Parker's nomination might have been given the nod by the Senate.

What of President Bush's political clout? It is true that he faced a Democratic majority in the Senate and in its Judiciary Committee, and that the Committee's chairman, Joseph Biden, was a liberal. This contrasts sharply with the Democratic majority enjoyed by President Carter and the Republican majority enjoyed by President Reagan for the first six years of his presidency. Still, Bush more often than not got his way in making judicial selections, although it is clear that Bush's success in this regard decreased after his troubles in securing Supreme Court Justice Clarence Thomas's confirmation. Court watcher Sheldon Goldman explains, "Of the 65 individuals nominated to lifetime district judgeships on or before October 24, 1991 [the time of the flap over the Thomas nomination], all but three were eventually confirmed, a rate of more than 95 percent. But of the 19 subsequent nominations in 1991, only 14 were confirmed, a 74 percent confirmation rate. Of the 59 individuals nominated in 1992 for lifetime district judgeships, only 24, or 41 percent, were confirmed" (1993, 284). Thus, the impact of President Bush's political clout vis-à-vis the Senate and its Judiciary Committee was a somewhat mixed one.

Our model suggests one final hurdle before a chief executive can have a significant ideological impact on the subsequent "output" of the judiciary—the current judicial-philosophical orientation of the other district and appellate court judges and justices with whom the president's new appointees must serve. Since U.S. federal judges serve lifetime appointments during good behavior, a president must accept the composition and orientation of the judiciary as it has been willed to him by his predecessors. What this means in practical terms is that if a new president faces a judiciary whose trial and appellate court judges already share his basic ideology, the impact of his new judicial appointees will be more immediate and substantial. Conversely, if a new chief executive is confronted with a majority of trial and appellate jurists who are committed to values radically different from his own, the impact of the subsequent judicial appointments will be much weaker and slower to materialize. New judges obviously must respect the existing judicial paradigm and are not free to make precedential decisions at will, lest they risk being overruled by a higher court.[36]

When Franklin Roosevelt became president in 1933, he was confronted with a lower-court judiciary that had been packed solidly with conservative Republican judges by his three GOP predecessors in the White House. Similarly, the Supreme Court contained a very stable working majority of justices who were greatly indisposed toward the major economic components of the New Deal. Indeed, it was not until the 1937 "switch in time" that the Supreme Court began to look with favor upon the major New Deal innovations. Thus, despite the ideological screening that went into the selection of FDR district judges, one may say that between 1933 and 1938 the Roosevelt trial judges had to restrain their liberal propensities in many of the cases that were tried in their respective courts. (This may explain why the Roosevelt judges' liberalism score of 47 is not much greater than the scores of his three Republican predecessors, whose scores averaged around 42 percent.)

Conversely, the highly conservative voting pattern of the Reagan judges may also be explained by this same reasoning process. When the Reagan jurists began to stream into the federal judiciary, they were greeted by a healthy number of Eisenhower-Nixon-Ford judges. By the end of Reagan's second term, not only a majority of Supreme Court justices but a majority of the lower court judges were Republicans, and this allowed the conservative Reagan judges to flow with the tide rather than against it. In fact, one may say that the impact of the Reagan appointments was to decisively change the ideological direction of the federal judiciary. This has made the role of George Bush much easier. While there were initially a few pockets of liberalism in the lower federal judiciary (in the form of Johnson and Carter holdovers), the Bush cohorts were really facing only a "mopping up" action; the liberal dragon received its mortal wound during the Reagan years. Thus, the Bush judges have been free to be as conservative as they like without much worry about being overruled by appellate court panels with different ideological values. Of course, this may change if President Clinton is reelected, and his moderate to liberal appointees begin to have a greater impact on the composition of the federal judiciary.

To summarize, we have contended that four general conditions must be met for a president to have maximum effect on the ideological direction of the judiciary. First, he must, of course, choose to make his selections on ideologically based criteria. Second, he must have the opportunity to make a sufficient number of judicial appointments so as to make a real impact on the judiciary as a whole. Third, the chief executive must have the political clout and skills to push through his nominations in the face of possible opposition in the Senate and/or its powerful Judiciary Committee. And, finally, his appointees must enter a judicial arena that is either ideologically "friendly" or at least one that can easily be made "friendly" with the addition of a few more appointments. Given these criteria, it is clear that, the Democratic majority in the Senate notwithstanding, George Bush's impact on the federal judiciary will be substantial as its center of gravity moves more and more to the right.

SUMMARY AND CONCLUSIONS

This chapter has focused primarily on the degree to which the voting behavior of federal district judges is influenced by the judges' (prior) political party affiliation and by the appointing president. We began by observing that between 1933 and 1987 Democrats on the trial court bench were 1.42 times more likely to decide cases in a liberal direction than were their Republican colleagues. We also noted that this has been true for the more specific case categories of criminal justice, labor and economic regulation, and civil rights and liberties—the latter category having invoked the greatest partisan differences over time. We then sought to account for partisan behavior in terms of the relationship between the district courts and the ideological composition and behavior of the Supreme Court. More specifically, as the Burger Court has slowly but consistently moved to the right between 1969 and 1986, so, too, have U.S. trial judges in their overall decisional patterns. Though Democratic trial judges maintained a more liberal voting record, their rear-guard action was limited by the massive conservative shift of the Burger Court.

The data also suggest that the ambiguity of a large number of the high court's rulings, many of which were closely split decisions, has given lower court judges the discretion necessary to assess the law and facts of a given case in terms of their own partisan lights. However, the most recent data also indicate that as the Burger and Rehnquist Courts have come to consolidate their majorities, this has tightened the noose on district judge discretion, and, as a consequence, partisan voting is being reduced. (Partisan differences were at the 20 percent level in 1984 but dropped precipitously to only 7 percent in 1986.)

The second focus of this chapter has been on presidential appointment effects. Such effects have been sizable and dramatic over time, as data from Presidents Wilson to Bush indicate. Looking more precisely at the cohorts of

Presidents Carter and Reagan, we noted that on all twenty-three issue categories the Carter team were more liberal than their Reagan counterparts. The differences were extremely high on the issues of racial minority discrimination, the right to privacy, and regulation of the economy by state and local governments. We then provided a preliminary assessment of President Bush's effect on the ideological direction of the district courts. We argued that presidents will have the greatest effect when they possess the desire to make ideologically based appointments and when they have an ample number of vacancies to fill. Such effects will also be great when they have the political clout to carry out their desires and when their appointees enter a judicial arena that is friendly toward their ideological orientation.

CHAPTER 3

The Influence of Geographic Factors on Judicial Voting Patterns

REGIONAL INFLUENCES

Almost three decades ago the classic observer of the American political scene V. O. Key Jr. noted that "in American politics the historical salience of place—as contrasted with class, occupation, religion, and other nongeographical categories—colors both intellectual analysis and popular decisions. Our national politics has been regarded as a process of reconciling the conflicting interests and ambitions of the great geographical sections of the country" (1964, 100).[1]

Sectional conflicts have long been part and parcel of the dynamics of American politics: they have affected how presidents, senators, congressmen, and voters have responded to the key issues of the day—for example, slavery, economic tariffs, and the gold standard.[2] The voting behavior of U.S. Supreme Court justices has likewise been influenced in the past by sectional cleavages. For example, in a study of fifty-two high court cases involving sectional rivalry between 1837 and 1860, John Schmidhauser found that party background was a major factor accounting for divisions among the justices. Because the four justices who were most supportive of southern regional interests were all southern Democrats and since the two justices with the strongest pro-northern voting patterns were northern Whigs, Schmidhauser concluded that the effects of party and region were virtually inseparable (1961, 615–640).

What about the present time? Are there still sectional differences in the United States that have significance for the political process, or have the influences of the mass media and social mobility muted virtually all traces of politically meaningful geographic variations? While no one would argue that sectionalism is as powerful today as in decades past, there is still substantial evidence that it does color the warp and woof of today's political culture. First of all, public attitudes and voting patterns on a wide range of issues vary from one region of the country to another.[3] As for national political officials, there is evidence that regionalism affects the voting patterns of congressmen and senators on many important issues, for example, agricultural policy, civil rights, and protection of the environment.[4] Furthermore, sectional considerations have their impact within each political party: on many significant issues northern Democrats are more liberal than their southern counterparts, and eastern Republicans are often more progressive than their GOP colleagues west of the Appalachians. Data collected by Stuart Nagel indicate that northern members of the federal independent regulatory commissions are more liberal than members with southern backgrounds (1969, 239).

Given the persistence of significant regional variations in the American political culture, what reasons are there to believe that they affect the decisional patterns of federal district judges? First, we note that spatial differences define different legal and democratic subcultures as well as variations in the content of judicial policy questions. Historically, U.S. trial judges have had strong affinities and ties with the state and region in which their courts are located; hence on many issues the decisions of the judges should reflect the parochial values and attitudes of the district. As Richardson and Vines have noted,

> A persistent factor in the molding of lower court organization has been the preservation of state and regional boundaries. The feeling that the judiciary should reflect the local features of the federal system has often been expressed by state officials most explicitly. Mississippi Congressman John Sharp Williams declared that he was "frankly opposed to a perambulatory judiciary, to carpetbagging Nebraska with a Louisianian, certainly to carpetbagging Mississippi or Louisiana, with somebody north of Mason and Dixon's line." (1970, 71)

Whether regionalism affects the voting patterns of U.S. trial judges is not just a matter of speculation: in recent years scholars have provided clear empirical documentation of this phenomenon. For example, studies have shown that judges in the South have had a unique—and usually more conservative—approach on issues such as race relations,[5] abortion,[6] and environmental protection.[7] Furthermore, we note that the legal context of cases may vary according to different regions of the country and/or different time periods, just as this has been true for the mix of cases coming before the U.S. Supreme Court.[8] For instance, there is a real difference between a southern school desegregation case in 1955, wherein segregation was mandated explicitly by state law, and an integration case in the North in the 1980s wherein separation of the races was a de facto function of segregated housing patterns. (This phenomenon, of course, creates a methodological as well as a substantial reason for comparing judicial voting patterns from one region and time frame to another.)

Finally, the Carp-Rowland study made the following observations about regional differences between 1933 and 1977:

> Regional differences occur within each [political] party, and party differences occur within each region. On the criminal justice dimension, North-South intra-

> party differences were initially small, but substantial change occurred after 1968 as northern Democrats and Republicans became more liberal than their counterparts in the South. Second, the split between the North and the South on the two composite variables of civil rights and liberties and also labor and economic regulation has been considerable and often volatile. Further, the data reveal that intraparty voting along North-South lines on these two sets of issues began to increase in 1969 after a remission during the Warren Court period. (1983, 100)

East-West differences during this same time period were found to be "minimal" (97).

In recognition of the fact that spatial effects flucuate over time, we have estimated regional effects for four eras: 1933–1953, 1954–1968, 1969–1977, and 1978–1988. Of particular interest is the most recent era, which begins at the end of our previous analysis and includes the periods of Supreme Court ambiguity identified in the previous chapter. What have regional differences been like in the most recent ten-year interval for which we have empirical data, that is, between 1977 and 1987?[9] Table 3-1 provides us with some key data to respond to this question.

In contrast to the 1969–1977 era, when there was a minor surge in regional voting patterns for all cases, there has been a sharp *decline* in the ten-year period after 1977. In the former era 9 percentage points separated liberal northern judges from their southern counterparts, and the odds ratio was a fairly significant 1.41. However, since 1977 the odds ratio has been a virtually insignificant 1.07, and only 2 percentage points separate the two geographic areas. It is also interesting to note that the closing of the gap has been caused mainly by southern jurists becoming more liberal rather than vice versa or by the two groups growing together. East-West differences continue to be minor, although there has been a modest widening of the gap during the more recent ten-year interval as western judges have become somewhat more liberal in their decision making than jurists in the East.

The issue dimension of criminal justice is particularly interesting in terms of what transpired during the post-1977 era. In the North the percentage of liberal decisions remained at the precise level that it had been in the prior era, 31 percent. However, in the South the percentage of liberal decisions jumped from 24 to 35 percent—an extraordinary change in so short a time interval. For East-West differences, jurists in the East went from 27 to 28 percent liberal for the two time periods, while judges in the western part of the United States became more liberal by 5 percentage points (30 to 35 percent) from one time frame to another.

For civil rights and liberties cases the findings for the most recent time frame are more in keeping with expectations. Both North and South have moved in a more conservative direction during this period, but their change

Table 3-1. Percentage of Liberal Decisions, Controlled for Region, 1933–1988

	1933–53	1954–68	1969–77	1978–88	All Years
All cases					
North	46	42	47	46	45
South	43	37	38	44	41
α	1.14	1.22	1.41	1.07	1.20
East	46	42	43	43	43
West	44	39	44	47	44
α	1.08	1.08	0.90	0.83	0.93
Criminal justice					
North	26	23	31	31	28
South	27	21	24	35	26
α	0.93	1.12	1.40	0.85	1.12
East	23	23	27	28	25
West	29	23	30	35	29
α	0.66	0.94	0.89	0.72	0.81
Civil rights and liberties					
North	39	39	53	48	47
South	45	42	45	41	43
α	0.79	0.88	1.39	1.30	1.20
East	39	39	51	44	44
West	42	41	49	46	46
α	0.80	0.86	1.00	0.90	0.92
Labor and economic regulation					
North	58	64	61	55	58
South	49	55	55	54	53
α	1.48	1.40	1.30	1.01	1.22
East	62	65	61	53	59
West	51	58	58	55	55
α	1.59	1.32	1.08	0.93	1.18

Source: Robert A. Carp and C. K. Rowland, *Policymaking and Politics in the Federal District Courts* (Knoxville: University of Tennessee Press, 1983), 97.

has been more in lockstep than with the previous issue dimension. From 1969 to 1978 8 percentage points had separated the two regions, while after 1977 the split is 48 to 41 with the North, as expected, being the more liberal. The odds ratio is 1.30 for the recent time frame—a bit more than the historical average of 1.20. East-West differences continue to be minimal, with only 2 points separating the two regions.

At this point we would look at two more specific issues within the broader category of civil rights and liberties that have been of interest to social scientists: cases involving the right to privacy and race relations cases. Privacy rights cases are selected for a closer look because recent research

Table 3-2. Percentage of Liberal Decisions for All Right to Privacy Cases by North-South Region

	Liberal		Conservative	
	%	(*n*)	%	(*n*)
North	64	(23)	56	(9)
South	36	(13)	44	(7)
Total	100	(36)	100	(16)

Note: Odds ratio = 1.38.

has indicated that this general variable differentiates both Americans as a whole and federal judges along North-South lines.[10] (The variable primarily comprises topics such as abortion, gay rights, search and seizure where "privacy" is the main issue, and so on.) Although the literature does not indicate that North-South differences are overwhelming it does suggest that the southern population in general and southern jurists in particular take a more conservative stand on privacy rights than do their respective counterparts north of the Mason-Dixon line.

Table 3-2 presents our data on right-to-privacy cases as decided by judges in the North and in the South. Although the numbers are fairly small for this recently created variable, they strongly suggest that U.S. judges in the South do take a substantially more conservative position on matters of personal privacy than do their colleagues in the North. In the southern states 36 percent of the published cases are liberal, while this figure is an impressive 64 percent in the North. This compares well with the Alumbaugh and Rowland study, which, using somewhat different methodology, examined only abortion cases in selected parts of the North and South since 1973. They concluded that "a district judge in the South is almost 70 percent more likely to resist *Roe* than is a judge in the North" (1990, 161). Our study reveals that on the broader issue of right-to-privacy for both regions in full, northern jurists are 77 percent more likely to support this right than are their southern colleagues.

The topic of race relations is also worthy of a closer look since it has been and remains an issue that clearly differentiates the citizenry along North-South lines.[11] Table 3-3 provides concrete evidence for the proposition that jurists in the North have been and still are more disposed to the claims of minority litigants than their colleagues in the South. Prior to 1954 the odds ratio indicates that northern judges were 1.32 times more likely to decide in favor of the minority litigants. For the next two eras this ratio increased to 1.50 and then to a high of 1.72 in the interval between 1969 and 1978. Whereas for the post-1977 era for *all cases*, North-South differences have dropped to almost nil (see Table 3-1), this has not been true for race relations cases. Here the odds ratio reveals that the North is still a hefty 1.67 more liberal for this issue dimension than is the South.

We now turn to an examination of intraparty cleavages by region and the intraregional cleavages by party for the four time periods between 1933 and 1988. East-West differences are minimal, and therefore we focus our discussion on intraparty cleavages within the North and the South.

When all cases are considered, Table 3-4 reveals that for the fifty-five-year period of our study northern Democrats have been the most liberal group of judges. This is followed by southern Democrats, northern Republicans, and then southern Republicans. The differences between southern Republicans and northern Democrats is 14 percentage points; that is, northern Democrats are 40 percent more liberal than southern Republicans. Among Democrats the North-South split increased for the time periods between 1954 and 1978, but in the most recent time frame the intraparty disparity has been almost negligible. For Republican judges the fairly large differences that characterized the periods between 1933 and 1978 have virtually disappeared in the most recent time period; northern Republicans are now only 2 percentage points more liberal than their GOP colleagues in the South. Thus, since 1977 for all cases, differences *between* the two parties have remained strong while intraparty differences have become almost negligible.

For the category of criminal justice cases the most recent time frame demonstrates a marked and substantively significant departure from the two previous time frames. That is, from 1954 to 1969 and from 1969 to 1978, the odds ratios for northern Democrats being more liberal than southern colleagues were 1.19 and 1.56, respectively; after 1977 the odds ratio dropped dramatically to 0.86. The dramatic closing of this gap came primarily from southern Democrats becoming more liberal: between 1969 and 1978, 27 percent of their decisions were liberal, but this jumped to 37 percent for the subsequent era. In fact, Democrats in the South actually became more liberal than their northern counterparts: 37 percent to 34 percent.

Table 3-3. Percentage of Liberal Decisions, Controlled for Region, for All Race Relations Cases, 1933–1988

	1933–53	1954–68	1969–77	1978–88	All Years
North	63	54	62	53	56 (1,044)
South	56	44	48	40	45 (1,528)
α	1.32	1.50	1.72	1.67	1.59

Table 3-4. Percentage of Liberal Decisions by Party and Region, 1933–1988

	1933–53			1954–68			1969–77			1978–88			All Years		
	Dem	Rep	α	Dem	Rep	α	Dem	Rep	α	Dem	Rep	α	Dem	Rep	α
All cases															
North	47	44	1.11	43	41	1.06	54	39	1.79	52	40	1.65	49	40	1.46
South	46	37	1.44	38	35	1.11	42	31	1.63	49	38	1.56	44	35	1.44
α	1.03	1.34	—	1.23	1.29	—	1.59	1.45	—	1.10	1.05	—	1.26	1.24	—
Criminal justice															
North	27	24	1.16	26	21	1.29	37	25	1.75	34	29	1.22	32	25	1.35
South	29	27	1.10	22	20	1.13	27	19	1.60	37	32	1.26	28	26	1.30
α	0.92	0.88	—	1.19	1.05	—	1.56	1.43	—	0.86	0.88	—	1.19	1.12	—
Civil rights and liberties															
North	40	38	1.10	42	35	1.35	63	42	2.29	55	38	1.97	54	39	1.83
South	49	39	1.53	41	45	0.84	50	36	1.81	49	32	2.02	48	35	1.75
α	0.69	0.95	—	1.06	0.66	—	1.69	1.33	—	1.28	1.32	—	1.26	1.21	—
Labor and economic regulation															
North	58	56	1.06	65	63	1.09	69	54	1.90	61	48	1.65	62	54	1.41
South	53	40	1.66	57	53	1.14	59	46	1.68	59	49	1.44	57	48	1.44
α	1.23	1.93	—	1.42	1.49	—	1.54	1.36	—	1.09	0.96	—	1.25	1.27	—

Source: Robert A. Carp and C. K. Rowland, *Policymaking and Politics in the Federal District Courts* (Knoxville: University of Tennessee Press, 1983), 98.

This same phenomenon is true for Republicans, where the pattern is almost identical. Between 1969 and 1978 only 19 percent of the southern GOP decisions were liberal on criminal justice matters, while in the following era this percentage jumped to 32 percent. In this most recent time frame, southern Republicans are actually *more liberal* on this issue dimension than are GOP colleagues in the North. This is all the more impressive since this phenomenon did not manifest itself with the issue dimensions of civil rights and liberties or with labor and economic regulation cases. A partial explanation for the dramatic regional shift can be traced to changes in the law and the prevalence of complex narcotics cases in Florida and Texas during this era. Despite the government's commitment to eradicate "drug kingpins," federal prosecutions in this realm typically include charges of trafficking, conspiracy, and other hard-to-prove elements of criminal jurisprudence. But a complete explanation for this surge in liberal criminal justice decisions in the South is beyond the scope of our inquiry and must be relegated to the realm of speculation pending future investigation by public law scholars. For example, it is possible that southern law enforcement officials (both federal and state) have been more poorly trained and/or less observant of proper criminal procedure than their counterparts in the rest of the nation. This would serve as a stimulus to more error-correction (i.e., liberal) decisions by southern federal judges than would be the case if they held court elsewhere in the nation. If this were true, our findings would not be a function of a surge in liberal criminal justice decision making in the South but rather an indirect commentary on federal and state law enforcement practices in southern states. Clearly, only additional research will resolve this puzzle.

For the issue dimension of civil rights and liberties it is clear that, for both Democrats and Republicans, their northern wings have been more supportive of these values. For all years the odds ratios have been 1.26 and 1.21, respectively. For Democrats there have been sizable fluctuations in intraparty cleavages over the years. The difference in odds ratio was as high as 1.69 for the 1969–1977 time frame, but for the most recent period the disparity backed off to 1.28. For GOP jurists there has been little change in recent decades, with odds ratios of 1.33 and 1.32 in the two most recent time periods.

Labor and economic regulations cases comprise the third case category, and historically the northern wings of both parties have been about one and a quarter times more likely to opt for the regulator and/or the economic underdog than have their southern counterparts. For Democrats the odds ratio for the first three time frames mounted from 1.23 to 1.42 to 1.54. However, in the most recent time frame the difference has suddenly dropped to the substantively trivial—1.09. This has come about entirely because the northern wing of the party has become more conservative—from 69 percent liberal between 1969 and 1978 to 61 percent liberal from 1978 and 1988; the southern contingent remained precisely at 59 percent. For Republicans the odds ratio has decreased for each of our four time periods to the point where there now are no significant differences between the two branches of the party on this issue dimension.

Upon review of the regional effects on each category, one overarching conclusion is in order. In comparing the 1969–1977 era with the post-1977 period, it is clear that there has been a generally consistent and substantial decrease in intraparty differences by region. This is all the more significant because partisanship on the whole during this most recent period has been as intense as ever (see Tables 2-4 through 2-6). What this strongly suggests is that since 1977 presidents have been able to impose more *national* appointment criteria for the selection of U.S. district judges. This aggregate evidence indicates that Presidents Reagan and Carter held stringent ideological standards for the selection of their judicial cohorts and that they were able meaningfully to impose their will in the selection process—even in the face of the tradition of senatorial courtesy. There is anecdotal evidence (to be discussed in chapter 4) revealing a weakening of the influence of home-state senators and/or local party bosses in the judicial selection process—particularly during the Reagan years. Our quantitative data support this thesis as well.

Table 3-5 compares the voting record of Reagan's judicial team with that

Table 3-5. Percentage of Liberal Decisions by Reagan Cohort versus Other Republican Presidential Cohorts by Region, 1981–1988

	Reagan Cohort	Other Republican Cohort	α
All cases			
North	36	40	0.82
South	35	39	0.86
Criminal justice			
North	29	26	1.17
South	28	32	0.80
Civil rights and liberties			
North	30	39	0.67
South	29	33	0.84
Labor and economic regulation			
North	46	52	0.81
South	46	49	0.88

of other Republican presidential cohorts for our several case categories from 1981 (the year Reagan began appointing judges) to 1988. If our thesis is correct that Reagan was able to apply national, conservative appointment criteria in his selection process, then his judicial cohort should be more conservative than that of other Republican presidential teams when region is controlled for.

For the most part Table 3-5 lends strong credence to our general hypothesis. With the exception of Reagan judges in the North for criminal justice cases, the Reagan cohort is significantly more conservative than the judicial teams appointed by other GOP executives. This is true when all cases are considered and when we examine our more specific case types with controls for region. Equally important, North-South differences for the Reagan team are virtually nil, whereas they are substantial for other Republican cohorts: for the issue dimensions of criminal justice and civil rights and liberties only 1 percentage point separates the Reagan judges in the North from those in the South, while there is absolutely no difference on the dimension of labor and economic regulation. On the other hand, for non-Reagan Republicans, 6 points separate the North-South contingents for criminal justice and for civil rights and liberties cases, and 3 points divide them for labor and economic regulation is sues.

Do these same phenomena prevail when one compares the Carter cohort with that of other Democratic appointees for the same time period?

First, we reiterate that the Carter judges are more liberal than other Democrats on the bench in both the North and the South. This pattern is true for all case categories with the exception of Carter appointees in the South, who, on the dimension of labor and economic regulation, are somewhat more conservative than other Democratic appointees. We have no ready explanation for the existence of this one deviation from the rule, although it is clear from the literature that the Carter team was recruited primarily for its attitudes on race relations and other Bill of Rights issues and not on matters of economic philosophy.

There is one difference between the phenomenon of Carter and other Democrats versus Reagan and other Republicans. While the Reagan team appears to have been cut out of whole ideological cloth, with North-South variations being almost nil, such is not the case when one compares the Carter cohort with that of other Democratic appointees. Table 3-6 indicates that while Carter was generally able to secure appointees more liberal than other Democrats on the bench, still, regional North-South differences were more significant in his appointment process than seems to have been the case during the Reagan years. This pattern would suggest that although Carter did not abdicate selection prerogatives to state nomination commis-

Table 3-6. Percentage of Liberal Decisions by Carter Cohort versus Other Democratic Presidential Cohorts by Region, 1977–1988

	Carter Cohort	Other Democratic Cohort	α
All cases			
North	54	49	1.23
South	50	48	1.09
Criminal justice			
North	38	27	1.66
South	40	32	1.43
Civil rights and liberties			
North	56	55	1.03
South	49	47	1.10
Labor and economic regulation			
North	63	58	1.23
South	57	62	0.82

sions, the presence of these institutions may have afforded Carter somewhat less control than was afforded Reagan by his more centralized institutional arrangements.

VOTING PATTERNS INFLUENCED BY CIRCUIT

Not only do judicial policy propensities vary from region to region, but studies also suggest that each circuit differs from others in its interpretation of the law and in its decisional tendencies.[12] Perhaps more than region, "circuit" combines elements of the legal and democratic subcultures. In his study of voting behavior on the United States court of appeals, Sheldon Goldman found evidence of "organized liberal-conservative voting patterns" by the judges and discovered that party affiliation was associated with voting behavior on economic liberalism issues. Nevertheless, Goldman was obliged to conclude that despite certain characteristics common to all circuits, "the eleven United States courts of appeals . . . differ in their rates of dissension and intracircuit conflict as well as the sources of conflict" and that "the institutional diversity of the appeals courts . . . imposed limitations on data collection and analysis" (1966, 382).

Interviews with district judges provided a host of specific examples of how judicial administration differed among circuits. For example, the following judicial policies were said to have been affected in whole or in part by unique appeals court decisions: the disposition toward the pleas of labor unions and of civil liberties advocates, the criteria for appointment of special masters in antitrust suits, the definition of what constitutes automobile theft, the interpretation of patent law, and whether or not it is desirable for trial judges to prepare *written* justifications for their decisions.[13] Each judge strongly asserted that the existence of differences in judicial output from circuit to circuit is common knowledge among federal judges.

The court of appeals is in a strategically powerful position to influence the nature and scope of the decisions of its trial judges. As James Eisenstein has noted, "Within the same circuit, of course, the behavior of district judges is even more similar. Since they all look to the same appellate body, the judges within a circuit look to and cite the same body of decisions and rulings" (1973, 146). This was supported in William Kitchin's study, in which he interviewed a large number of U.S. trial judges about their judicial behavior and perceptions. In discussing the importance of precedent to these jurists, Kitchin concluded that "most district judges . . . considered precedent as binding only if it were from their own circuit or from the U.S. Supreme Court" (1978, 77).

The institutionalized power of circuit courts to define the law within their boundaries has been enhanced by the dramatic increase in case filings delineated in chapter 1. Losing litigants have a right of appeal from district courts to their circuit court of appeal. This right does not attach in any meaningful sense to appeals from the circuit to the Supreme Court. Moreover, the number of cases heard by the Supreme Court has remained relatively static in the face of the increased case pressures below. Therefore, res judicata is increasingly achieved in the circuit.

Circuits also follow important sectional lines that mark off historical, social, and political differences that give them a distinctly regional character. Some of the circuits are entirely regional, such as the Fourth, Fifth, and the Eleventh (only southern states), and the Seventh (only midwestern states). Others are predominantly regional but include one or more outside states, such as the First, which contains New England states and Puerto Rico, and the Eighth, which takes in six midwestern states, a border state (Missouri), and a southern state (Arkansas). (A United States map divided according to circuits is found in Appendix C.) To the extent that circuits incorporate extralegal influences from the democratic subculture as well as legal influences, differences among circuits may be expected to increase. Thus some of the circuit-to-circuit variance may be caused by extralegal political and environmental influences on the district judges rather than by appellate court rulings.[14]

Our previous study of circuit-to-circuit differences among U.S. trial judges, covering the period 1933 to 1978, offered three general conclusions.

First, we noted generally that, across time, some circuits have been substantially more liberal in their decision making than others. For example, 51 percent of the First Circuit's decisions had been liberal whereas only 38 percent of the Tenth Circuit's rulings had been in a liberal direction. In this same context we concluded that "the relatively small eta[15] suggests that for all cases across all years, knowledge of circuit adds slightly more than knowledge of region to one's ability to discriminate between liberal and conservative policy decisions; that is, differences among circuits are only slightly greater than differences within circuits" (Carp and Rowland 1983, 101–102).

A second observation pertained to the consistency of individual circuits from one time frame to another. Some have varied little over time in terms of ideological orientation (e.g., the Ninth Circuit), whereas others have fluctuated widely over time (e.g., the Washington D.C. circuit). Some, such as the Fifth, have been becoming more liberal over the years, while others, such as the Third, have moved in a more conservative direction.

A final observation dealt with diachronic changes in measures of intercircuit differences: these indices more than doubled from the first time frame to the third. We concluded that "variances in judicial voting patterns from one circuit to another seem to have increased over time, and this trend appears to have accelerated." We ascribed this phenomenon partly to "the inconsistency and ambiguity of legal cues from the Burger Court," which "enhanced the judges' discretion to respond to the environmental influences, which vary from circuit to circuit." In addition, we suggested that the enormous increase in the workload of the courts of appeals in recent decades has made it impossible for the Supreme Court adequately to screen and oversee the cases that are appealed to it from the circuit courts. Because of these two factors, we reasoned that each of the appeals "courts may now be somewhat more independent and autonomous than it was in previous decades. This phenomenon would subsequently manifest itself in differences among the . . . groups of district judges" (Carp and Rowland 1983, 102). What has transpired in the decade since this earlier study was performed?

First, as Table 3-7 reveals, in the most recent era there are still wide variations in the liberal-conservative orientations of the circuits. In the D.C. Circuit, for example, 58 percent of its decisions have been liberal in nature, while this has been true for only 40 percent of the rulings in the Second and Eighth Circuits. When all years are considered, the D.C. Circuit has the record for being the most liberal, with a liberalism score of 53 percent. This is contrasted with the Fourth Circuit, whose index is only 37 percent. In comparing the liberal-conservative trend of the 1978–1988 era with the preceding time frame for each circuit, no clear pattern emerges, as some have moved to the right of center while others have tilted in a more liberal vein:

Table 3-7. Percentage of Liberal Decisions by Circuit for All Cases, 1933–1988

Circuit	1933–53	1954–68	1969–77	1978–88	All Years (*n*)
First	52	48	53	48	50 (2,344)
Second	45	42	44	40	42 (7,988)
Third	47	40	36	43	41 (6,321)
Fourth	42	30	35	43	37 (3,958)
Fifth	40	41	48	48	45 (5,153)
Sixth	43	42	48	50	47 (3,644)
Seventh	45	42	54	48	49 (4,095)
Eighth	48	38	38	40	40 (3,892)
Ninth	47	45	45	52	47 (3,842)
Tenth	38	43	32	48	44 (1,465)
Eleventh	—	—	—	49	49 (775)
D.C.	47	43	57	58	53 (2,059)
M	45	41	45	47	45
S	3.9	4.5	8.3	5.2	4.2
Eta	0.06	0.09	0.14	0.09	0.09

Source: Robert A. Carp and C. K. Rowland, *Policymaking and Politics in the Federal District Courts* (Knoxville: University of Tennessee Press, 1983), 101.

since 1977, six circuits have become somewhat more liberal; three have become more conservative; and one remained at the same level.

Second, the decrease in the regional effect since 1977 (depicted in Tables 3-1, 3-3, 3-4, and 3-5) is further manifested in Table 3-7. The standard deviation for the 1978–1988 time period is 5.2—a major decline from the preceding period, when it was at a high of 8.3. Just as the overall differences between North and South—both overall and intraparty—have decreased since 1977, so, too, have the variations in voting patterns among the several circuits. This reduction in intercircuits is contrary to expectations derived from the reduction in the percentage of circuit court decisions reviewed by the Supreme Court, and it suggests that countervailing trends, such as the nationalization of appointment and the domination of the federal judiciary by Reagan/Bush nominees, have mitigated the institutional effects of reduced Supreme Court supervision.

Is this consistent pattern maintained when one examines intraparty differences by circuit since 1977? Table 3-8 reveals that the answer is clearly affirmative. For Democrats the standard deviations for the first three time periods went from 4.3 to 5.2 to 12.0. After 1977 the trend reverses sharply as the standard deviation drops back to 4.6. For GOP jurists there is a similar pattern—at least for the last two time frames, when the standard deviation drops from 7.3 to 5.2. The eta scores for Republican judges have been more symmetrical, as they have swung upward for the first three eras (.10, .12, and .15) and then fallen back to .09 in the most recent time period.

Table 3-8. Percentage of Liberal Decisions by Party and Circuit for All Cases, 1933–1988

	1933–53			1954–68			1969–77			1978–88			All Years		
Circuit	Dem	Rep	α	Dem	Rep	α	Dem	Rep	α	Dem	Rep	α	Dem	Rep	α
First	51	45	1.27	54	44	1.47	72	37	4.44	55	43	1.66	59 (1,009)	41 (1,187)	2.03
Second	45	43	1.12	44	41	1.10	48	38	1.45	43	38	1.23	45 (3,875)	39 (3,770)	1.25
Third	51	44	1.34	37	43	0.79	39	35	1.92	48	41	1.34	43 (2,704)	39 (3,188)	1.17
Fourth	41	34	1.19	35	26	1.50	48	21	3.39	53	38	1.82	45 (1,817)	30 (2,091)	1.93
Fifth	44	34	1.52	40	45	0.82	50	41	1.42	52	41	1.52	48 (3,595)	41 (1,449)	1.32
Sixth	43	30	1.80	43	37	1.33	50	44	1.32	56	40	1.91	50 (2,526)	40 (1,097)	1.49
Seventh	51	34	1.97	41	46	0.82	60	40	2.30	52	36	1.91	53 (2,444)	39 (1,451)	1.81
Eighth	47	48	1.01	36	40	0.85	39	37	1.07	48	31	2.07	42 (2,210)	37 (1,591)	1.26
Ninth	46	47	0.96	46	43	1.12	46	44	1.06	56	47	1.47	49 (2,244)	45 (1,430)	1.19
Tenth	42	40	1.08	41	44	0.89	29	33	1.03	52	46	1.27	45 (899)	42 (566)	1.11
D.C.	51	49	1.09	47	40	1.35	66	49	1.97	61	51	1.50	60 (967)	49 (861)	1.57
M	47	41		42	41		50	38		52	41		49	40	
S	4.3	6.6		5.2	3.6		12	7.3		4.6	5.2		5.9	4.5	
Eta	0.06	0.10	—	0.08	0.12	—	0.18	0.15	—	0.09	0.09	—	0.09	0.09	—

Source: Robert A. Carp and C. K. Rowland, *Policymaking and Politics in the Federal District Courts* (Knoxville: University of Tennessee Press, 1983), 104.

The phenomena outlined here are quite consistent with the decline in intraparty *regional* differences for the time period since 1977 (see Table 3-4). Just as the disparity between northern and southern Democrats and their regional counterparts in the Republican Party have decreased in the most recent time frame, so, too, have differences within party cohorts in the several circuits. This occurs at the same time that differences *between* party cohorts were at record levels. We regard this as further evidence for the nationalization of presidential appointment criteria—a theme we shall continue to articulate.

Table 3-8 also reveals that since 1977 partisan conflict has been greatest in the Eighth, Seventh, and Sixth Circuits, where the odds ratio (of Democrats being more liberal than Republicans) have been, respectively, 2.07, 1.91, and 1.91. Such conflict has been least common in the Second, Tenth, and Third Circuits, where the ratios have been 1.23, 1.27, and 1.34. When all years are considered, partisan conflict has been greatest in the First, Fourth, and Seventh Circuits, where the odds ratios have been 2.03, 1.93, and 1.81, respectively. Interparty clashes have historically been least prevalent in the Tenth, Third, and Ninth Circuits, for which the odds ratios have been 1.11, 1.17, and 1.19.

VOTING PATTERNS INFLUENCED BY LEVEL OF URBANIZATION

Behavioral Differences Between Urban and Rural Areas

The final geographic variable to be related to judges' decisional patterns is the extent to which they live in an urbanized area. In essence we shall set forth and test the proposition that the level of urbanization is associated with more liberal voting patterns by the judges. Before examining the empirical data to test this hypothesis, we shall briefly summarize the literature that lends credence to this hypothesis.

First of all, in terms of basic attitudes and values the social science literature is replete with data indicating that those living in metropolitan areas are more likely than their small-town and rural neighbors to be associated with liberal political orientations. For example, the more urban the residents, the more likely they are to favor public enterprise in regulating the power industries and in seeing that everyone is provided with adequate housing, to support the idea that "the government ought to help people get doctors and hospital care at low cost," to oppose curbing the power of labor unions, and to believe that "the government in Washington ought to see to it that everybody who wants to work can find a job" (Key 1964, 112–113). Moreover, there is evidence that persons living in rural areas are more likely than their urban counterparts to oppose American involvement in the international community of nations (114).[16]

In summarizing a vast amount of data on urban-rural differences Erikson, Luttbeg, and Tedin recently concluded that "small-town and rural America have been long thought to be the bastion of conservatism . . . with liberalism being the hallmark of the large cities." They attribute much of this variation to what they term a "compositional effect." Citing the data from the National Election Studies conducted by the Center for Political Studies at the University of Michigan, they observe,

> City residents show up as relatively liberal in surveys because they have large proportions of people with liberal group characteristics, such as blacks, Jews, and Catholics. . . . Small towns and rural areas are conservative because they are predominantly Protestant and, outside the South, contain few blacks. But there is something to city life independent of composition that leads to liberalism (perhaps exposure to social diversity). If we compare white Protestants living in rural areas in 1988, the city dwellers are typically 5 to 7 percent more liberal on the issues contained in the 1988 National Election Study than their brethren in the countryside. (1991, 195–196)

Not only does community size affect the values and behavior of ordinary citizens, but it influences the voting patterns and behavior of public officials. For instance, in a study of differences in the distribution of constituency among all Democratic and Republican representatives in a particular session of Congress, Randall Ripley noted that "Democrats were more likely to come from poorer, more urban districts with a relatively large non-white population and Republicans were more likely to come from richer, more suburban districts with a relatively small non-white population" (1978, 290).

Why Judges in Metropolitan Areas Are Hypothesized to Be More Liberal

While the literature suggests that the general public, bureaucratic officials, legislators, and so on tend to be somewhat more conservative in rural areas than they are in more urban centers, what reason is there to believe that this phenomenon is also true for judges, particularly U.S. trial judges? Because we have discussed this subject at some length elsewhere (Carp and Rowland 1983, 125–130), we shall merely summarize the main propositions we have previously set forth.

First, the sociological impact of the community, in combination with an appointment process that tends to ensure that judges are representative of the local political culture, causes us to believe that judges are likely to be (at least somewhat) representative of their respective communities. Scholars have long documented the fact that federal district judges tend to preside in the judicial district in which they were born and raised. (Such was the case for 57.7 percent of the Richardson and Vines's sample [1970, 72] and for 70 percent of the Carp and Wheeler sample [1972, 366].) If the urban culture as a whole tends to be more liberal than the rural environment, and if judges are likely to serve in districts where they were born and raised, then it is likely that they will reflect the attitudes and mores of their respective districts. Furthermore, the greater homogeneity of smaller communities may create even greater pressures on their judges to conform to conservative local values than is the case with jurists in more pluralist urban centers.

Second, the evidence suggests that articulate, well-financed liberal judicial lobbying groups are more prolific and active in metropolitan areas than in America's small-town and rural areas.[17] Whether they appear as actual litigants or as "friends of the court," liberal groups are more likely to be found in large cities, where, in turn, they initiate or sponsor litigation. Labor unions, women's rights groups, the American Civil Liberties Union (ACLU), gay rights organizations, the American Jewish Congress, and the National Lawyers Guild are examples of groups more likely to be strong and active in the nation's urban centers. What Richardson and Vines concluded over two decades ago about the consequences of these facts is equally true today:

> In the same region there are sharp contrasts in decision making activities among district courts because litigation is sparse in some courts, such as that of southern Mississippi, compared to districts such as eastern Louisiana [New Orleans], where litigation is more frequent. Cases are simply not brought in some districts, notably those with low urban populations, because the motivation, skills, and facilities required to carry on litigation are lacking. The eastern Pennsylvania district [Philadelphia] with its large urban and industrial population presents an example in which such litigation occurs more frequently than in any of the Southern districts. (1970, 95–96)

In their sample for the same time period, the Southern District of Mississippi had 2 labor cases and 4 civil liberties cases; in the Eastern District of Pennsylvania there were 145 labor cases and 48 civil liberties cases. According to Richardson and Vines,

> Although one may expect that Southern districts such as southern Mississippi would be a prolific source of civil liberties (which included civil rights) litigation, the absence of much litigation indicates the inactivity which the federal judiciary can exhibit in an area unless initiative is taken by interested participants. For all practical purposes, during our sample period, the federal district courts—and as a result much of the higher judiciary—were silenced on important topics by the failure of litigation to develop. (1970, 96)

Even though liberal judicial lobbying groups are more active and prolific in the metropolitan areas, cities do not automatically become centers of liberal decision making. Still, there can be no victories for liberal causes unless and until the appropriate cases are brought to court. Progressive-minded judges in small-town and rural areas would have little effect if presented with no cases through which they might manifest their liberal values. Likewise, conservative jurists in urban areas would be under scant intellectual pressure to be more disposed toward liberal plaintiffs if they were not confronted frequently with teams of articulate, well-organized attorneys representing liberal causes. Thus, while the presence of liberal lobbying groups in the larger cities does not ipso facto cause judicial liberalism, their effects may at least create the opportunities for liberal decisions to be rendered.

The literature on the behavior of small groups provides a third reason for hypothesizing more liberal and independent behavior from jurists in large multijudge urban centers than from their more isolated colleagues in smaller communities. A well-developed body of literature demonstrates that persons are much more likely to make risky and independent decisions when acting as part of a collegial group than when acting as separate, isolated individuals. The literature gives two reasons for this. One is that members of a group tend to give each other needed psychological reinforcement when faced with the prospect of making a risky, potentially dangerous decision; second, group decisions buffer the individual members from individual accountability.[18]

Although decision making by U.S. judges in metropolitan areas is still, of course, performed on an individual basis, nevertheless there is reason to believe that jurists in multijudge cities do receive the necessary psychological support and anonymity to allow them to be more independent (i.e., liberal) in their decisions.[19] Obviously, it is not urbanism per se that is the liberal impetus here; rather, it is that populous urban centers by their very nature require more judges than do smaller communities, and hence a state of affairs is created wherein the manifestations of small-group behavior might appear.

In earlier works (Carp and Rowland 1983, 125–130) we have provided ample empirical and anecdotal information that jurists in the larger, multijudge cities, unlike their isolated colleagues in rural areas, do obtain needed psychological support from their fellow trial judges when they render innovative and/or unpopular liberal decisions.[20] Likewise, we have shown that a large urban environment provides the anonymity required for independent judicial decision making (again, see Carp and Rowland 1983, 125–130). We demonstrated that such anonymity provides an additional psychological incentive for judges to take the initiative in rendering unpopular, liberal decisions—especially in the areas of criminal justice, and civil rights and liberties.

In sum, we hypothesize a positive relationship between urbanism and liberal judicial opinions because (1) metropolitan areas tend to be more liberal than small-town and rural areas; (2) judges tend to preside over district courts in the same environments in which they were born and socialized, and thus those who come from more pluralist, liberal metropolitan centers ought to be more liberal than jurists in more homogeneous, conservative, less urban districts; (3) articulate liberal interest groups lobby more actively in large urban centers; and (4) jurists in multijudge cities are provided with two factors that, according to small-group theory, foster bolder, more independent (liberal) decision making, namely, mutual psychological support and a greater degree of anonymity.

Literature Review of the Relationship Between Community Size and Liberal-Conservative Judicial Decisions

Most of the early studies of a possible correlation between judges' decisions and whether they were in an urban or rural setting dealt with sentencing patterns, but the conclusions of these studies have been rather ambiguous and often contradictory. During the 1960s Stuart Nagel performed several studies of the relationship between community size and judicial sentencing behavior. Using a sample from 194 counties in all fifty states, his investigation yielded these observations: (1) In rural areas, 50 percent of the defendants sentenced to prison in felonious assault cases received terms of more than one year, whereas in urban areas only 37 percent were given such terms; and (2) in rural areas, 61 percent of those sentenced to prison in grand larceny cases were required to serve more than a one-year term, whereas in urban areas only 54 percent were so required (1969, 106–107). When the federal courts were examined, the results were more ambiguous. For the cities he studied, 70 percent of those convicted in federal assault cases were sentenced to prison terms of more than one year, but in rural areas only 63 percent were accorded such punishment (109). Nagel suggests that at least at the time of his study, urban areas placed a greater stigma on assault, whereas the rural citizen had more negative views about grand larceny. He contends that the "assault differences may be based on notions of self-defense associated with more agricultural societies, as opposed to the defense by professional police associated with more industrialized societies (100). In interstate larceny cases, 54 percent of those sentenced in metropolitan centers, as opposed to 48 percent in the more rural areas, were obliged to serve terms of more than one year. However, for this same offense, defendants in rural areas were more likely to be found guilty (86 to 83 percent) and more apt to receive a prison term rather than a suspended or probated sentence (52 to 46 percent) (110).

In the wake of Nagel's inconclusive findings, the Federal Judicial Center conducted a study of sentencing practices in the U.S. Second Circuit almost two decades ago. Its findings suggested that urban judges may be *more severe* in their sentencing practices than their colleagues in more pastoral settings. For example, it was noted that "sentences in the Eastern District [of New York–Brooklyn] tend on the whole to be somewhat more severe than the median sentences for the entire circuit in particular cases, that sentences in the four smaller districts tend to be less severe, and that sentences in the Southern District [New York City] are about equally distributed around the median" (Partridge and Eldridge, 1974, 32). However, the scholars at the Federal Judicial Center acknowledged that their statistical tests "do not suggest that the differences among districts are particularly strong," and they add that "it also seems clear that the venue is a good deal less important than the identity of the individual judge" (32). (It would be interesting to see whether such differences have continued to hold since the congressional passage of the Sentencing Act of 1987 designed to eliminate or at least minimize sentencing disparities among federal judges.)

Evidence *in support* of the proposition that rural areas are associated with more severe sentencing practices came from Beverly Cook's study of draft offender cases. She found, inter alia, that jurists in rural settings were more severe in their sentencing practices than colleagues in medium-sized and smaller cities. She found that the average severity index was 20.2 for U.S. trial judges in cities of more than 500,000 persons, 23.5 for jurists in cities of between 50,000 and 500,000, and 29.9 for judges in cities of fewer than 50,000 (Cook 1973, 612). In her discussion of her findings she compares her results with those of Walter Markham, whose study of the same subject also found that the size of the district population correlated positively and significantly with the percentage of offenders sentenced to prison. However, Markham did not find a correlation when he examined the length of the prison term nor sentence disparities within districts (Markham 1971, 179–180).

Elaborating on Cook's study, David Danelski made this observation:

> Judges in large communities tend to be less severe than those in small communities probably because (a) judicial attitudes underlying sentencing behavior vary with population size and (b) local opinion varies with population size and influences sentencing behavior. . . . Judges who hear few draft cases and judges who sit alone and hence take all of the draft cases in their courts give significantly more severe sentences because they tend to serve in small communities, which means (a) they tend to be conservative, and (b) local opinion in those communities tends to support severe sentences. (1972, 664)

Our 1983 examination of the relationship between the size of the district court and the decisional propensities of the trial judges provided several conclusions.[21] On the whole the data generally supported the "basic hypothesis that urban centers are more liberal than rural ones. Nevertheless the data also reveal that the relationship is relatively weak and that the phenomenon is much more complicated and subtle than we had imagined" (Carp and Rowland 1983, 132). The primary conclusion of this earlier study was that

> prior to 1954, urban-rural differences on the whole appear to have been negligible. . . . After 1953, however, a basic pattern began to emerge which was true not just for all cases taken together but also for the categories of criminal justice and of civil rights and liberties: more liberal decisions were rendered in the courts with two judges than in those with only one; a noticeable drop in liberal voting occurred in the courts with three to six judges; and in the courts with seven or more judges there was a modest upswing in the number of liberal decisions. In all cases for all years, 41 percent of the single-judge court opinions were liberal; this jumped to 46 percent at the two-judge level but dropped back to 41 percent at the districts with three to six judges; for cities with seven or more judges, 43 [percent] of the decisions were liberal. (132)

This study also found that the correlation between liberalism and court size was greatest for issues involving labor and economic issues and was weakest on the dimensions of criminal justice and of civil rights and liberties. The reason for the falloff in liberal voting on these latter two dimensions was hypothesized to be a function of the judicial selection process—particularly in the North. In northern cities the political bosses, who traditionally had enormous power under Democratic administrations, were usually very liberal on labor and economic issues but quite conservative on dimensions involving the Bill of Rights and the Fourteenth Amendment. It thus appeared that judicial nominees supported by these party bosses mirrored these same attitudes, and hence those two liberalism indices fell when they reflected judges in the large northern cities. In the South, on the other hand, where federal judicial selection has not historically been a product of party boss machinations, the correlation between liberalism and court size was substantial on all three issue dimensions (Carp and Rowland 1983, 132–138).

Research Findings of This Study

Table 3-9 brings up-to-date our previous research on this topic. When the most recent time period (1978–1988) for all cases is compared with the previous time frame, it is apparent that the dramatic increase in liberalism from one- to two-judge cities has virtually vanished. While the spread had been

Table 3-9. Percentage of Liberal Decisions by Number of Judges Assigned to the District Court, 1933–1988

	One Judge	Two Judges	Three to Six Judges	Seven or More Judges
All cases	44	43	46	46
1933–53	36	44	40	43
1954–68	36	44	40	43
1969–77	43	49	40	43
1978–88	45	46	47	46
All years	42	46	44	45
Criminal justice				
1933–53	26	24	28	24
1954–68	21	25	21	25
1969–77	28	35	27	28
1978–88	34	36	35	30
All years	27	32	27	29
Civil rights and liberties				
1933–53	42	45	39	37
1954–68	38	43	38	43
1969–77	51	52	47	49
1978–88	44	45	44	48
All years	45	48	44	47
Labor and economic regulation				
1933–53	55	50	56	61
1954–68	54	65	64	65
1969–77	58	62	57	60
1978–88	53	53	58	55
All years	55	56	59	58

Source: Robert A. Carp and C. K. Rowland, *Policymaking and Politics in the Federal District Courts* (Knoxville: University of Tennessee Press, 1983), 133.

some 6 percentage points between 1969 and 1977, the current disparity is only 1 percent. At the next cutoff point—three to six judges—there is an additional 1 percent in liberal voting, although this gain is given up at the seven-or-more level. Thus in the aggregate for the current time period the relationship is in the expected direction, but it would be difficult to maintain that it is substantively significant.

For criminal justice cases since 1977 there has been a modest increase in liberal decision making as the court size increases, but also an abrupt falloff at the seven-or-more level, where the liberalism index falls from 35 to 30. Perhaps the increase in crime—particularly violent crime—in America's cities in recent years has negatively impacted judges' responses to the pleas of criminal defendants.

For the civil rights and liberties dimension our hypothesis finds some support in the most recent era. Forty-eight percent of the large-city judicial decisions support a broadening position on Bill of Rights and Fourteenth Amendment issues, while this is true of only 44 percent of decisions in the most rural districts.

Finally, in the realm of labor and economic regulation our hypothesis has some validity—particularly in the difference between court points with only two judges, where the liberalism index is 53, and three- to six-judge cities, where the index jumps to 58. In cities with more than seven jurists there is a small conservative turn, and it is interesting to note that decision making in this realm has grown generally more conservative in recent decades: during the past three time frames the liberalism index for America's largest cities has dropped from 65 to 60 to 55 percent.

In Table 3-10 we break our database down into North-South regions, and this continues to provide some useful insights just as it did in our previous study. For all cases in the North in the most recent time period, a very interesting phenomenon is observed: without exception, for all of the case categories the relationship between liberal voting and court size is curvilinear. That is, liberalism increases progressively as one goes from one district size to another, but then at the seven-or-more-judge level there is a dramatic falloff. Using "all cases" as an illustration of this phenomenon, the liberalism index goes from 44 to 48 to 54 and then back to 43.[22] Why this is so for *northern* cities in recent years is certainly not readily apparent and should become a subject of future research and analysis. It is possible to suggest that as the quality of urban life in the North's larger cities has declined in recent years because of increasing poverty, pollution, crime, lack of funds to maintain the infrastructure, and so on, this has triggered a conservative backlash among upper-middle-class federal jurists who have "had enough" of crime, civil disorder, and counterproductive bureaucratic regulations. Another possibility is that in jurisdictions with enough judges, small-group psychology suggests that a large conservative cohort would be emboldened to go against the ideological grain of a liberal urban jurisdiction. But this is only speculation.

The South, on the other hand, had in our previous studies provided the best example of a direct relationship between court size and liberal voting. Between 1933 and 1978 as one moved from small to larger court districts, the liberalism index went from 38 to 40 to 41 to 49. Since 1977, however, the differences between one court size and another appear almost random—or at least more complex than our capacity to analyze. Still, two items do readily stand out to the observer.

One is an increase in liberal voting on criminal justice issues in one-judge courts after 1977, where the index jumped from 21 to 41 percent.

Table 3-10. Percentage of Liberal Decisions by Number of Judges Assigned to the District Court According to North-South Regions, 1933–1977 and 1978–1988

	One Judge		Two Judges		Three to Six Judges		Seven or More Judges	
	1933–77	1978–88	1933–77	1978–88	1933–77	1978–88	1933–77	1978–88
North								
All cases	43	44	48	48	41	54	43	43
Criminal justice	27	31	31	39	25	41	26	28
Civil rights and liberties	46	47	54	48	44	52	44	47
Labor and economic regulation	56	50	59	53	60	63	62	53
South								
All cases	38	46	40	43	41	41	49	48
Criminal justice	21	41	26	33	29	31	33	35
Civil rights and liberties	45	40	40	42	49	38	57	48
Labor and economic regulation	52	56	53	54	54	52	56	56

Note: For this study, southern states are Ala., Ark., Del., Fla., Ga., Ky., La., Md., Miss., Mo., N.C., Okla., S.C., Tenn., Tex., Va., and W.Va.; the northern states consist of the remaining thirty-three.

Source: Robert A. Carp and C. K. Rowland, *Policymaking and Politics in the Federal District Courts* (Knoxville: University of Tennessee Press, 1983), 137.

(The other court sizes also show increases but not as dramatic.) We had observed this same phenomenon from a different vantage point in our analysis of Tables 3-1 and 3-2 where we found that for *both* Republicans and Democrats in the South there had been a sizable increase in liberalism on the issue dimension of criminal justice. Now we know where this increase primarily came from—the rural and small-town areas of southern America. What are we to make of this? In theory there are several possibilities. One is that for some reason Carter and even Reagan intentionally appointed judges in the rural South who would be particularly liberal on criminal justice matters. Of course there is absolutely no reason, empirical or intuitive, to believe this. Another possible reason is that the criminal justice cases coming before rural southern judges in recent years have contained inordinately egregious violations of criminal justice procedures and protections, and/or small-town southern judges have been obliged (perhaps by more vigilant appellate courts) to bring local federal practices up to national standards. We believe that one or both of these latter two explanations come closer to the truth than the unlikely notion that both Carter and Reagan intentionally selected criminal justice liberals for their rural southern trial court vacancies. Still, this topic warrants much greater study and analysis than we have provided here.

A second item worthy of note is that there are currently, as in past years, significantly more liberal victories for civil rights and liberties in large southern cities than there are in the rural and small-town areas. Forty-eight percent of such decisions were liberal for seven-or-more-judge cities, while this was true of only 40 percent of the rulings in southern hinterlands. We think the theoretical reasons articulated earlier in this chapter for greater liberalism in urban areas account for this phenomenon. Still, if southern cities begin to experience the same social and economic upheavals that now plague America's urban centers in the North, the liberal flare of urban Dixie may quickly fade.

In the final segment of this analysis we wish to identify and highlight those specific case types that have best responded to our proposition that increasing urbanization is associated with greater liberal decision making. In Table 3-11 we see that three issues provide the best fit for our hypothesis about the relation between court size and liberalism: issues pertaining to state and local economic regulations, suits brought by the NLRB, and disputes between a company and its labor union(s). Interestingly, all three of these specific issues deal with labor and economic issues and not with criminal justice or Bill of Rights matters. One reason for this is the abrupt falloff in liberal voting by judges in the large northern cities (discussed earlier), which effectively excludes criminal justice and civil rights and liberties from being related linearly to the size of the district court. We would further note

Table 3-11. Percentage of Liberal Decisions for Selected Issues by Number of Judges Assigned to the District Court, 1933–1988

	One Judge	Two Judges	Three to Six Judges	Seven or More Judges
	Perfect Linear Relationship			
Local economic regulation	63	67	67	72
NLRB cases[a]	52	56	59	69
Union vs. company	48	48	49	53
	Strong but Uneven Relationship			
Age discrimination	37	47	50	44
Environmental protection	55	64	62	63
Voting rights cases	45	52	50	47
Freedom of expression	51	56	53	59
Race discrimination	47	50	46	53
U.S. commercial regulation	66	69	72	69
Excess profits and rent control	57	60	66	63

[a] This category dealt with suits brought by the NLRB or the Secretary of Labor against either an employer or a labor union. Technically this category ended in 1985 when we split it into two separate ones depending on who was being sued—the employer or the union.

that local economic regulation is a subject for which district judges have an inordinate degree of discretion plus great immunity from appellate court review (see discussion in chapter 2), and thus it is no surprise to see it listed among those issues for which extralegal variables have great explanatory power.

Cases involving civil rights and liberties do emerge on our list where there appears a "strong but uneven relationship" between size of the district court and liberal voting patterns. In comparing one-judge courts with those of seven or more jurists for the issues of age discrimination, voting rights, freedom of expression, and race discrimination, the respective percentage differences are 7, 2, 8, and 6. (As expected, the percentage differences are often greater when one deletes the effect of conservative northern cities and ends with court points of three to six judges. Here the respective percentage differences are 13, 5, 2, and 6.)

The environmental protection variable is further evidence for what social scientists have long known and documented: concern with the environment is generally less intense in rural and small-town areas than in urban areas. U.S. commercial regulation cases and issues involving excess profits and rent control are also given more liberal treatment as the size of the court increases; however, as with many other case types, there is a conservative trend at the level of seven or more jurists.

SUMMARY AND CONCLUSIONS

Several conclusions about the data in this chapter warrant special emphasis. In terms of regional influences on district judge behavior, the primary differences are between judges north and south of the Mason-Dixon line rather than between jurists in the East and West. Still, we observed that in the aggregate, variations between judges in the North and South have markedly declined since 1977 although they are still to be found for some specific case types, such as privacy rights and race relations.

In terms of intraparty variances by region we noted that historically northern Democrats have been the most liberal group, followed by southern Democrats, northern Republicans, and southern Republicans. Equally interesting, however, is that since 1977, intraparty differences have decreased dramatically, particularly for Republicans—despite record-level interparty disparities. We accounted for this phenomenon by setting forth a proposition that we shall continue to articulate throughout this text: that since the late 1970s there has been a *nationalization* of appointment criteria for federal district judges and a concomitant decrease in the impact of sectional influences in their selection and subsequent voting patterns. This proposition was clearly substantiated when we compared the Reagan cohort with that of fellow Republicans for the most recent time frame (Table 3-5), although this phenomenon was less dramatic for Democrats (Table 3-6). Reagan appears to have been almost completely successful in establishing truly national appointment criteria, whereas Carter had to temper his search for liberals with greater concessions to North-South regional influences.

We then continued our analysis by focusing on circuit-by-circuit variations, and the findings matched rather precisely those dealing with North-South differences. First, we noted that historically there have been sizable variations in the decisional patterns between jurists in one circuit and another, and that major substantive differences still exist today. Nevertheless, the standard deviation for the most recent time period (5.2) is some 60 percent less than what it had been in the previous era (8.3). Equally important, since 1977 intraparty variation by circuit has declined significantly, and this phenomenon has been more true for Carter and Reagan judges than for their partisan cohorts. This is further evidence that these two presidents (especially Reagan) were able to set and enforce national standards in their selection of district court judges in a way not achieved by previous administrations.

Finally, we examined the degree to which urbanization influences district judge behavior. In the aggregate there is still good evidence that jurists in urban centers are more liberal than colleagues in rural or small-town settings, but this generalization must be accompanied with a myriad of caveats and more precise commentary. First of all, we noted that since 1977 urban-rural differences appear to be on the whole less substantial than they were previously. This may well be further evidence for the decline in regional effects generally that has been observed after 1977.

Second, as with our 1983 analysis of this phenomenon, we found it useful to break down our analysis of the urbanization effect according to North-South region. Our prior study revealed that in the North liberalism was related to level of urbanization on the broad issues of labor and economic regulation but that for criminal justice and Bill or Rights matters there was a falloff in liberal voting in cities with seven or more judges. We attributed this in part to the influence (in the judicial selection process) of big-city party politicos who tended to be liberals on labor and economic issues but conservative on questions of criminal justice and civil liberties. Since 1977 in the North this phenomenon has continued, but the conservative falloff in the nation's largest cities now includes labor and economic issues as well. We speculated that (1) the decline in the quality of urban life in recent years may have triggered a conservative backlash among judges in big-city courts that now takes in *all* types of issue dimensions, and (2) conservatives with a large number of like-minded colleagues may be emboldened to impose their conservatism on liberal litigants.

In the South our predictive model works somewhat better—particularly with cases involving civil rights and liberties, where jurists in the largest cities are some 20 percent more liberal than colleagues in rural and small-town areas. Disrupting our aggregate statistics but intrinsically important was our finding a surge in "liberal" voting on criminal justice matters in single-judge courts. (The 41 percent liberalism score is almost twice as high as it had been historically, and was the product of both the Reagan and Carter judge cohorts.) Our belief is that this phenomenon was not the result of appointing liberals to rural southern court points. Rather, we attributed it to either or both of these two possibilities: that violations of criminal procedures by federal law enforcement officials in the South have been comparatively more egregious and thus provided better opportunities for "liberal" voting; and/or that U.S. appellate courts are becoming more insistent that southern trial judges no longer turn a blind eye toward violations of federal criminal justice procedures.

Finally, we identified three specific case types that historically have engendered the greatest amount of liberal voting as the size of the district court has increased. These case types, all in the labor and economic realm, are: state and local economic regulation matters (an area of maximum district judge discretion), suits brought by the NLRB, and disputes between a company and organized labor.

CHAPTER 4

The Politics of Home-State Recruitment

While judicial recruitment has always been talked about by political scientists and by the popular press, in recent decades it has been given relatively little attention. This is because presidents such as Jimmy Carter and Ronald Reagan so dominated the judicial appointment process and became so closely identified with it in the public eye that topics such as "senatorial courtesy" and home-state politics have been downplayed. Scholars and journalists have now come routinely to refer to the "Carter bench," the "Reagan effect," or the "Bush team" just as if the chief executive himself had personally handpicked each district judge and all other appointment variables were *de minimus*.

Given the close correspondence between the values of recent presidents and the ideological content of their judges' voting patterns, it is not surprising that many court watchers have tended to oversimplify cause and effect in this realm. But to attribute presidential appointment effects exclusively to the chief executive is to ignore the very real influence of home-state politics and politicians on the appointment of district judges. This is unfortunate, because despite the importance of "presidential appointment effects," there is still considerable evidence to suggest that the "blue-slip" convention used by hostile senators and local political machinations have been every bit as important in the judicial selection process as the values and attitudes of the president in whose name the appointment was made.

Although the scope and significance of the blue-slip procedure have fluctuated over the last fifteen years (Chase 1972; Slotnick 1980a, 1980b), during the first six years of the Reagan administration it meant that Republican home-state senators had virtual veto power over unacceptable district court nominees in their states (Short interview, 1986). Thus, although it was true that only the president could nominate district judges, it was equally correct that President Reagan could nominate only persons whose legal and political credentials were acceptable to the Republican senators in the state where the judge would serve. Moreover, even in states with no Republican senators, Reagan was dependent on in-state political operatives to identify and recruit politically and legally acceptable judicial candidates.

Given the formal and informal avenues by which home-state politics can influence judicial selection, one cannot fully understand the politics of appointment or the link between such politics and jurisprudence without first understanding the dynamics of home-state judicial recruitment and without examining the links between recruitment politics, selection, and judicial outcomes.

HOME-STATE RECRUITMENT PATTERNS

It is somewhat surprising that so little scholarly attention has been devoted to the increasing politicization of the appointment process in recent decades and the growing recognition that appointment politics help shape judicial policy outcomes—the first link in the connection between politics and jurisprudence. In fact, it is no exaggeration to say that until the last ten years virtually no attention was devoted to recruitment per se. On the rare occasions when researchers did look at home-state recruitment and the role of home-state politicos in the selection process, it was from the perspective of presidents seeking senatorial support for their judicial nominees.

The tendency to view home-state recruitment from a presidential perspective is perhaps best exemplified by Neal McFeeley's excellent study of the Johnson administration (1987). McFeeley describes with great clarity and insight the importance that Johnson, the ex–senate majority leader, attached to individual senators' recommendations. He notes that this apparent deference was extended not only to Democrats but to some Republican senators such as minority leader Everett Dirkson, whose political stature and acumen made him a valuable ally and a dangerous enemy. However, despite its important insights into Johnson's appointment strategies and the ability of key senators to influence that strategy, McFeeley's work tells us very little about what happened back home *before* negotiations began between the president and the senator(s). We know nothing, for example, of the process by which Senator Dirkson identified potential candidates for judicial vacancies in Illinois, nor do we know what political and/or legal criteria were used to define acceptable candidates in that state.

The presidential perspective exemplified by McFeeley is consistent with previous studies of the Kennedy and Johnson administrations (Chase 1972), and extends to studies of other presidencies. Most notable in this vein are Navasky's study of the Kennedy administration (1971) and Jackson's study of the Nixon administration (1974). Navasky delineates from the perspective of Robert Kennedy's Justice Department a compromise between Kennedy and James Eastland, the Democratic chair of the Senate Judiciary Committee. This compromise gave Eastland and other southern segregationists control over district court nominations in their home states in return for Eastland's support of Thurgood Marshall and other liberal Kennedy nominees to appellate courts.

Jackson describes the Nixon administration's strategic response to the Democratic majority in the Senate and, most importantly, on the Judiciary Committee. According to Jackson, the administration's strategy was built upon idiosyncratic compromises between Nixon and Democratic senators. For example, a "deal" between Nixon and Democratic Senators Tunney and Cranston in California gave the senators every fourth appointment in return for their support of the president's next three nominees.

The work by McFeely, Chase, Navasky, and Jackson tells us a great deal about how some home-state senators interact with different presidential administrations. By providing a clear focus on the politics of presidential nominations, they delineate the evolving politicization of the nomination process and identify the appointing president as the most important predictor of politicized outcomes. However, this presidential perspective tended to ignore the importance of what happened *before* the chief executive's involvement. Fortunately, this focus of inquiry has been broadened somewhat by recent scholarly attention to the Carter and Reagan administrations. President Carter mandated the use of merit selection panels for the recruitment of candidates for appellate judges and encouraged strongly the creation of such panels for district court vacancies. When Carter introduced incentives for senators to create "merit" selection commissions for judicial vacancies, he explicitly involved his administration in the home-state recruitment of judges. This explicit presidential involvement, in turn, created an incentive for scholars (even those working from a presidential perspective) to determine why some states adopted merit commissions while others did not, and whether those states with commissions contributed to the president's goal of generating a greater number of female and minority judicial candidates.

Among the most visible studies of judicial recruitment during the Carter administration was Alan Neff's comparison (1981) of commission and noncommission states. His study was based primarily on questionnaire responses from commissioners and, secondarily, on supplemental interviews with senate staffers and interest group representatives. He depicted on a state-by-state basis the twenty-eight recruitment commissions created during the Carter administration and examined the implications of these commissions for senators' power to shape the composition of the federal bench in the state. Neff found that, although whether to utilize a nominating commission was left to the discretion of the state's senator(s), senators who chose to abandon the traditional prerogatives typically offered very little structural or procedural guidance after creating a commission. Indeed, although most commissions filtered their recommendations through the senator, who then forwarded them to the president, Neff concluded that many senators rubber-stamped commission recommendations and/or forwarded the commission's selections directly to the president. These findings led Neff to conclude, "Senatorial discretion remained theoretically broad but diminished in practice" (1981, 151).

To many scholars familiar with the reluctance of senators to abandon their political prerogatives, Neff's picture of abdicated influence seemed counterintuitive. Particularly troubling was the fact that his findings were based primarily on the observations of commissioners and judicial candidates, rather than senators and their staffers. It was not surprising, therefore, when parallel work by Elliot Slotnick (1979, 1984) suggested that whatever perceptions commissioners may have had about their own influence, most senators and their staffers continued to perceive judicial recruitment as a process dominated by senators and other home-state politicos. Slotnick's inquiry, which was based on interviews with senators, senate staffers, and others involved in the recruitment process, was primarily an investigation of the responses by home-state recruiters to the creation of judicial selection commissions. He did not, therefore, offer detailed descriptions of state-by-state differences in commission structures, recruitment procedures, or strategy. He did, however, offer important insights into matters such as senators' perceptions of their role in the recruitment process, what senators perceived to be the proper balance between presidential and senatorial prerogatives, and what they believed to be the correct balance between legal and extralegal appointment criteria. Slotnick found, inter alia, that most senators perceived recruitment for district court vacancies as primarily a senatorial prerogative and perceived the recruitment process as an interactive, bargaining process in which senators and presidents anticipate each others' preferences and incorporate this anticipation into their selection strategies and criteria. According to Slotnick's respondents, this process often includes senatorial lobbying on behalf of preferred candidates. In addition, most respondents openly acknowledged a propensity to favor political partisans, and they defended using a candidate's legal and political philosophy as legitimate selection criteria. A substantial minority were also willing to consider a candidate's stand on relatively specific policy issues, particularly if the president was viewed to feel strongly on the policy issue(s).

Contrary to Neff, Slotnick concluded that whether a state did or did not utilize a merit selection commission tells us very little about the power of senators to dominate judicial recruitment in that state. The creation and staffing of district court commissions remained, after all, a senatorial prerogative, and most senators retained ultimate control over the final submission of recommendations to the president. Furthermore, Slotnick found that many senators created commissions not to secure meritorious judges but for political reasons, such as the symbolic insulation of senators from the appearance of partisanship. Perhaps the consensus of Slotnick's respondents was summarized best by an anonymous respondent on the Senate Judiciary Committee staff:

> The commissions are only as good or as bad as the senators who have set them up. A selection commission is only a little more pomp and flair on the underlying senatorial participation. The results of [our senator's commission] were appointments as good as he would have made himself. Other commissions come up with appointments [*sic*] as bad as the senator would have made himself. . . .
>
> We're quite happy with the commission because it does help to insulate the senator. (quoted in Slotnick 1980b, 124)

It would be an exaggeration to conclude from Slotnick's work that home-state senators exert unfettered influence over the recruitment of candidates for judicial vacancies in their states. Slotnick's work also tells us that the quality and quantity of influence exerted by home-state senators is, to some degree, a function of the partisan and ideological composition of the Senate Judiciary Committee. When the committee was chaired by Senator Eastland, a segregationist Democrat, the blue-slip convention was used to give home-state senators a virtual veto over nominees, especially those whose segregationist credentials were suspect. When Senator Kennedy, a liberal northern Democrat, became chair, the blue slip was relegated to advisory status, that is, the Judiciary Committee incorporated senators' personal objectives into its deliberations but was not unequivocally bound by them. Nonetheless, as depicted by Slotnick, senators in both commission *and* noncommission states not only considered selecting federal judges to be a senatorial prerogative, but they also willingly acknowledged political, as well as legal, recruitment criteria. Moreover, as anticipated by anecdotes from previous studies, they were willing to lobby the White House for the appointment of their own preferred candidates.

That this activist pattern extended to the Reagan administration is clear from Gary Fowler's study (1983) of recommendation procedures during the early days of that administration. Perhaps the most striking distinction between recruitment during the Carter and Reagan administrations was found in states with no senators from the president's party. Carter encouraged Republicans in states with no Democratic senators to establish bipartisan commissions; if they did so, he would accept nominations from the commission. Of course, the prudent recruiter anticipated presidential prerogatives by submitting names that were within the bounds of presidential acceptability (Slotnick), but the process did accommodate bipartisan participation in the process (Neff). President Reagan, by contrast, accommodated only Republican senators or their panels. If the state had no Republican senators, the president generally either relied on the state's Republican congressional delegation as a quasi commission or created a panel of party officials and loyalists to identify acceptable candidates. Thus, unless Republican senators invited their participation, Democratic senators were effectively left out of the recruitment process.

The virtual exclusion of Democratic senators from the selection process was facilitated by the Senate Judiciary Committee's version of the blue-slip convention during the first six years of the Reagan administration. Under the chairmanship of Strom Thurmond, a conservative Republican from South Carolina, blue slips were sent *only* to home-state Republicans. Unless they were members of the Judiciary Committee, home-state Democrats could rarely influence the confirmation of appointees to their state unless their evaluations were solicited by their Republican counterpart and incorporated into his or her evaluation of the candidate. As a result, the Reagan administration felt little need to consider out-party senators in recruitment.

Despite the deference of the administration to home-state Republicans, Fowler also identified a recurring tension between the Reagan White House and many Republican senators. The White House urged Republican senators to submit three to five names for review by the Justice Department's Office of Legal Policy and the Department of Justice Select Working Group chaired by the attorney general. After review, these committees were to submit evaluations to a White House working group, chaired by White House Counsel Fred Fielding. They would then select one preferred nominee pending investigation by the American Bar Association and the Federal Bureau of Investigation (Markman interview, 1987). However, many Republicans resisted the White House and insisted on maximizing their control over nominations by submitting only one name per vacancy.

More recent journalistic accounts indicate that if the senator was a philosophical as well as a partisan ally of the president (e.g., Republican Phil Gramm of Texas), wranglings over appointments were of no substantive significance. But when the recalcitrant Republicans were ideologically out of step with the president, judicial selection squabbles often resulted in major appointment gridlocks, with the senator(s) refusing to submit a name acceptable to the president, who in turn declined to nominate the candidate(s) submitted by the senator(s). The best example of such a standoff was Pennsylvania, where six vacancies went unfilled until President Reagan and Senators Heinz and Spector finally were able to reach a compromise under pressure from the Pennsylvania bench and bar (Markman interview, 1987).

In combination with subsequent work that documents the tendency of President Reagan to nominate and secure confirmation of white male conservatives (Goldman 1989), Fowler's attention to the balance between senatorial and presidential prerogatives is revealing. It reminds us that, even with a Republican majority on the Senate Judiciary Committee, the president must occasionally be willing to reach ideological compromises with senators of his party. And it suggests implicitly that these compromises may be reflected subsequently in the aggregate ideological direction of judicial outcomes in that state.

Although the literature on recruitment politics is rather small and constrained by the lack of a comparative perspective, a comparison of recruitment during different administrations offers some important insights into the recruitment process and the political boundaries of that process. The first is that the dynamics of home-state recruitment vary fundamentally from one administration to another. These differences are most obvious when a new party takes the White House, but they extend also to intraparty shifts, as exemplified by differences in the Kennedy and Johnson administrations in their judicial appointments in the South. Thus, while scholars may have overemphasized the role of the president in the district judge appointment process, still their research did underscore the reality that only the president can nominate judges and that judicial recruiters must work within the parameters of anticipated presidential appointment criteria.

A second insight to be gleaned from the literature is that the absolute and relative influence of presidents and senators on recruitment parameters fluctuates in tandem with changes in the composition, leadership, and norms of the Senate Judiciary Committee. Again, these shifts are most obvious in the wake of a partisan shift in the committee's majority and, therefore, its chair. We saw this phenomenon demonstrated in 1987, when the conservative Republican Senator from South Carolina, Strom Thurmond, was obliged to give up his chairmanship on the Judiciary Committee to Joseph Biden, the liberal Democrat from Delaware. However, *intra*party changes can also alter significantly the dynamics of the confirmation process as observed a decade earlier after conservative Democratic James Eastland of Mississippi gave over his chair's post to liberal Democratic Senator Edward Kennedy of Massachusetts.

In combination, the senatorial and presidential constraints outlined here suggest that the politics of home-state recruitment, like the politics of presidential appointment, can best be under stood in the context of "selection eras," each of which is marked by changes in leadership in the White House and/or the Judiciary Committee. However, the third insight to be gleaned from these recruitment studies is that, although recruitment procedures and criteria may be constrained by the president and the Judiciary Committee for a given selection era, the procedures and criteria that drive home-state recruitment are subtle and may also vary from state to state during the same era. This idiosyncratic variation was vividly illustrated in California under the Nixon administration when the president (as previously noted) was obliged to appoint one liberal Democrat for every GOP judge he selected; it was also exemplified in the subtle variation among state selection commissions during the Carter administration. Moreover, it is exacerbated by the occasional idiosyncratic differences among recruitments by the *same* senator(s) in the *same* state during the *same* recruitment era. Such idiosyncrasy can be illustrated by the persistent tendency of many new senators to award the first available judicial vacancy to a college friend or roommate (Rowland 1991).

In sum, despite the insightful contributions of recent recruitment research to our understanding of variation in aggregate recruitment patterns, we remain largely uninformed about state-by-state variation in recruitment procedures and criteria during a given era. For example, although Neff does a good job of distinguishing interstate variance in the structure of recruitment, his premature perceptions of diminished senatorial influence suggest insufficient attention to the criteria by which senators and other politicos identify acceptable candidates. On the other hand, although Slotnick documents very well the influence of political criteria and the perception by most senators that judicial recruitment is a senatorial prerogative, his research does not include a discussion of state-by-state variations. (Part of the cost of acquiring his data was his promise not to identify sources on a state-by-state basis.) And while Fowler provided valuable glimpses of the recruitment environment during the early days of the Reagan administration, he relied primarily on anecdotes rather than examining systematically interstate variation in judicial recruitment. The result was a valuable series of snapshots of judicial selection during the early days of the Reagan presidency. Still, such glimpses, however vivid, do not provide us with a comprehensive, coherent picture of interstate variation in procedures and criteria during the Reagan and Thurmond selection era.

AN EMPIRICAL EXPLORATION OF HOME-STATE RECRUITMENT

How do senators or other home-state recruiters identify and evaluate candidates for judicial vacancies? What is the relative involvement of the state's legal and democratic subcultures in the recruitment of federal district judges, and what legal and political criteria are used to distinguish acceptable candidates? We examine these questions not from the perspective of the president but from the perspective of key home-state recruiters. We begin with a discussion of our research methodology.

In recognizing that recruitment dynamics vary across eras defined by presidential administration and control of the Senate Judiciary Committee, we concentrated on recruitment during the Reagan and Thurmond era (1981–1986) and focused on qualitative differences among fifteen specified states.[1] These states were selected for their economic, political, and geographic diversity and include states with and without Republican senators. We also included states that used selection commissions as well as those that relied on traditional, personal recruitment by the senator.

To depict accurately the politics of recruitment within individual states and facilitate comparisons across states, we relied on several data sources. Our primary source was interviews with Senate and House staff members who were actively involved in judicial recruitment. In states with Republican representation in the Senate these staffers were identified simply by contacting the senator's Washington office and asking for the person(s) responsible for judicial nominations. In states with no Republican representation in the Senate, House staffers and other key operatives were identified by contacting the Office of Legal Policy (OLP), the highly politicized arm of the Justice Department with responsibility for screening the legal and political credentials of judicial candidates, and asking that office to identify key home-state liaisons.

Secondary sources included key "back-home" operatives identified by staffers, and journalists who covered appointments for home-state newspapers. A typical home-state operative would be the chair of a recruitment commission appointed by the senator or the chair of a key state bar association committee. Interviews with in-state sources were sometimes tailored to determine specifics left unanswered by staff respondents—for example, whether attorneys on a commission were designated by the state bar association or appointed by the senator. The most informed journalists were Washington correspondents for large urban newspapers, such as the *Los Angeles Times* or the *Houston Chronicle*, who had done feature stories on controversial recruitments by their state's senator(s).

To clarify the recruitment picture we needed to know how states went about recruiting judicial candidates, and the legal or political criteria that served as prerequisites to recruitment. To identify key procedures and criteria we asked our respondents three sets of open-ended questions.

First, we asked them to describe in detail their state's recruitment process from the time a judicial vacancy was created to the time one or more candidates for that vacancy were recommended to the White House. Included within this line of inquiry were questions about how many names were submitted per vacancy; submission of more than one name was treated as deference to presidential prerogative, while submission of a single candidate was viewed as an exercise of Senate prerogatives. Respondents were also asked to estimate the involvement of the political and legal subcultures.

The legal subculture's participation was designated as significant to the extent that state and local bar associations or their official representatives were formal participants in the identification and/or evaluation of candidates. In states with Republican senators, the political subculture's involvement was deemed significant unless the senator(s) delegated responsibility for selection and evaluation of candidates to the bar or bar-dominated commissions; in states with no Republican senators, political involvement was significant to the extent that elected Republican officials or campaign officials were involved in the process.

After outlining the recruitment process and the relative involvement of the legal and political subcultures in that process, respondents were asked to estimate the importance of candidates' legal and political backgrounds as recruitment criteria. To ascertain legal criteria each respondent was asked whether each of four variables was significant: judicial experience, trial court experience, judicial temperament, and whether the candidate had the support of the bar association. To ascertain the importance of political backgrounds, respondents were asked to estimate the significance of partisan affiliation and activity and of the level of political conservatism.

Finally, respondents were asked about the importance of ideology and whether specific policy preferences were important criteria. Whatever the answer to this question, it was followed by probes to determine the significance of four policy preferences identified by the Reagan administration as important appointment criteria: opposition to abortion, opposition to affirmative action, support for capital punishment, and support for reduced government regulation of commercial activity.

AN OVERVIEW OF HOME-STATE RECRUITMENT

A state-by-state overview of variation in recruitment patterns is presented in Table 4-1. Before looking at the specifics of this table, however, we would first emphasize that our findings fully support those of other studies which revealed that judicial recruitment is a very idiosyncratic phenomenon. The observation is well illustrated by the decision of Texas Senator Phil Gramm, a highly partisan, conservative Republican, to recommend as his first judicial recruit a moderate Democratic congressman for a district court vacancy. At first blush this choice seemed a refreshing abandonment of partisan priorities; however, according to press accounts (*Houston Chronicle* 1983), the purpose was purely political—namely, Gramm thought that by securing the Democrat's appointment to the federal bench he would enable a Republican to fill the *congressional vacancy* created by the appointment. (As it turns out, Gramm was wrong. The ex-congressman was confirmed, but another Democrat won the special election to replace him.)

Since each state—indeed, each recruitment—included enough political maneuvering, legal assessment, and negotiation to justify a case study, it is not surprising that scholars have eschewed interstate and intrastate comparisons in favor of a presidential perspective, which serves to organize and aggregate inquiry for a given era. However, despite the prevalence of richly variegated interstate and intrastate recruitment, it is also true that our respondents revealed some common patterns of home-state recruitment during this era. The first, and most significant, generalization is to confirm Slotnick's observation that knowing whether or not a state utilizes a judicial selection commission tells us little about the political influences on judicial recruitment in that state. Some commissions are dominated by the legal subculture and rely heavily on legal criteria. For example, when a vacancy occurred in Oregon, Senators Hatfield and Packwood solicited three names from the Oregon bar association and forwarded all three names to the Justice Department, where a single nominee was selected after a review of legal and political credentials (Higgins interview, 1986). Other commissions were dominated by political actors and political selection criteria, while some incorporated both sets of influences. In California, for example, Senator Wilson established two commissions for each of the state's four federal judicial districts. Responsibility for the initial identification of candidates with strong legal credentials rested with a "legal commission" made up primarily of prominent attorneys and bar association representatives. But the legal commission's recommendations were filtered through a highly partisan "political committee" that reviewed each candidate's partisan background and policy preferences. The political committee, whose membership was confidential, recommended to the senator only those candidates who were politically as well as legally acceptable. The senator, in turn, reviewed these names and forwarded to the Office of Legal Policy a single candidate for each judicial vacancy (Glass interview, 1986). Thus the presence of a "merit" selection committee did not prevent the process from becoming highly political and personal.

If we conclude that the presence of a selection commission per se tells us very little about judicial recruitment, the reader may very well ask: What, then, *does* account for the presence or absence of selection commissions in the first place? If commissions do not distinguish merit and politicized recruitment strategies, why do some senators establish commissions while others do not? The answer to these questions is both surprising and commonsensical.

The best predictor of a commission was neither a political nor a legal

Table 4-1 (a). Summary of Recruitment Procedures and Criteria: States with Republican Senators

	Recruitment Process				Criteria							
					Importance of Legal Criteria				Importance of Political Criteria			
	Commission	Level of Bar Involvement	Level of State Party Involvement	No. of Names to White House	Judicial Experience	Trial Experience	Judicial Temperament	State Bar Support	State Party Affiliation	Activism	Conservatism	Policy Preferences
CA[a]	Yes	No	No	1	High	High	Low	Low	High	Moderate	High	—
CO[b]	No	No	No	1	Moderate	Low	Moderate	Low	High	Low	High	Yes
CT[c]	No	No	No	1	Low	High	—	No	No	No	No	No
FL[d]	Yes	No	No	?	High	Moderate	—	No	High	Low	High	No
MN[e]	No	Moderate	Low	1–3	High	High	—	High	Moderate	Low	Low	"No!"
MS[f]	No	No	No	1	Low	High	Moderate	Low	No	No	Low	"No!"
OR[g]	No	High	No	3–5	—	—	—	High	No	No	No	"None"
NC[h]	No	Low	Low	1	High	Moderate	Low	Low	High	High	High	Yes!
PA[i]	Yes	Low	Low	1	Moderate	High	High	Low	High	No	No	None
TX[j]	Yes	Moderate	Low	1	High	Low	—	Moderate	High	High	High	Yes

Table 4-1 (a) *Continued*

Comments:

[a] Two commissions per district—one legal, one political. Both quite informal. Both made up of Wilson loyalists; membership confidential, but reputed to include active federal judges, which has caused controversy. Deny importance of policy preferences, but acknowledge preference for candidates with judicial experience and a record of support for victim rights.

[b] *Very* personal. Senator Armstrong familiar with pool of potential candidates. Contacts personally, reviews opinions, etc. Generally supportive of administration but against capital punishment and imprisonment of most nonviolent offenders.

[c] *Very* personal. Identifies good candidate via their litigation experience and contacts, then persuades them to become judge and persuades administration to accept them. Not very partisan; consults with Dodd; says "specific policy agenda would hurt candidate's chances."

[d] Committee very personal, made up of attorneys who share Senator Hawkins's political and judicial conservatism. But committee proceedings fairly formal, with questionnaires and interviews. No specific policy preferences, but conservatism very important, and specifics dictated by "shared views with OLP." The five names may or may not be ranked, but "Senator has always gotten her first choice.

[e] Informal; two Republican senators tend to alternate recruitment initiatives, but process varies idiosyncratically from nomination to nomination. Emphatic refusal to consider policy preferences has created conflicts with OLP.

[f] Personal. When vacancy occurs, Senator Cochran does the investigation, makes calls to litigators and judges, etc. He looks for moderate civil rights and minimizes partisan criteria, staff acknowledges anticipation of OLP on key policy issues.

[g] Recruitment delegated to state bar. Bar reps not very forthcoming, but they forward three to five names to Hatfield, who "reviews" but forwards to White House without interviews, etc. Rationale for this abdication is fact Hatfield is not attorney.

[h] Informal; dominated by Senator Helms, who likes to recruit members of his staff and "conservatives with good legal credentials." Primacy of political criteria reflected in enthusiastic commitment to candidates who are "correct" in busing, states' rights, law-and-order, abortion, and prayer.

[i] Formal commission—questionnaires, interviews, etc.—of fourteen members. Seven appointed by each senator, but Specter, the ex-litigator, is most active in process of reviewing and selecting candidate. Both staffs cited conflicts with Justice and were very critical of Justice's "shallow overreliance on political favors."

[j] Most personal of commissions; one for entire state; all members are attorneys close to Gramm; includes a husband and wife and overrepresents Republican areas. Gramm relies on commission to identify qualified candidates because "he is not attorney." But he is very active in final selection of candidate via personal interview. Ideology very important to senator, as are victim rights and law-and-order. Abortion less important, but anticipates OLP.

Table 4-1 (b). Summary of Recruitment Procedures and Criteria for States Without Republican Senators

	Recruitment Process				Criteria							
					Importance of Legal Criteria				Importance of Political Criteria			
	Commission	Level of Bar Involvement	Level of State Party Involvement	No. of Names to White House	Judicial Experience	Trial Experience	Judicial Temperament	State Bar Support	State Party Affiliation	Activism	Conservatism	Policy Preferences
AR[a]	No	None	None	3	Low	Low	9	None	Low	Low	A	"Not Really"
IL[b]	No	High	High	3	None	High	—	High	Moderate	Moderate	Moderate	No
LA[c]	Yes	None	High	2/3	None	None	None	None	High	Moderate	High	White House
MA[d]	Yes	Low	High	16	None	High	Moderate	Moderate	High	High	High	White House
MI[e]	Yes	High	High	3/5	—	Moderate	Moderate	Moderate	Moderate	Moderate	Moderate	White House

Comments:

[a] Very informal and personal; the state's Republican congressmen divide the state geographically and rely on personal political contacts and "reputation in community" to identify good candidates. Policy preferences not very important.

[b] Most candidates self-nominated. They fill out formal questionnaire and submit to committee made up of Republican Congressional delegation and chaired by Representative Michel, the senior Republican, whose presidential support score was 85. Questionnaires are evaluated by state and local bar association, then Republican representatives select top three.

[c] Recruitment of judges done unabashedly by patronage committee. Members include Reagan/Bush campaign chair and state representatives to national party. Justice sometimes conducts own search, which did not bother respondents, all of whom share president's policy criteria.

[d] Massachusetts selection committee headed by state chair of Reagan/Bush campaign and includes as ex officio member the general counsel for the National Republican Committee. State's lone Republican representative (Conte) had minimal role, presumably because his 1984 presidential support score was 36, which is barely half the Republican average (68). The 16 names are extraordinary and give White House almost total discretion.

[e] A 25-30 member judicial recruitment committee is appointed by state party chair; includes representatives of all bar associations, including minority and female, and state party officials. Judicial recruitment committee sends each candidate questionnaire, checks with bar grievance committee, and interviews all "serious" candidates. Senior representative Broomfield (support score = 73) acts as liaison between judicial recruitment committee and Republican Congress delegation, which reviews judicial recruitment committee recommendations and between delegation and White House. Deference given to representative(s) from district with vacancy, but number of names ensures that White House will indeed "take care" of policy preferences.

variable but rather whether the state's population was large or small. Indeed, states *with* commissions (such as California, Florida, Illinois, New York, and Texas) were all much more populous than their noncommission counterparts. However, as will become clear in the state-by-state analysis, even though senate-appointed commissions are concentrated in populous states, the presence of a commission says little about the involvement of the legal subculture or the importance of political selection criteria. Even in states with Republican senators, the selection format ranged from being highly politicized to one dominated by legal criteria and the legal subculture. It would seem, therefore, that Republican senator(s) relied on commissions when sheer numbers made personalized systems impractical and time-consuming, but that the structure of the recruitment system was relatively unrelated to the politics of recruitment.

The second general conclusion we may draw from our interviews is that, as anticipated by Fowler's description of the blue-slip convention during the early years of this era, recruitment was much more partisan than during previous eras. Despite notable exceptions (such as in Connecticut), Democratic senators were almost never consulted by their Republican counterparts or by partisan commissions during the recruitment process. Rather, they learned the identity of judicial candidates from the press or when they were contacted during the OLP's background investigation. The distinction between this circumvention of out-party senators and the collaboration of previous eras is exemplified by the experience of Senator Bentsen (D. Texas). During the Carter administration Senator Bentsen utilized a statewide selection commission that accepted and solicited recommendations from the "politically active legal community." Before he recommended a candidate to the White House, Bentsen always consulted informally with his Republican counterpart, Senator John Tower. This consultation, which staffers described as cordial, mirrored exactly the courtesy extended Bentsen by Tower during the Nixon and Ford era. But the courtesy that characterized previous eras disappeared with the election of Republican Phil Gramm as the state's junior senator and the dawn of the Reagan and Thurmond selection era. During this period Senator Bentsen and his staff learned the identity of nominees for district judgeships in Texas *not* during the recruitment process, *not* during the OLP review process, but only *after* the formal submission of a nominee to the Senate Judiciary Committee. Usually this notice came after a hearing had been set, which staffers say afforded insufficient time for a meaningful review of the candidates' credentials (Sanchez interview 1986; Madden interview 1986).

Although the Bentsen experience approximates very closely the experience of most Democrats during the era, it should be noted that the partisan dynamics of recruitment changed when the Democrats regained their majority on the Judiciary Committee in 1987. At that time a Judiciary Committee analogue to the OLP was created. The committee conducted independent investigations and shared the results with Democratic senators. Although no formal blue-slip policy was established, the head of that committee said that the blue-slip powers of home-state Democrats were expanded significantly; moreover, if Democrats had not been notified before the submission of a name to the Judiciary Committee, hearings were delayed until the out-party senator had sufficient time to evaluate the nominee and express his or her support or opposition (Metalitz interview, 1987; Markham interview, 1987). Thus, the extreme partisanship of the Reagan and Thurmond era is at least partially attributable to the institutional dynamics that defined the era.

A final general observation relates to the potential for intraparty conflict during this era in states with two Republican senators. Given the patronage value of federal judgeships and the absence of formal recruitment guidelines, one would anticipate occasional conflicts *between* home-state senators. This anticipation is buttressed by the disagreements between Ohio's Democratic Senators Glenn and Metzenbaum during the Carter administration. However, despite the potential for conflict, our interviews identified no intrastate partisan disagreement. The process of cooperation varied in other states, however. In some the senators appointed equal numbers of commissioners to an independent commission while in others they simply consulted informally. Elsewhere they divided primary recruitment responsibilities sequentially, or among the state's judicial districts. But in no state was the division of authority contentious.

Having presented an overview of home-state recruitment in an era dominated by partisanship and intraparty cooperation, we turn now to a more focused, state-by-state assessment of recruitment procedures and criteria. Given the attention of previous research to presidential involvement and our ultimate goal of estimating the extent to which recruitment politics affect the link between presidential appointment and aggregate judicial judgment, it is useful to organize our discussion around a distinction between states in which presidential discretion is constrained by the prerogatives of Republican senators and states without Republican representation in the Senate.

Recruitment in States Without Republican Senator(s)

Six of our sample states were without Republican senators—Arkansas, Hawaii, Louisiana, Illinois, Massachusetts, and Michigan. As anticipated by the absence of Republican senators and the constraints of senatorial courtesy, the White House was able to exert substantial unfettered influence in each of these states. This dominance is evidenced most clearly by the fact that each of these unrepresented states forwarded at least three names to the Justice Department for each district court vacancy. Massachusetts offered as many as sixteen names! These multiple submissions give the Justice Department, and ultimately the president, tremendous latitude to identify and nominate a candidate who meets the administration's political criteria.

Despite the uniformly high level of the chief executive's influence on these states, it is also true that the nature of presidential dominance depends on the quantity and quality of the state's representation in the House of Representatives. For instance, executive domination was greatest in the two states with no Republican House members—Louisiana and Hawaii.

Hawaii represents the extreme of White House domination. Neither the state bar nor the state Republican Party was a meaningful recruiter; rather, the Justice Department recruited its own candidates on the basis of the same substantive criteria it used to evaluate candidates for nomination. This external domination is illustrated by the "recruitment" and nomination of Albert Sousa. Born in Hong Kong, Mr. Sousa had ties to Hawaii that were limited to an eight-year stint as general counsel for the telephone company. For the five years preceding his nomination in 1985, he had been acting head of the Federal Energy and Resource Commission (FERC) in Washington, D.C. However, his most important experience had been in California, where he had been public utilities commissioner when Reagan was governor (Nakamura interview, 1986).

More typical of presidential dominance in unrepresented states is Louisiana. As with most states with no Republican representation, the White House assumed a quasi-senatorial role and created a Patronage Committee whose duties included, inter alia, the recruitment of district judges. The committee included the chair of the state's Reagan and Bush campaign committee and several state party leaders who demonstrated loyalty to the ticket in 1980 and 1984. The committee's procedures were quite informal, but they included the development of a Political Activities Summary for each serious judicial candidate. The purpose of this report was to ensure that the candidate's philosophy and policy preferences were consistent with the Reagan platforms and to help the Patronage Committee meet its avowed goal of "reversing the liberal activist trend on the federal bench in the 11th Circuit" (Smith interview).

A step down the dominance ladder were states with a small number (one or two) of Republican representatives, in which the state's degree of procedural and substantive independence was a function of support for the president in Congress. This distinction is illustrated in our sample by the differences between Massachusetts and Arkansas.

In 1984, Massachusetts Congressman Conte's *Congressional Quarterly*

Presidential Support Score was 36; the average support score for Republicans was 68. It is not surprising, therefore, that judicial recruitment in Massachusetts paralleled closely recruitment in Louisiana and other states with no Republicans in Congress. The White House established a selection commission chaired by the chairman of the state's Reagan and Bush campaign committee. The committee included as an ex officio member the general counsel for the Republican National Committee. The committee was given no formal instructions, but members said it was clear from the committee's composition that it was to locate and recruit "conservatives committed to judicial restraint" (Conway interview, 1986). Although this might appear to be easier said than done in the only state that supported George McGovern, it was facilitated by the extraordinary submission of sixteen names to the Justice Department, a procedure that essentially shifted the selection process to Washington. (It is interesting to note parenthetically that one of this committee's first recruits was the attorney who had argued the losing side in several Boston desegregation cases presided over by Judge Garrity, a liberal Democratic appointee. Ironically, the vacancy for which he was recruited was created by Garrity's retirement.)

The contrast between Arkansas and Massachusetts could not have been greater. For most of this era Arkansas was represented in the House by two Republicans—Congressmen Bethune and Hammerschmidt—both of whom were loyal, highly visible supporters of the Reagan administration. It is hardly surprising, therefore, that these two supporters were entrusted with judicial recruitment for most of the era. Indeed, these congressmen became quasi senators—namely, they divided the state east and west, accepted unsolicited names informally from large law firms and political allies, evaluated the candidates informally on visits to their districts, and submitted three names to the Justice Department for each vacancy (Reed interview 1986). Here it is interesting to note that Congressman Bethune was a candidate for federal judgeship during the Ford administration. He was "blue-slipped" by Democratic Senator Bumpers, which may have contributed to the complete exclusion of Bumpers from judicial recruitment during the Reagan administration.

The two remaining states in our "unrepresented" sample are similar geographically, demographically, and politically. However, unlike our other unrepresented states, Michigan and Illinois each had a relatively large Republican delegation in the House, and each delegation was led by a senior congressman who was supportive of President Reagan's policy initiatives. It is not surprising, therefore, that recruitment patterns in the two states are somewhat similar to each other and quite distinguishable from those in other unrepresented states. In both states the senior congressman acted as a liaison between his state and the White House. In both states the Republican congressional delegation reviewed and evaluated candidates before three to five names were forwarded to Washington. Moreover, despite some variation in emphasis, recruiters in both states said that, although partisanship was important, consideration of policy preferences was largely delegated to Justice Department gatekeepers.

Despite the overall structural similarities between Michigan and Illinois, these general patterns should not be allowed to obscure important functional and structural differences between the two states. Judicial recruitment in Michigan was considerably more formal and included more diverse elements of the legal and political subcultures than did recruitment in Illinois. In Michigan a twenty-five-member Judicial Review Committee appointed by the state Republican chairman included token representatives of diverse bar associations. Vacancies were advertised in the newspapers and bar publications. Candidates identified by these ads were sent questionnaires asking them to detail their relevant qualifications and experiences; moreover, their backgrounds were checked through bar grievance committees. Only after the Review Committee had reviewed each questionnaire and interviewed each candidate were the candidates rated, ranked, and their names forwarded to the Republican congressional delegation for final evaluation. After the background check, the delegation, usually in consultation with the state party chair and the state Reagan and Bush chair, reviewed the candidates with "an eye for good Republicans but no policy specifics" (Sinclair interview 1986).

Because he was the senior Representative, Congressman Broomfield chaired the Michigan delegation's meetings and acted as White House liaison; however, particular deference was shown representatives from districts where the prospective judge would preside. For example, when a vacancy occurred in the western district, Bloomfield delegated his role to Congressman Henry, whose congressional district coincided closely with the western judicial district.

As did most states without Republican senators, Michigan sent multiple names—usually three to five—to Washington without preference ordering. It did so, however, with the expectation that the White House *would* ask questions about "ideological preferences" and the expectation that individual supporters, including some members of the Review Committee or congressional delegation, would lobby the White House on behalf of their preferred recruit.

Illinois differed significantly on two counts from its neighbor. First, the recruitment *process* was more overtly partisan and exclusive. Illinois did utilize a candidate questionnaire and did submit the candidates' names and responses for review by the Illinois State Bar Association and local bar associations. Absent from the process, however, was participation by an analogue to Michigan's large Review Committee and representatives of diverse bar associations. Furthermore, most candidates were identified not on the basis of media announcements but from a list of candidates compiled by former Senator Charles Percy.

Second, Congressman Michael, Illinois's senior representative and House minority leader, was much more proactive in recruitment than was his Michigan counterpart, Congressman Bloomfield. In situations comparable to those where Bloomfield delegated primary recruitment responsibility, Congressman Michael was simply "attentive to the opinions" of representatives from the district where the recruit would be seated (Yard interview 1986).

Illinois's relatively inclusive model is significant not only because it differs somewhat from that of its neighbor but because it varies from the model followed by Senator Percy before his defeat in 1984. Percy used a commission that included formal representation of adverse groups though he did *not* include the Republican congressional delegation in his recruitment process (Westal interview 1986). Thus, the differences between Illinois and Michigan may reflect reactions to idiosyncratic variances in previous recruitment eras as much as they reflect more fundamental strategic differences in processes or criteria.

Although idiosyncratic differences distinguished recruitment in Michigan and Illinois, they should not be allowed to obscure the more fundamental regularities identified not only for Michigan and Illinois but for all states without Republican representation in the Senate. First, as noted for the larger sample, the presence or absence of a commission had no substantive or procedural significance per se. Second, absent Republican senators, the degree of presidential involvement was a function of the quantity and quality of the state's Republican representation in the House of Representatives. The White House was deferential only to home-state recruiters whose ideological preferences resembled closely those of the president. Finally, despite the procedural and participatory variation among states, President Reagan was able to structure recruitment in these states in ways that enhanced presidential influence over policy preferences. (This was true even in Michigan, which institutionalized bar involvement and eschewed direct questions about policy preferences.) Multiple names were always sent to the Justice Department, with the understanding that the OLP would ensure that when the prospective list was winnowed to a single candidate, he or she would be committed to the president's priorities.

We do not expect the persistent pattern of presidential domination to be repeated for states with Republican senator(s). The norms of senatorial courtesy guaranteed that home-state Republican senators could, if they wished, exert substantial influence on judicial selection. In the following section we look at procedural and substantive variation in the exercise of this influence.

States with Republican Senators

As with unrepresented states, recruitment in states with Republican senator(s) varied across two general dimensions—procedural and substantive. Moreover, qualitative variation along both dimensions offers insights into the causes and consequences of state patterns. Therefore, we will first discuss differences in recruitment procedures and then turn our attention to variations in substantive criteria. The chapter's conclusion will explore links between a state's recruitment patterns and judicial outcomes in that state's federal courts.

The primary procedural distinction between represented and unrepresented states derives directly from the powers conferred upon home-state senators, especially senators from the president's party, by the convention of senatorial courtesy. Because the president cannot nominate a candidate whom the senator finds personally objectionable, the potential of the White House to influence the in-state recruitment process in represented states is distinctly diminished. The senator(s) may create a very personalized process or may delegate control of the process to selection commissions, bar associations, or even politically active law firms, but White House influence on these *procedural* decisions is minimal. Even when senators delegated recruitment responsibility, they selected their own delegates, and with little interference by the president or state Republican officials. Thus, in our sample of represented states the formal involvement of state party officials or Reagan and Bush campaign officials was minimal.

The uniform procedural immunity of Republican senators does not mean that recruitment procedures were uniform among the represented states. To the contrary, they varied along several important dimensions. The most obvious was whether the senator(s) personally chose the judges or whether they created a selection commission. As noted earlier, commission systems were concentrated in the more populous states. Indeed, the four most populous states in our sample (California, Florida, Pennsylvania, and Texas) all utilized commissions, while the other six (Colorado, Connecticut, Minnesota, Mississippi, North Carolina, and Oregon) did not. Moreover, as anticipated by Slotnick's research, tremendous procedural and substantive variation was found among the commission states. For example, some commissions acted as highly personalized agents of the senator(s), while others were designed to maximize participation by highly disparate elements of the legal and political subcultures. Some commissions specifically rejected consideration of political criteria; others were highly and unabashedly politicized. Likewise, some senators without commissions emphasized political criteria, while others depended heavily on bar associations and legal criteria.

Although the variance between commission and noncommission states tended to be "a distinction without a difference," variation across other, more subtle procedural dimensions was more meaningful. Of particular significance for the link between recruitment and judgment were three procedural variations. First, states differed substantially in the quantity and quality of bar association involvement. Individual members of the bar or influential law firms were frequently part of the process, but in six of our ten represented states organized bar association involvement was nil. In the other four states the degree of bar involvement varied almost randomly. It is interesting to note, however, that the extremes of bar involvement tended to be found in small, uncommissioned states such as Oregon and Colorado. In Oregon, Senator Packwood, who was not an attorney, virtually delegated recruitment responsibilities to the Oregon state bar. In Colorado, Senator Armstrong, who had strong personal opinions about capital punishment and the incarceration of nonviolent offenders, rarely involved the bar or other interested organizations.

Second, states varied substantially in the degree of personal involvement by senator(s) in the recruitment process. This variation was most apparent in noncommission states. To extend the Colorado example, Senator Armstrong frequently took advantage of the two-hour time difference to make evening recruitment calls to Colorado candidates and references (Welcher interview 1986). Likewise, Mississippi Senator Cochran was described as "close to the vest" in his evaluation of judicial recruits (Slade interview 1986). However, this variation in personal involvement extended to states with commissions, some of which were rather independent, while others were highly personal extensions of senatorial involvement. In Texas, for example, Senator Gramm personally interviewed every recruit who cleared his handpicked commission (Madden interview 1986). In Pennsylvania, by contrast, analogous interviews were conducted by a fourteen-member commission whose appointments were divided evenly between the state's Republican senators.

Finally, states varied significantly in the number of candidates recommended to the White House. As indicated previously, most Republican senators sent a single recommendation to the White House. Moreover, according to their staff members, senators limited their recommendation for a given vacancy to a single name because they considered judicial recruitment an important senatorial prerogative and considered the submission of multiple names a threat to that prerogative. As for Minnesota and Oregon, the two states that submitted multiple names, both have high or moderate bar involvement; thus the multiple submissions may be indicative of senatorial decisions to shift recruitment prerogatives from the political to the legal subculture.

When one turns from procedures to questions of substantive selection criteria, it is much more difficult to generalize across states. States varied a great deal in their proffered balance between legal and political criteria and in their willingness to acknowledge explicitly the importance of political criteria. They also differed significantly in the extent to which they anticipated and accommodated the president's substantive selection criteria. Variation in attentiveness and deference to presidential criteria are paralleled by variation in the extent to which senators delegate procedural responsibility and whether commissions or bar associations specify the substantive criteria to be applied by their designees. Some establish very specific political and legal criteria, while others lean over backward to avoid even the appearance of such specifications. Most, however, fall somewhere in between—that is, they do not specify selection criteria, but political as well as legal criteria are implicit in the identity of the commissioners or other designees. As one anonymous commissioner put it, "We weren't told specifically to look for Republicans who agreed with Senator [X] on certain issues, but we are all conservative Republicans and we know that [the senator] wants conservatives who believe in judicial restraint." Given this rich variation in substantive criteria, the sample states can be compared systematically on several legal and political dimensions.

Legal Criteria

Interstate variation on this dimension occurred primarily in response to questions about the influence of state bar associations and questions about attention to legal and judicial experience. The rather ambivalent role of the bar in all levels of state and federal judicial selection led us to ask recruiters how important the backing of state bar associations was to the selection of recruits in their state. The answer varied substantially. Bar support was very important in only two states—Minnesota and Oregon, both of which formally involve the bar in the recruitment process. But for Texas, where bar support was only moderately important, the significance of bar support as a selection criteria was rated as "low" while in other states it was "nonexistent." States where bar support was unimportant included commission and traditional states, and they ranged from the highly informal (e.g., Colorado) to the formal (e.g., Pennsylvania). In general, however, one can say that the influence of bar associations over recruitment in these states was rather limited and symbolic. When we turn our attention to courtroom experience, a rather different picture emerges.

Recruiters in all of these states demanded as a legal selection standard that the potential judge have some type of prior courtroom experience. However, the relative importance of this criterion varied greatly. For instance, California and Minnesota highly prized prior judicial and trial experience, while other states were more ambivalent about such matters. In Connecticut, for example, trial experience was important but judicial experience was not; in Texas, judicial experience was important but trial experience was not. An obvious question raised by this finding is why some states would emphasize bench experience while others would eschew this factor and concentrate instead on experience as a trial attorney. While our data do not offer a complete answer to this question, a tentative conclusion will emerge when we explore the pattern of political criteria.

Political Criteria

As with legal criteria, the emphasis on the "political correctness" of the judicial nominee varied greatly from one jurisdiction to another. In some states, there was an unabashed commitment to using overt political selection criteria, while in other states there was an explicit agreement to ignore such considerations. It is not surprising, therefore, that the responses of home-state recruiters to questions about political selection criteria were more diverse and more guarded than were their responses to questions about legal criteria.

The most politicized states—that is, those most overtly and unapologetically committed to the inclusion of partisanship and policy preferences as selection criteria—tended to be large states with judicial selection commissions. This pattern was typified by Texas and California, whose selection commissions were instructed explicitly to review the partisan history and policy preferences of legally qualified recruits. In California preference was given to seated judges with strong proclivities for expansion of victims' rights, and in Texas recruits were told before their interviews that "everything discussed will remain confidential, but the senator feels free to ask questions about ideology, law-and-order and other things" (Madden interview 1986).

It is also noteworthy that both Texas and California emphasized judicial experience as a legal selection criteria. The reason for this counterintuitive combination became apparent during the interview process—namely, experienced trial judges have established a track record on key issues such as crime control and due process. Thus, in large states where personal knowledge of each recruit is precluded by the size of the candidate pool, recruiters can have more confidence in their substantive political assessments if the candidate has a judicial track record.

The explicit embrace of political criteria extended also to North Carolina, a noncommission state. Senator Helms, a strong conservative, not only supported President Reagan's judicial selection criteria in North Carolina but lobbied against nominees from other states if he disagreed with their positions on issues ranging from abortion to criminal justice. It is no surprise, therefore, that his own recruitment strategies included a predilection for judicial experience and a preference for choosing his own staff members who were, of course, "correct on busing, states' rights, abortion, law and order, and prayer" (Fryar interview 1986).

One step below on the politicization ladder was Colorado, where Senator Armstrong was concerned that only fellow members of the GOP and/or conservatives be appointed to the bench. However, the Colorado picture was complicated by the fact that two of the senator's policy stands—opposition to capital punishment and to imprisonment of most nonviolent offenders—put him at odds with the administration. Furthermore, as head of the Republican Senate Policy Committee, he demonstrated his independence by refusing to endorse Attorney General Meese's demand that Armstrong and other Republican senators submit multiple names to the White House (Welcher interview 1986).

At the opposite end of the spectrum were states that either rejected political criteria outright or assigned low priorities to them. Indeed, two of the sample states emphatically rejected political recruitment criteria altogether. In Oregon the denigration of political standards was part of a larger transfer of recruitment prerogatives to the legal community in general and the state bar in particular. In Connecticut the rejection of political criteria was an extension of Senator Weicker's highly personalized recruitment system and the ideological disjuncture between Connecticut Republicans and the Reagan administration. So committed was Weicker to avoiding the stigma of partisanship and politicized appointment that he regularly solicited the opinions of his Democratic counterpart. As one of his aides quipped, a "sagebrush" political agenda would have hurt a recruit's chances (Elliot interview 1986).

Mississippi, another highly personalized system, appears at first blush to be rather apolitical. Neither party affiliation nor activism was deemed important by staffers. Ideology was assigned some weight, but Senator Cochran was said to be looking for political moderates rather than for ideologues. But a closer look revealed that although ideological purity was not paramount in the selection process, the judicial search was hardly apolitical. Rather, Senator Cochran was uniquely successful in using judicial appointments to broaden his political base among moderates and blacks in Mississippi. One of his first appointments, for example, was Henry Wingate, a highly respected, somewhat apolitical, black prosecutor in Hinds County (Jackson).

Finally, two commission states with moderate Republican senators acknowledged only minimal reliance on political criteria. In Pennsylvania it was important that recruits be Republicans, but neither ideology nor specific policy preferences were considered salient recruitment criteria. In Minnesota, a state with a similar climate of political moderation, partisanship and conservatism were of some importance, but policy preferences were explicitly rejected. Indeed, the failure to consider candidates' views on reproductive privacy led to a pitched battle among the Minnesota delegation, the White House, and conservative Republican members of the Judiciary Committee over the nomination of Judge Doty, whose wife was alleged to be an active supporter of Planned Parenthood! (Moore interview 1986).

In sum, home-state recruiters varied a great deal in the extent to which they are willing to acknowledge the importance of political recruitment criteria. They also differed in the relative importance assigned to party affiliation, activism, ideology, and policy preferences. And there was variance in the extent to which target preferences coincided with administration priorities. But it was equally the case that state selection systems in represented and unrepresented states tended either to reinforce or retard administration selection priorities. In the concluding section of this exploration of home-state recruitment, we control for this distinction and then examine the effect of home-state recruitment on the link between presidential appointment and home-state jurisprudence.

CONSEQUENCES OF HOME-STATE RECRUITMENT

As with recruitment procedures and criteria, the consequences of home-state recruitment have received very little scholarly attention. One notable exception is Slotnick's inquiry (1984) into the effect of recruitment systems on the demographic composition of the district-court bench. To organize his inquiry he first devised a four-part typology for home-state recruitment systems: (1) Personalized Panels, in which senator(s) eschew commissions and rely on personal contact to recruit candidates for judicial vacancies; (2) Supervised Panels, where senators appoint commissions but screen panel recommendations before forwarding names to the White House; (3) Independent Panels, in which senators allow their panels to submit names directly to the White House without screening by senator(s); and (4) Presidential Panels, limited to districts (e.g., Puerto Rico and the District of Columbia) without representation in the Congress. To facilitate inquiry he also identified for each state the "key actor" for judicial recruitment. Key actors ranged from the senior Democratic senator in personalized states to commission chairs in states with independent panels.

Given President Carter's reasons for encouraging selection commissions, Slotnick expected greater demographic diversity in commission states than in states that maintained traditional, personalized recruitment patterns. However, contrary to expectations, Slotnick found that the selection system had very little impact on judicial demography. Moreover, although President Carter's affirmative action selection criteria were slightly more visible in systems with independent panels, neither the type of panel nor the identity of "key actors" had a substantial impact on judicial backgrounds.

Slotnick's findings suggest that the more obvious structural and procedural differences among state recruitment systems may not be predictive of recruitment outcomes. But to say that demographics do not vary significantly across selection systems is not to say that variation in the substance and politics of recruitment will not be associated with subsequent, recruitment-related variation in judicial outcomes. To the extent that recruiters in these states are relatively independent from White House control, we would expect to find some independent relationship between recruitment politics and the political jurisprudence of district judges in these states. Moreover, although very little research has focused directly on the link between recruitment and aggregate outcomes, a variety of studies suggest indirectly that politicized recruitment may be linked more closely to outcomes than to demographics. For example, our 1983 study of Johnson and Kennedy appointees' support for civil rights found that, although those two cohorts were virtually indistinguishable in the North, Johnson's southern appointees were much more supportive of civil rights than were Kennedy's southern appointees. Given Kennedy's well-documented deference to Senator Eastland and other segregationist senators in the South (Navasky 1971), the best explanation for this finding is that the politics of recruitment and confirmation mitigated presidential effects on civil rights jurisprudence in this region.

Indirect evidence of recruitment effects is buttressed by our 1984 study (with Ronald Stidham) of support for criminal defendants by federal district judges in California. (Recall that Nixon "sacrificed" every fourth nomination to the state's liberal Democratic senators in return for their promise to support the law-and-order president's next three nominees.) For this state we expected to find a disparity in support for criminal defendants between President Nixon's Republican and Democratic nominees, and these expectations were fulfilled. The Democrats, selected without interference from the White House, supported the claims of criminal defendants 36 percent of the time, while Republicans, chosen without interference from the liberal home-state senators, supported such litigants only 14 percent of the time.

Given the indirect evidence from previous studies, one would expect presidential appointment effects to be enhanced in traditional and commission states where recruitment is dominated by the president's agents and/or when home-state recruiters share the president's extralegal recruitment criteria. On the other hand, presidential effects would be mitigated in states where home-state senators delegate recruitment prerogatives to the legal subculture and/or when they resist the president's political recruitment criteria.

We shall now test our expectation that presidential effects on jurisprudence will be less evident in "mitigating" states, where the president was forced by the norms of senatorial courtesy to nominate compromise candidates, than in "enhancement" states, where home-state recruiters reinforce presidential priorities. However, before reporting the results of this test it is important to note that, as with many unexplored avenues connecting politics and district court jurisprudence, specification of recruitment effects is made problematic by some inherent design difficulties. Thus three caveats are in order.

The most obvious derives from the nature of recruitment data. As was reflected in the description of procedural and substantive variation in recruitment patterns, many aspects of home-state recruitment vary idiosyncratically from state to state. This qualitative variation makes it very difficult to organize recruitment programs into isomorphic categories or to measure interstate variation along a single recruitment dimension. The difficulty is exemplified by unique differences between Mississippi Senator Cochran and Colorado's Senator Armstrong. Both men conducted highly personalized recruitments and were generally supportive of presidential selection criteria. However, anecdotal evidence suggests that Cochran was uniquely committed to recruiting acceptable black candidates as a means of enhancing his support among minority voters, while Armstrong was committed for personal reasons to recruiting "law-and-order" judges who were nonetheless opposed to the death penalty. Thus, each senator was uniquely independent.

A second, related caveat is based on anecdotal evidence that recruitment strategies and priorities may vary substantially, not just from state to state but from recruitment to recruitment within the same state. As discussed previously, the highly partisan Senator Gramm of Texas used his first judicial vacancy to appoint a Democratic congressman to the bench. (He hoped that the congressional vacancy would be filled by a Republican.) Senator Helms often showed a predilection for trusted members of his staff regardless of their political party identification. This intrastate variation makes it difficult to generalize about a state's recruitment cohort, even during a single recruitment era.

A final caveat derives from the fact that expected recruitment effects are, by definition, limited to a recruitment era. This means that the number of published cases susceptible to such effects will be especially limited if one includes in the sample of home-state recruitments a representative set of smaller, less litigious states, and that these limitations will make it virtually impossible to impose controls for specific case types and/or examine state-by-state differences.

Notwithstanding the caveats inherent in our research design and data, one can explore tentatively recruitment effects for this sample of states during this era by dividing our states into "enhancing" states and "mitigating" states and comparing presidential effects under controls for enhancement and mitigation. Two states have been dropped from the analysis. Colorado is difficult to designate as mitigating or enhancing. On the one hand, Senator Armstrong shared many of the Reagan administration's selection criteria; on the other hand, he was quite independent on key issues, such as capital punishment. In Oregon, the standoff between state recruiters and administration selectors resulted in a dearth of published opinions. Thus, although Oregon is clearly a mitigating state, it too has been dropped from the analysis.

Based on the descriptions of remaining recruitment programs, four of our states will be designated as mitigating—Connecticut, Minnesota, Mississippi, and Pennsylvania. Although these four states vary substantially in recruitment procedures and criteria, the Republican senator(s) in each of these states disappointed the White House either by delegating recruitment prerogatives to the legal subculture or personally resisting key segments of the administration's political criteria. Nine states will be designated as enhancing. The "enhanced" category also varies from small, unrepresented states to large states with Republican senator(s), but the nine enhanced states—Arkansas, California, Florida, Illinois, Louisiana, Massachusetts, Michigan, North Carolina, and Texas—share a common commitment by their key recruiters to President Reagan's selection criteria or a procedural deference to administration prerogatives.

To initiate an exploration of recruitment effects we will limit our analysis to published opinions between 1981 and 1986 and will compare liberalism differences between Carter and Reagan appointees in enhanced states with these same differences in mitigating states. Because of the data limitations discussed previously, this comparison will be limited to all cases and the large subset of civil rights cases. The results of the comparison are presented in Table 4-2. Our expectation that Reagan effects would be more pronounced in enhanced states receives qualified support from the findings reported in Table 4-2. Liberalism differences between the two presidential co-

Table 4-2. Comparison of Appointment Cohert Liberalism in Enhancing and Mitigating States, 1981–1986

	All Cases		Civil Rights	
	Enhancing	Mitigating	Enhancing	Mitigating
Reagan	33 (669)	39 (247)	25 (249)	31 (62)
Carter	54 (2,002)	52 (542)	54 (637)	51 (145)

horts are greater in the enhanced states than in the mitigating states, and these disparities are maximized for civil rights cases, a category that encompasses many of the administration's appointment priorities, such as opposition to affirmative action and a woman's right to choose. Moreover, these differences are accounted for entirely by the greater conservatism of Reagan appointees in enhanced states.

SUMMARY AND CONCLUSIONS

Although the disparities between cohorts would seem at first to confirm our expected recruitment effects during the Reagan-Thurmond era, many questions remain. What, for example, accounts for the remarkable consistency of the Carter cohort across recruitment models and case cohorts? Absent more detailed knowledge about recruitment in these states during the Carter-Kennedy era, answers must remain speculative. Less speculative is the degree to which recruitment procedures and criteria sometimes vary idiosyncratically from state to state and within states over time; state recruitments also vary systematically along several dimensions. Moreover, we have documented several other dimensions of variance, the most important of which is the extent to which recruitment is primarily an extension of the presidential selection strategies or primarily an exercise of perceived senatorial prerogatives. Thus, one may hypothesize from these data that recruitment effects do interact with presidential effects, and that interstate differences in appointment effects are at least partially a function of analogous differences in home-state recruitment priorities. Specification of the scope and quality of these recruitment effects awaits future research that includes more states, more recruitment eras, and more qualitative attention to the temporal and spatial vagaries of individual recruitments.

CHAPTER 5

Appointment Effects on Unpublished Decisions

In the previous chapter we explored a realm of public law about which we have little systematic knowledge, namely, home-state appointment effects. In this chapter we turn to another area of the legal process into which scholars have seen only "as through a glass darkly"—the nature and political significance of unpublished U.S. trial court opinions. Well over 90 percent of district court opinions are never formally published, and, as noted in chapter 1, at least half of those decisions that do find their way onto the printed page are never regularly studied by public law scholars. Many published opinions (e.g., those dealing with matters such as patents, land condemnation hearings, copyright disputes) are not thought to contain underlying political variables, while other published cases are thought to be only "routine" and unworthy of major social science analysis (e.g., contract disputes or disputes over Social Security benefits).

Regardless of the logic behind whether trial court opinions should be published or whether those that are in print should be studied by social scientists, we have little systematic, substantive knowledge about these substantive outputs of the U.S. trial courts. While this lacuna calls to mind a myriad of questions, some are particularly troublesome for students of public law: Are published opinions a random sample of the universe of district court decisions or at least a random sample of the politically more important decisions? Are the links that have been established between published trial court opinions and political variables (e.g., appointing president and geographic region) equally true for nonpublished opinions? While limiting inquiry to published opinions is obviously much easier for the researcher than trying to collect and analyze those that are not printed and disseminated, such an endeavor can be justified only if there is reason to believe that published and nonpublished decisions bear enough inherent congruity so that generalizations about one category are equally true of the other, or if unpublished opinions are unimportant for meaningful social science analysis.

WHY SOME DECISIONS ARE PUBLISHED AND OTHERS ARE NOT

The atypical character of published judgments derives primarily from formal and informal publication norms. Since time constraints make it virtually impossible to publish all decisions, it is not surprising that in a common-law system where precedent-setting decisions must be explained to appellate courts, trial judges would select for publication primarily those decisions that require the exercise of substantial discretion. Nor is it surprising that most appellate courts explicitly discourage the publication of routine, typical cases and encourage judges to publish only those decisions that encompass the exercise of judicial discretion and, therefore, make an original contribution to the *corpus juris* (Songer 1988). These formal and informal publication constraints mean that published decisions should, by design, constitute an atypical subset of complex, ambiguous, or unprecedented disputes that require judges to explain the legal or factual basis of their decisions in a way that would guide other judges in similar cases.

The selection bias engendered by formal and informal publication guidelines is exacerbated by West Publishing's publication policy. Generally speaking, West publishes in the *Federal Supplement* any opinion submitted to it by the district judges (or their law clerks). Thus, despite the restraint urged by appellate court guidelines, the publication decision is ultimately a function of idiosyncratic determinations made by the trial judges themselves.

Emerging empirical evidence adds to our suspicion that written decisions are atypical and somewhat idiosyncratic representations of federal court decisions. Anecdotal evidence indicates, inter alia, that judges occasionally submit for publication rather whimsical decisions that are surely neither precedent-setting nor exercises of much judicial discretion. (For examples, see Carp and Rowland 1983, 16.) Still, such trivial items constitute only a very small percentage of the universe of cases, and they appear to be quite randomly distributed and thus pose little problem for the general validity of our data set. The real potential problem stems from evidence that judges sometimes *fail* to publish opinions that, according to appellate guidelines and common-law norms, should be published. Several observers have found that judges often fail to submit opinions that *do* meet the appellate guidelines (Vestal 1966a, 1970–1971, Songer 1988). Failing to submit important cases for publication is deleterious because it can lead to inconsistencies among courts and engender confusion and uncertainty among litigants. For example, Vestal (1966a) found over twenty years ago that when trial judges failed to codify their interpretations of statutes and the reasoning behind them, inconsistencies among courts were exacerbated and the ability of litigants to calculate the consequences of strategic decisions was compromised.

In this study our primary concern is not whether judges' failure to publish important cases disrupts the chain of common-law consistency; rather, our concern is whether there is any relation between political effects and the decision to publish or not. In other words, are political effects equally evident in those opinions that are and are not selected for publication? Recent work by political scientists offers some helpful, albeit ambivalent, insights into this question. In a comparison study of reversal rates for published and unpublished federal district court decisions, Donald Songer (1988) found that, although published decisions engendered somewhat higher rates of reversal and dissent on the courts of appeal than did unpublished decisions, unpublished decisions engendered much more intercourt and intracourt disagreement than would be predicted by an assumption that unpublished decisions were limited to nondiscretionary judgments unlikely to engender disagreement among jurists. All this would suggest that we may be missing something important by not including nonpublished opinions in our overall data set. However, because most district court decisions are neither published nor appealed (Posner 1985), Songer's comparison of published and appealed decisions with unpublished and appealed decisions was a comparison between two atypical decision sets. Conspicuously absent was attention to routine decisions that are neither appealed nor published.

Fortunately, such routine decisions were included in a recent comparison of published and unpublished district court decisions by Susan Olson (1992). Although Olson reports a very limited relationship between the probability of publication and the litigating attorneys' assessments of the cases' importance (Olson 1992), she found that the published decisions were unique and that their uniqueness was predictable from the federal publication guidelines—that is, they explained the discretionary interpretation of facts and evidence. Thus, her conclusions reinforce conventional wisdom that the population of published district court decisions cannot be treated as a sample of all decisions because it systematically overrepresents cases that require new or ambiguous judgments.

In sum, studies have suggested that publication is occasionally idiosyncratic and even whimsical, and recent inquiries by political scientists have found that publication is *not* necessarily a function of a case's importance if that is defined by litigators' criteria, such as defendant's exposure to damages or punishment. Indeed, Songer's comparison of appellate outcomes for published and unpublished decisions argues persuasively that many discretionary judgments are not opined. Nonetheless, as determined by Olson, publication is typically a function of a judge's need to explain and defend the exercise of legal judgment. Thus, although many decisions that should be published are not, and a few that should not be published are, it is still fair to say that published opinions generally do represent an atypical population dominated by nonroutine cases that require the exercise of judicial judgment.

To say that published opinions are more important and precedent-setting than those that are not published raises many questions about how and why written judgments are unique, such as, to what extent do publication rates vary from one time and place to another? Questions such as these have been the focus of some sociolegal scholars (Eisenberg 1989). Most relevant for our inquiry is a recent study of published and unpublished employment discrimination decisions by Siegelman and Donohue. The express purpose of this work was to ascertain "how district court cases with published opinions differ from those without them" (1990, 1135). There are some methodological problems in comparing their study with those performed by political scientists. (For example, they used Lexis rather than the *Federal Supplement* as the source of their data, and their dependent variable was the rather narrow one of employment discriminations cases.) Still, their findings, based on a sophisticated longitudinal sampling of discrimination filings in multiple districts, do add several important pieces to the publication puzzle.

First, the probability of publication appears to have increased over time. Indeed, the publication rate for employment discrimination cases increased from 6 percent in 1974 to 27 percent in 1980. Although the authors' purpose and methodology limit their capacity to account for this increase, they speculate reasonably that the increase is a function primarily of changes in the legal context of discrimination and the concomitant increase in discretion associated with such changes.

Second, as predicted by previous work that focused on macro case categories (Vestal 1966a), publication rates for this class of disputes varied significantly among jurisdictions. Among the seven urban districts studied, the publication rate for 1973–1977 ranged from 5.5 percent in Atlanta and New Orleans to 30.1 percent in New York. Moreover, those districts with the highest publication rates for employment discrimination cases also tended to have the highest overall publication rates. Again, although it was not the authors' purpose to specify the correlates of these differences, they point out that the spatial differences in publication rates coincide with spatial differences in the complexity of case content, as well as differences in local legal culture (Church 1978).

The third, and most relevant, precursors of publication identified by these authors are factual and legal ambiguity. Specifically, they found the following "factual complexity" variables to be correlated with publication rates: the number of plaintiffs, the certification of a class action, and claims of continuous (rather than one-shot) discrimination. Likewise "legal ambiguity" factors such as these also affected publications rates: whether or not the case arose under the Age Discrimination in Employment Act and other relatively new dispute categories where case law and statutory interpretation are relatively unsettled. In sum, Siegelman and Donohue generally found that the greater the complexity and/or novelty of the case, the greater the likelihood that it would be offered for publication by the judges. This is entirely consistent with the earlier findings by Eisenberg and Schwab: "The general criterion for publication is that the case be noteworthy rather than routine or obvious, and thus will contribute to the development of the law" (1989, 535).

Publication and Appointment Effects

In previous chapters we contended that with certain types of cases judges have an inordinate amount of room for maneuver and discretion, such as instances where controlling precedents are either absent or conflicting, situations where the arguments and case law favor each side about equally, or cases that encompass new areas of the law. In such cases political variables are more likely to manifest themselves in the judges' behavior than in "routine" cases where their discretion is more circumscribed by the "legal subculture." In this chapter we summarize evidence suggesting that cases with factual complexity and/or legal ambiguity were more likely to be submitted for publication than were cases without those characteristics. If all this is true, then logically it would follow that political variables (e.g., the judge's party identification or appointing president) would more likely be found in published opinions than in ones that are not submitted for publication. That is, the case characteristics that engender political decision making by the judges are the same characteristics that are positively correlated with case publication. If this is true, then we might expect higher levels of partisan differences in published than in nonpublished opinions. While we have overall confidence in these assumptions, there are several caveats that should be acknowledged at the outset.

First, as noted in chapter 1, psychometric models have demonstrated rather conclusively that judges' personal policy preferences are a major factor influencing their decision making (Carp and Rowland 1983; Gibson 1983, 1991; Segal and Spaeth 1993; Rowland 1991; Schubert 1974). If this is so, then *all* of their decisions—whether published or not—should reflect to some degree factors such as presidential appointment effects and judges' personal attitudes and values.

Furthermore, sound empirical studies have in fact demonstrated that many types of cases that we would consider routine or mundane, and hence unworthy of publication, have nonetheless engendered sharp partisan cleavages among trial judges. For example, between 1975 and 1984 there was a 412 percent increase in the number of cases involving Social Security recipients (Galanter 1988). This was a result of a policy initiative of the Reagan administration that curtailed and restricted benefits to be paid out by the administration. Judicial decision making in these cases was highly partisan, with Democratic jurists significantly more likely to decide in favor of the potential claimant than were Republican judges. Still, the number of *published* Social Security cases during this ten-year time span did not markedly increase because the judges (correctly) did not consider their decisions to be unusual or precedent-making and thereby worthy of publication. Because of this and other examples, we thus fully recognize that many "ordinary" or "routine" types of cases may still serve as battlegrounds that manifest the effects of the democratic subculture on judicial decision making.

Second, many unpublished decisions reflect judges' rulings on litigants' motions made during a trial and on litigants' petitions to settle a dispute prior to a final court verdict. While it is tempting to regard such unpublished decision making as routine and unreflective of the political subculture, the evidence suggests otherwise. To begin with, we note that the vast majority of disputes in the federal trial courts (as in all American courts of general jurisdiction) are resolved without a judges's verdict at the end of a formal trial (Posner 1985; Kritzer 1993). Decisions for early settlements are made by the litigants themselves (Priest and Klien 1984), and although they must be approved by the court, they are recorded technically as litigants' motions rather than judges' decisions. Such "out-of-court" negotiated settlements are almost never appealed. The apparent absence of the judge's influence in such matters is deceiving, however. A wealth of scholarship indicates that the path to pretrial settlement offers multiple avenues for formal and informal judicial involvement, much of which greatly influences the direction and substance of the out-of-court settlement (Resnick 1982; Kritzer 1993).

Nowhere is the potential for judicial influence on settlement decisions greater than with judges' interim rulings in response to pretrial rulings. Such rulings can change dramatically the balance of probable trial outcomes and, therefore, of each side's incentives to settle a case. For example, a judge's decision to limit a defendant's affirmative defenses would dramatically increase the probability of the plaintiff's victory at trial and thereby push the defendant toward a pretrial settlement. Many of these interim rulings require the exercise of substantial fact-finding discretion as well, and findings of fact are generally not reviewable by the appellate courts. Thus trial judge influence in pretrial settlements not only is substantial in its impact but is largely immune from appellate court contradiction—facts not unknown to experienced trial attorneys. It is hardly surprising, therefore, that more than half of the 1,380 civil litigators interviewed during the Civil Litigation Research project felt that judges influenced in important ways the ultimate outcome of their settled cases (Kritzer 1990, 1993).

Despite the importance of judges' decisions in out-of-court settlements and in pretrial rulings, such decisions are rarely published. This is especially true of rulings in support of motions that prolong litigation, such as denials of motions for summary judgment or dismissal, or other interim judgments that do not conclude a case. The degree to which these pretrial settlements and rulings manifest judges' presidential appointment effects and personal values is largely unknown, but there is good intuitive reason to believe that they are not immune from such influences. We shall endeavor to explore this subject later in this chapter.

There is a third reason for our refusing automatically to believe that unpublished opinions are ipso facto devoid of political content or significance. Some research in recent decades indicates that a president's judicial cohort tends to be more supportive of that president's domestic policies than they are of other chief executives' programs (Ducat and Dudley 1989; Kritzer 1978). Since this tendency is true for both published and unpublished cases, this would suggest that political variables manifest themselves to some degree in all decisions, whether or not they are found on the printed page.

In sum, while the discipline is beginning to accumulate a good deal of information about the similarities and differences between published and unpublished opinions, there are still some large gaps in our knowledge about this general phenomenon. We will therefore turn our attention in the remainder of this chapter to an analysis of data that we have collected about opinion writing by trial jurists appointed by several recent presidents. In the following analysis we shall examine questions such as these: Are appointment effects mirrored equally in opinions that are published and unpublished? For unpublished opinions, why do judicial appointment effects manifest themselves more strongly with certain types of cases than others? We now turn to an empirical exploration of these questions by comparing the support of Nixon, Carter, and Reagan appointees for Reagan administration litigants.

The Effects of Reagan Appointment on Unpublished Decisions

To test the effect of Reagan appointment on unpublished opinions we sampled cases in two urban jurisdictions—Detroit, Michigan, and Kansas City, Missouri. To maximize the representation of Reagan administration litigants and Reagan appointees, we drew a weighted random sample of cases from the docket sheets and a smaller, nonrandom sample from case files in each jurisdiction. The docket sheet sample was weighted to enhance representation of 1985, 1986, and 1987 cases, which in turn created a balance among the three appointment cohorts. Although we are interested in aggregate support patterns in every jurisdiction, explanations of independent jurisdictional effects fall outside the scope of our research. Therefore, the substantive foci differed on two counts. First, only the Kansas City sample included settlement decisions. Because the coding of these decisions is tedious and labor-intensive, the Kansas City sample is smaller. Second, because the coding protocols encouraged a larger sample, key subcategories were drawn entirely from Detroit. This sample enabled us to maximize the quantity of information in the larger jurisdiction, and to maximize the quality of information in the smaller jurisdiction. From this database we were able to compare aggregate support patterns across both jurisdictions and support patterns for specific case categories and interim judgments within each jurisdiction.

JUDICIAL LIBERALISM

We begin by aggregating into a single category the several types of cases that had evinced liberal/conservative appointment effects for published decisions, namely, civil rights, criminal justice, civil liberties, labor, and economic regulation. We then took this measure of "judicial liberalism" and compared it with the appointees of Reagan, Carter, and Nixon judges for both published and unpublished opinions in each jurisdiction.

Keeping in mind that unspecified differences in legal context preclude systematic examination of contextual effects that might account for aggregate differences in judicial liberalism *between* districts, we turn our attention first to the differences among appointment cohorts in Detroit. As indicated in Table 5-1, the Detroit pattern for published opinions is a familiar one. Judicial liberalism varies greatly among the three cohorts. The variation is in very predictable directions. The Carter appointees are approximately four times as supportive of judicial liberalism as are the Reagan appointees. The Nixon appointees fill a familiar niche in between their more extreme successors.

When attention is shifted to Detroit's unpublished decisions, two related patterns emerge, both of which are consistent with the notion that unpub-

Table 5-1. Appointment Effects on Liberalism of Published and Unpublished Decisions in Detroit and Kansas City, 1981–1987 (in percentages)

	Detroit		Kansas City	
	Published	Unpublished	Published	Unpublished
Nixon	35 (86)	30 (623)	—[a]	—
Carter	64 (94)	33 (1,143)	56 (75)	14 (267)
Reagan	14 (28)	29 (654)	43 (30)	21 (294)

[a] Insufficient representation for calculation.

lished decisions afford judges less discretion to interject their appointment-based personal preferences. First, the polarization of the Carter and Reagan appointees is replaced by a remarkable moderation by both cohorts. The Reagan appointees are much less conservative, the Carter appointees much less liberal.

The moderation of unpublished opinions may initially appear somewhat inconsistent with research suggesting that published employment discrimination cases tend to be significantly more liberal than their unpublished counterparts (Siegelman and Donohue 1990). This apparent inconsistency may be a function of jurisdictional differences or variations between our general judicial liberalism cases and employment discrimination cases. A more likely explanation is the failure of sociolegal scholars to control for appointing president. Given the large number of decisions by Carter appointees and the fact that Carter appointees' published decisions were much more liberal, failure to differentiate between appointing presidents would have led us to identify a relationship between publication and liberalism rather than the relationship between publication and moderation that emerges with the imposition of presidential controls.

Whatever the causes for the moderation of unpublished decisions, the consequence of that moderation is the virtual disappearance of intercohort differences in judicial liberalism in this city. The fact that this pattern of similarity is based on more than two thousand cases suggests that it is not a statistical or legal artifact. Therefore, at least for Detroit the differences between appointment effects on published and unpublished judicial liberalism are consistent with the argument that judicial discretion is a prerequisite for publication and appointment effects on judicial judgment.

The pattern in Kansas City, however, is somewhat different. First, differences in published judicial liberalism are much smaller than in Detroit; second, the diminished disparities are accounted for almost entirely by the relative liberalism (43 percent) of the Reagan cohort's published opinions in Kansas City. Third, as predicted by Siegelman and Donohue (1990), the published opinions of both cohorts are significantly more liberal than either cohorts' unpublished opinions. Finally, although the magnitude of differences is small, the Reagan appointees' unpublished opinions are actually more liberal than the Carter appointees by an intriguing 33 percent. The Kansas City patterns are surprising on several counts—not the least of which is the relative liberalism of the Reagan appointees.

How does one explain the contrast between Detroit's expected and Kansas City's unexpected patterns of appointment effects? Differences between the political and legal cultures of the two cities may in part account for this, but we possess no hard data for this possibility. Still our analysis of the unpublished decisions suggests a couple of meaningful clues. First, and most obviously, those aggregate patterns may hide important differences in the magnitude of appointment effects on specific case categories, especially those that engendered the most significant effects on published opinions. If so, the apparent similarities among appointment cohorts in Detroit and the apparent differences between cohorts in Kansas City may be artifacts of each jurisdiction's case mixture. The disparities in unpublished judicial liberalism also raise the possibility that the Detroit and Kansas City patterns are surrogates for judges' support for the administration that appointed them. Do Reagan appointees, for example, support the Environmental Protection Agency during this time period regardless of whether the EPA is defending itself against an environmental plaintiff or suing hazardous-waste generators? If so, the differences or similarities among appointment cohorts may actually hide the direct support for a presidential administration found in studies that relied on published opinions.

To better understand the link between politics and unpublished opinions, we first explore differences in support for two politicized case categories—claims made by criminal defendants and civil rights disputes. Then we compare the support of Nixon, Carter, and Reagan appointees for Reagan administration litigants.

CRIMINAL RIGHTS AND CIVIL RIGHTS

To estimate political effects on these case categories we first compared appointment cohorts on published and unpublished prisoner petitions and habeas corpus claims, and then replicated the comparison for civil rights claims in each jurisdiction. The results are presented in Table 5-2.

We begin by noting a couple of general patterns that distinguish these particular subcategories: first, as with civil rights discrimination claims re-

Table 5-2. Appointment Effects on Liberalism of Published and Unpublished Criminal and Civil Rights Decisions, 1981–1987 (in percentages)

	Criminal		Civil Rights	
	Published	Unpublished	Published	Unpublished
Detroit				
Nixon	17 (12)	2 (78)	36 (33)	8 (47)
Carter	45 (20)	6 (164)	56 (34)	7 (103)
Reagan	25 (4)	1 (93)	11 (18)	11 (65)
Kansas City				
Carter	46 (15)	1 (194)	53 (28)	38 (13)
Reagan	20 (5)	2 (177)	19 (32)	13 (48)

ported in other studies, published opinions in both these case categories tend to be substantially more liberal than unpublished ones (Donohue and Siegelman 1989). Second, presidential effects tend to be substantially greater for published opinions in both case categories than for their unpublished counterparts. However, exceptions to each pattern will become apparent as we focus on each jurisdiction.

In Detroit, the patterns of appointment effects on published opinions resemble the national patterns reported in previous chapters. Indeed, although all three cohort's published decisions are somewhat more supportive of criminal claimants in Detroit than in most jurisdictions, the disparities in published civil rights opinions reflect almost exactly the national pattern for these cases. Moreover, as we had expected, appointment effects on both patterns of unpublished decisions are virtually nil. However, despite its overall predictability, the Detroit pattern includes a perplexing anomaly. Reagan appointees support civil rights claimants 11 percent of the time in this jurisdiction regardless of whether or not the decisions are published. Not only does the Reagan pattern contrast sharply with the Nixon and Carter cohorts, it is also inconsistent with the conventional wisdom that only written opinions are characterized by a legal context that allows the imposition of political preferences on judicial decisions.

In Kansas City, as in Detroit, the pattern for published and unpublished criminal cases is as anticipated. However, when attention shifts to civil rights decisions, two anomalies emerge. First, although both cohorts' published opinions are more liberal than their unpublished decisions, the probability of a Carter appointee's unpublished civil rights decision being liberal is 300 percent greater than that of a Reagan appointee. Moreover, when juxtaposed with the similarity of responses to unpublished civil rights cases in Detroit, these differences appear to be primarily a function of the relative liberalism of Carter's cohort in Kansas City. Second, although it is greater than it was in Detroit, the difference between the Reagan administration's published and unpublished support for civil rights remains relatively small.

The anomalous patterns identified for civil rights decisions in both jurisdictions are problematic if one wishes to maintain the assumption not only that disputes that engender publication are different but that the differences break the chain linking politics with jurisprudence. Our results reinforce the notion that unpublished disputes are somewhat singular for criminal cases, but they leave us ambivalent about the scope of political effects on the more highly politicized case categories such as civil rights. It is possible that our findings about civil rights cases are just an anomaly based on chance—a function of a relatively small n. Still, their concentration in a highly politicized case category cautions against this interpretation. Perhaps they simply reflect decisions by Kansas City judges not to publish decisions that would be published in Detroit. However, despite the variation in publication rates identified in previous research (Eisenberg and Schwab 1989), our data indicate a greater proclivity to publish in Kansas City than in Detroit.

A more probable explanation for the absence of clear distinctions between published and unpublished civil rights decisions derives from the context of the typical contemporary case. Unpublished civil rights cases frequently involve a contest over the relevant facts of the dispute wherein the judge defines his legal rationale as following "the plain language of the law." Let us examine a typical such case in which a fight occurs between a minority employee and a nonminority supervisor, and the worker is fired from his job. The legal question focuses on the question of who started the altercation. If it were the employee, then by law the dismissal is a legitimate business practice; on the other hand, if the supervisor were the instigator, then the dismissal is a mere pretense for racial discrimination—a clear violation of the employee's civil rights. Faced with conflicting testimony about the origins of the altercation, the judge becomes free to construe the "facts" in a variety of ways, and his fact-finding essentially answers the "routine" legal question of whether or not the firing was a legitimate business practice or an obvious civil rights violation. Such typical disputes afford the trial judge tremendous fact-finding discretion. Moreover, the jurist's personal and professional experiences readily influence the exercise of this discretion. Yet to the judge such a case is not novel or unusual and therefore not a candidate for writing up the findings with an eye toward its publication.

The anomalous patterns associated with the relatively small number of civil rights cases raise the possibility of similar differences among the Reagan, Carter, and Nixon cohorts' support for Reagan administration litigants during Reagan's presidency. We now explore this possibility by looking first at overall support in both jurisdictions and then by focusing on differences in support for the large category of recovery and Social Security claims in Detroit.

Support for Reagan Administration

As noted earlier, judicial cohorts tend to support the domestic policies of their appointing president (Ducat and Dudley 1989). However, this phenomenon has so far been documented only from the analysis of published judicial decisions, and we do not know if it likewise holds for unpublished cases. To explore this matter we first isolated those decisions in which the federal government—which for this study meant the Reagan administration—was a plaintiff or a defendant. Then we compared support for federal litigants among the presidential appointment cohorts in each jurisdiction. The results are reported in Table 5-3 (a).

Table 5-3 (a). Support for Reagan Administration by Nixon, Carter, and Reagan Appointees in Detroit and Kansas City, 1981–1987 (in percentages)

	Detroit	Kansas City
Nixon	65 (335)	—[a]
Carter	62 (603)	86 (44)
Reagan	64 (312)	83 (54)

[a] Insufficient cases.

As indicated, variation among appointment cohorts in overall support is virtually nil. Moreover, as will become apparent, what appears to be variation between the two jurisdictions is actually an artifact of the large number of Social Security and recovery claims in the Detroit sample. Absent these cases, the aggregate support levels as well as the patterns of similarity are virtually identical for the two jurisdictions. Therefore we turn our focus to Social Security cases in a single jurisdiction—Detroit.

Social Security

After the Reagan administration chose to restrict Social Security benefits for thousands of beneficiaries, their only avenue of appeal was to the federal district courts. It is not surprising, therefore, that the number of Social Security filings increased by over 400 percent during the Reagan era (Galanter 1988). These eligibility reviews and removal policies became the center of much political controversy and debate. According to one account, the reviews "were halted in response to criticism from many members of Congress, *federal judges* [emphasis added], and governors" (Pear 1986). Thus, even if Galanter's characterization of these disputes as prosaic "collection-agency" actions is accurate, the Social Security cases spring from a highly politicized policy decision that impinged upon significant numbers of Americans. Is decision making in these cases reflective of judges' political values, and are Reagan judges inordinately more likely to support his administration's policy on Social Security? To explore these questions we examined a random sample of Social Security cases from Detroit, the results of which are presented in Table 5-3 (b).

Contrary to expectations, decision making in Social Security cases does not appear to be similar to judicial decision patterns in other "routine" categories, such as prisoner petitions, in which judges are significantly more likely to reflect the values of the administration that put them on the bench. Despite the fact that every one of these cases was essentially an appeal of administrative decision that implemented Reagan administration social welfare policy, Reagan appointees were not significantly more likely—or less

Table 5-3 (b). Support for Social Security and Contracts Claims During Reagan Administration by Nixon, Carter, and Reagan Appointees, Detroit, 1981–1987 (in percentages)

	Nixon	Carter	Reagan	Total
Social Security	49 (152)	54 (227)	50 (115)	51 (494)
Contracts·	37 (297)	41 (371)	39 (166)	38 (834)

likely—to support the government than were Carter or Nixon appointees. Indeed, the range of variation is a minuscule 4 percentage points.

The independence of unpublished Social Security decisions is perhaps best appreciated in juxtaposition with unpublished contracts decisions. Contracts cases almost never evoke the platform-based policy preferences that engender appointment effects on categories of published opinions. To the extent that judges look for opportunities to support the domestic policies of their appointing president, one would expect more appointment effects on Social Security cases than contract cases. Yet the disparities in support for plaintiffs in contract cases among the Nixon (37), Carter (41), and Reagan (39) cohorts resemble very closely the patterns of support for the Social Security cases. Thus, the clear message of Table 5-3 is that the strength of appointment effects on these case categories is virtually nil. In fact, although the Reagan cohort is very slightly more supportive of the administration's Social Security decisions than is the Carter cohort, the margin of difference for recovery cases is actually the same as for contracts, a category with no theoretical or empirical expectation of appointment effects.

To this point the evidence suggests that Reagan appointees in Detroit are no more supportive of their appointing administration than are other appointment cohorts. Turning back to Kansas City, we now ask whether the anomalous appointment effects on unpublished civil rights outcomes extend as well to criminal defendants' interim petitions.

Interim Motions

Among the most common motions filed in trial courts are those to dismiss and for a directed verdict, both of which ask the judge preemptively to resolve the dispute. Equally important, however, are motions in *limini* that ask the judge to shape the adversarial balance of power. For example, the judge is frequently petitioned to admit or exclude key testimony that may not fit unambiguously within federal rules of evidence. Judicial responses to contested motions usually shape the context of litigation in ways that favor one side over the other—for example, the probability of the plaintiff's prevailing at trial can be reduced significantly by a judge's decision to grant the defendant's motion to exclude from evidence a damaging memo from a corporate defendant's attorney. Because they shape the balance of *probable* outcomes, judicial responses to these interim motions may influence litigants' decisions to settle or adjudicate a dispute and the favorability of settlement for one side or the other (Kritzer 1993; Priest and Klien 1984). If this is so, then what appears in official archival records as a litigant's voluntary decision to abandon litigation may in fact be the indirect product of judicial responses to a much more complicated, highly contested set of motions in *limini* or other interim judicial rulings.[1]

The intrigue surrounding pretrial motions is elevated by the fact that these motions frequently blur the distinctions between factual and legal judgments. Many motions in *limini* require judges to evaluate the quality of evidence relative to appropriate federal rules (or, in diversity cases, state rules of evidence) rather than to make factual determinations. For example, whether to qualify a potential expert witness depends primarily on the judge's qualitative assessment of the witness's qualifications. Or a judge's ruling on the admissibility of testimony in a sexual harassment case may depend on perceptions of whether a double entendre was part of an ongoing pattern of a defendant's behavior or a mere inadvertent slip of the tongue.

As with Social Security and civil rights cases, extant theoretical and empirical frameworks leave us ambivalent about expected appointment effects on these judgments. On the one hand, many motions in *limini* can be expected to evoke appointment-based preferences in a judicial and legal context that accommodates substantial judicial discretion. Moreover, since many of these judgments hinge on the judge's evaluation of "facts" (e.g., expert qualifications), they are buffered from appellate review. On the other hand, previous research leads us to expect little or no presidential influence on the interim judicial judgments in our sample because they are unpublished—namely, unpublished responses to motions are assumed to be routine and, therefore, to afford judges no opportunity to interject their policy preferences. With no clear-cut theoretical expectations of the expected outcome, we now turn to our data on this topic and look in the direction they point.

The collection of data on interim criminal court motions is inordinately labor-intensive, often requiring cross-referencing of docket sheets and case files. Therefore, to test political effects on unpublished responses to interim motions, we concentrated our efforts in Kansas City because of its proximity and accessibility. Prior research suggested that appointment effects on procedural decisions would be concentrated in cases with "underdog litigants" (Rowland and Todd 1991); therefore, we isolated a subsample of case categories that pit "underdog" plaintiffs against corporate or federal defendants for the years 1981–1987. Included in this underdog category were per-

Table 5-4. Percentage of Support by Carter and Reagan Appointees for Underdog Plaintiffs' Motions, Kansas City, 1981–1987

	Overall	Civil Rights	Criminal	Federal Defendants
Carter	65 (352)	75 (50)	21 (105)	91 (86)
Reagan	59 (409)	63 (82)	20 (116)	65 (41)

sonal injury cases, product liability claims, recovery, forfeiture and Social Security claims, civil rights cases, and the claims of criminal defendants. Because Kansas City had no active Nixon appointees, we initially compared the Reagan and Carter cohorts' support for underdog claimants' motions. Then, after comparing overall support for underdog motions, we replicated the comparisons under two sets of controls. First we isolated two specific categories with underdog claimants—criminal petitions and civil rights—to determine whether the aggregate pattern of effects on interim motions was replicated for these specific categories. Finally, to the extent permitted by the imposition of multiple controls on a relatively small data set, we tentatively explored appointment effects on support for presidential administration by examining intercohort differences in aggregate responses to motions filed against federal defendants during the Reagan years. In sum, we compared Carter and Reagan appointees' support for (1) the aggregate of underdog claimants' motions, (2) underdog motions in two specific case categories, and (3) motions filed by, and in opposition to, the Reagan administration. The results of these comparisons are presented in Table 5-4.

Absent controls for case category or federal involvement, overall appointment effects on interim judgments are modest. Nonetheless, the Carter cohort's overall support for underdog motions, as with its support for civil rights claimants, is noticeably greater than Reagan's for these plaintiffs. The source of these differences is apparent when one compares the support patterns for the control categories. As predicted from the outcome data, differences for criminal motions are nil. However, when one focuses first on civil rights cases and then on controls for government participation, some interesting patterns emerge.

The differences in support for plaintiffs' civil rights motions are substantially smaller than the previously reported differences for published decisions (Rowland and Todd 1991), but they are comparable to the variations reported here for unpublished civil rights decisions in Kansas City. Moreover, the differences are in the direction predicted by appointment effects on substantive outcomes in this highly politicized case category. It would appear, therefore, that appointment politics may indeed be linked not only to civil rights outcomes but to the interim decisions that shape the probable outcomes of civil rights cases in this jurisdiction.

At this juncture one can only speculate about the reasons for this moderate effect on interim civil rights judgments in Kansas City. On the one hand, this case category includes disputes, such as discrimination in the workplace, that offer substantial fact-finding discretion and evoke politicized appointment criteria. Moreover, because answers to legal questions—about the admissibility of evidence, for example—are usually contingent upon the trier of fact's evaluation of that evidence, these motions give judges an opportunity to decide in a legal context that recognizes and values the exclusive discretion of trial judges to evaluate the factual foundations of motions in *limini.* Thus, except for the fact that the judges' decisions were not published, the prerequisites for appointment effects seem to be in place. On the other hand, given our small data sample, our findings may stem from such various factors as forum shopping by attorneys, unspecified attorney strategies, or the idiosyncratic inclinations of individual judges. To help clarify the picture we look at cases defended by the Reagan administration.

When one looks at the subset of cases filed against the Reagan administration, the Carter cohort supports plaintiffs' motions 91 percent of the time whereas the Reagan appointees do so only at the 65 percent level. (Unfortunately, a separate examination of the criminal and civil rights motions is precluded by the small number of cases in our data set.) Intuitively, one would expect the 30 percent difference in support for defense motions against the Reagan administration to be a function of Reagan appointees' support for the defense; it is interesting to note, however, that the difference is actually a function of a dramatic increase in the Carter cohorts' support for plaintiffs when the federal government is the defendant. In fact, the Reagan cohort becomes slightly *more* supportive of underdog motions when the government is a defendant. Thus, appointment effects on the motions of underdog plaintiffs are maximized for all dispute categories when Carter appointees rule on plaintiffs' motions filed against the Reagan administration.

A full explanation for the unanticipated Carter effects is beyond the scope of our aggregate data. However, a perusal of case files in Kansas City does suggest partial explanations, each of which could be subjected to empirical test in the future. First, although deterrence cannot be measured quantitatively, it appears that claimants may have been less likely to file motions against the Reagan administration when the motion was to be heard by a Reagan judge. If so, the Carter cohort may have been responding to a qualitatively different set of legal and factual stimuli. Second, an inordinate number of the cases where Carter appointees ruled on interim motions aimed at Reagan administration litigants may have been rather symbolic. In one case, for example, Judge Scott Wright, a Carter appointee, granted the plaintiff's contested motion for a continuance in a federal habeas corpus dispute. It is not clear that this continuance had an impact comparable to, for example, the suppression of evidence. Nor was it clear from the file how vigorously the government contested the motion. It is clear, however, that the underdog won a symbolic interim victory that may or may not have gained him concessions from the government. Thus, as with all findings reported in this chapter, the results are more suggestive than definitive, and the conclusions outlined in the following are more tentative than conclusive.

SUMMARY AND CONCLUSIONS

Our research provides mixed findings for the direction and intensity of appointment effects for judges situated in Kansas City and in Detroit. In Detroit such effects are virtually nil for all case categories. Moreover, the absence of appointment effects includes a missing link between Reagan appointees and Social Security disputes engendered by the Reagan administration. The Detroit data do, however, include the somewhat perplexing finding that the Reagan cohort's support for unpublished civil rights decisions (4 percent) is exactly equal to its support for published decisions in this case category. In Kansas City moderate appointment effects were most obvious for civil rights decisions. However, appointment effects in this jurisdiction also extend to two categories of interim motions in *limini.* Reagan judges are somewhat more resistant to motions filed by underdog civil rights claimants than are Carter judges, and Carter judges are substantially (60 percent) more supportive of underdog motions against the Reagan administration than are Reagan judges. Thus, although the magnitude and consistency of appointment effects on unpublished decisions do not compare with appointment effects on published decisions, the link between political appointment and jurisprudence appears to extend to unpublished civil rights cases and underdog motions in Kansas City.

How is one to explain these patterns? First, we must acknowledge that this was an exploratory excursion into the link between appointment politics and unpublished judgments. As such it was limited to archival data for selected case categories and case types in two courts for one judicial era. Thus, we must concede that these results could possibly be artifacts of our data limitations, and therefore not generalizable. But these jurisdictions are by no means atypical. And our case categories and time frame were based on expectations derived from previous research and conventional theoretical wisdom.

A second possible explanation to be offered is that appointment effects on these trial judges increase when they are engaged in discretionary fact-finding. The factual judgments that precede rulings on motions are virtually immune from appellate review, and they are rarely published. If, for example, a district judge views a computer animation and finds it inflammatory, his "routine" decision as trier of fact to exclude it from evidence is rarely codified and is an unlikely candidate for appeal.

Initially, the crucial role of fact-finding discretion seems consistent with adaptations of attitudinal models to trial settings. According to these adaptations (Gibson 1983; Carp and Rowland 1983), discretion is indicative of a legal context that allows activist judges, who are assumed to be motivated by the policy preferences that secured their appointment, the opportunity to impose these personal values on their decisions. By definition this legal context must have been present for civil rights disputes and underdog motions in Kansas City, but not present in Detroit or for other cases in Kansas City.

On closer examination, however, the attitudinal model's explanation is troubling on two counts. First, it is one thing to say that Supreme Court justices' legal interpretations are a function of their policy beliefs; we expect justices to interpret the Constitution as what they believe it means. But it is a different and troubling thing to assume that trial judges' *fact-finding* is motivated by their personal policy preferences. The attitudinal model discourages the qualitative analysis of individual judgment protocols that would help us understand the mixed pattern of appointment effects on unpublished judgments.

To overcome the empirical and theoretical limitations of available explanations, future research must, of course, devote idiographic attention to individual judges and qualitative examination of unpublished data, especially from other jurisdictions and times. Moreover, the rich information gleaned from our exploratory review of case files suggests strongly that future research into this question should include systematic qualitative analysis of case files and supporting materials, such as briefs, pleadings, and judicial interviews. But this empirical expansion should, in our opinion, be preceded by a more basic reevaluation of the theoretical underpinnings of this study. Specifically, we need to take seriously the primacy of district judges' role as fact finders and ask whether research should continue to be based on theories which assume that fact-finding discretion is exercised in response to personal preferences. Therefore, in the concluding section of the book we turn to a critique of the dominant contemporary theory of trial judges' decision making and the introduction of an alternative framework that would accommodate evidence of political links to fact-finding without assuming that fact-finding is somehow motivated by personal preferences.

CHAPTER 6

A Critique of Behavioral Models of Trial Judging

If the study of political jurisprudence is to move beyond its current comfort zone, we must develop a theory of judicial behavior that can accommodate political and jurisprudential influences without assuming away the judicial reasoning process. The traditional legal paradigm is an unlikely candidate for two reasons. First, and most obviously, it cannot accommodate the overwhelming empirical evidence that judicial decisions are often a product of variables quite independent of the facts and legal doctrines inherent in individual cases. Indeed, because it assumes away the influence of judges' personal discretion, mechanical jurisprudence cannot even accommodate inquiry into extralegal links to judicial decision making. Second, and less obvious, the legal paradigm includes a set of implicit assumptions about the relationship between trial and appellate judges that is equally unable to accommodate evidence of political jurisprudence. It assumes a strict hierarchical structure in which trial judges respond to guidelines promulgated by their appellate superiors who dictate unambiguous directions for the resolution of an infinite number of factual disputes. Evidence is composed of "facts" that can be "found." U.S. trial courts are unrealistically viewed as judicial institutions subordinate to appellate tribunals and buffered from external influences.

Social scientific studies of these courts and trial judge behavior have, of course, eschewed reliance on the legal paradigm and its associated approaches to understanding judicial decision making. In its place, scholars have developed organizational models of the courts and behavioral models of judicial decision making. These models accommodate evidence of extralegal effects on decisions at all levels of the federal judiciary as well as evidence that the federal district judges are neither purely subordinate to the appellate courts nor buffered completely from their social environment. Although these paradigms have facilitated rapid increases in our knowledge of extralegal influences, many of their axiomatic assumptions are inappropriate and anomalous when applied to the institutional context of the federal district courts and the behavioral context of its judges. As a result, many potentially important questions are assumed away, and extant models constrain the scope of scholarly inquiry in ways that impede rather than encourage scholarly innovation and growth.

ORGANIZATIONAL MODELS OF TRIAL COURTS

As noted, the legal paradigm has viewed district courts and judges as somehow institutionally and individually isolated from their social, political, and economic environments. In a reaction against this view, scholars turned to organizational models to explain mounting evidence that courts were in fact shaped by their environment and that jurists were not independent decision makers. This transition from a legalistic to an organizational perspective was most cogent for scholars who sought to explain the realities of plea bargaining and related phenomena in criminal trial courts.

When faced with compelling evidence that the vast majority of criminal dispute resolutions did not fit the legal paradigm's adversarial model, scholars developed alternative organizational models of judicial decision making (Packer 1968; Eisenstein and Jacob 1977; Jacob 1983). Their great strength was their recognition that the vast majority of criminal justice decisions were neither unique nor adversarial. Rather, they were routine decisions by members of a courtroom work group composed of the prosecutor, the judge, the defense attorney, and courtroom support personnel, all of whom shared common organizational goals, such as efficiency and cost-effectiveness. Thus, most criminal justice decisions could be understood not as the product of an adversarial process but as the output of an organizational process driven by the shared interests of its major participants (Eisenstein and Jacob 1974).

Organizational models of state criminal courts have been adapted to the federal district courts, and they have helped us understand the causes and consequences of changes in the quantity and quality of demands on these institutions (Heydebrand and Seron 1990). Although these models share with their criminal justice predecessors an emphasis on case processing and disposition, they depict federal district courts as large-scale organizations in which judicial discretion is constrained less by the symbiosis of work-group incentives than by constraints imposed by the larger political economy. Particularly important has been their depiction of the federal district courts not as courtrooms dominated by judges but as organizations, analogous to administrative agencies and state criminal courts, in which "a new technical-instrumental rationality designed to achieve results (effective case disposition) undermines . . . the formal rationality of law . . . and adjudication" (Heydebrand and Seron 1990, 13).

Organizational models have contributed significantly to our appreciation of the triangular linkage among the district courts' institutional imperatives, their position in the larger political economy, and changes in the quality and quantity of their caseload. However, organizational models have contributed little to our understanding of the link between politicized appointment and political jurisprudence in the district courts. Indeed, their depiction of these courts as organizations and their conceptualization of dispute resolution as an organizational process in which judges are less important than social forces or other legal actors tends to minimize artificially the importance of discretionary judgment. In addition, they have diverted our attention not only away from judges as individuals but away from the political influences on their major policy decisions that would help us link jurisprudence with appointment politics. Moreover, in sharp contrast with the legal paradigm, this perspective largely ignores (or assumes away) the importance of the federal judicial hierarchy and the explicit and implicit influences of appellate courts on trial judges' decisions.

In sum, organizational models that assume judicial behaviors to be the product of organizational or environmental influences on the courts cannot, by definition, guide inquiry into behavioral variation within the same or similar institutional environments. Nor can models that conceptualize courts as institutions driven by "technical-instrumental rationality" accommodate the complexity and nuances of the limited constraints on individual discretion imposed by the appellate courts. Because organizational models offer little guidance in learning more about the individual exercises of constrained discretion that create the aggregate links between politics and jurisprudence, refinements are necessary. We must develop concepts that accommodate evidence of individual variation in a context of constrained discretion if we are to conceptualize adequately the link between appointment politics and the exercise of judicial discretion. The model offered in the next chapter seeks to address this challenge.

ATTITUDINAL MODELS

In an attempt to link appointment politics with district court output, some public law scholars have adapted attitudinal models of Supreme Court justices' individual decisions to the study of trial judges. These attitudinal models had their roots in psychology's behavioral paradigm and in Coomb's theory of data. They evolved as a means of explaining the mounting evidence that individual justices' support level for specific constitutional issues (e.g., civil liberties) tended to be persistent and predictable over time and that differences and similarities among justices displayed similar properties (Pritchett, 1948). From these patterns of persistent and predictable "judicial votes," researchers were able to infer basic preference points and derive value dimensions—for example, civil liberalism—underlying appellate judges' decisions. From these derivations they concluded that differences in voting patterns among Supreme Court justices were the product of differences not in the law or legal interpretation but of variations in justices' personal values and beliefs (Schubert 1974; Segal and Spaeth 1993). Not only were differences the product of preferences, but the votes that produced the differences were *motivated* by the justices' personal preferences (Pritchett 1948). Indeed, it soon became basic dogma among attitudinal model scholars that the justices were motivated primarily by their extralegal belief systems: "There is, according to the [attitudinal] model, complete isomorphism between the configuration of ideal points in the psychological space and the belief systems of judges that *motivate* [emphasis added] their voting in Supreme Court decisions (Schubert 1974, 18).

Schubert's formulation of the belief-based judicial "vote" was subsequently refined by Rohde and Spaeth (1976), who expanded his focus on basic beliefs to include concern about policy-related attitudes and proximate policy preferences. However, as exemplified by Rohde and Spaeth's explication, these refined "attitudinal" models left the primacy of personal motives intact: "Each member of the Court has preferences concerning the policy questions faced by the Court, and when the justices make decisions they *want* the outcomes to approximate as nearly as possible those policy preferences" (Rohde and Spaeth 1976).

Although attitudinal models were developed in response to Supreme Court voting patterns, and designed by their architects as models of justices' behavior (Segal and Spaeth 1993), their generalization to lower levels of the judiciary was inevitable. This general application has been stated most succinctly by Gibson: "Judges' decisions are a function of what they prefer to do, tempered by what they think they ought to do, but constrained by what they perceive is feasible to do" (1983, 9). Thus trial judges, like their appellate colleagues, are assumed to be motivated primarily by their personal preferences. However, because trial judges are at the bottom of the judicial hierarchy, their preferences must be tempered by expectations of the trial judge's role and constrained by perceptions of the legal boundaries defining a given case.

Unlike traditional legal approaches and organizational models, adaptations of attitudinal models to trial court settings accommodate nicely the empirical link between appointment politics and political jurisprudence in the federal trial courts. Indeed, in the past we have relied on the logic of this model to explain persistent patterns of presidential appointment effects on federal district judges: because presidents appoint judges on the basis of their extralegal policy preferences, the appointing president becomes a surrogate for an appointment cohort's shared preferences. When these preferences are evoked by a dispute, judges are motivated to manifest them in their decisions—unless perceptions of the judicial role or the dispute's legal context deny them the discretion to do so (Carp and Rowland 1983; Rowland and Carp 1983b). Thus, according to trial court adaptations of attitudinal models, the link between appointment politics and judicial judgment is secured by individual judges who are motivated primarily by the preferences that secured their politicized appointment to the federal bench.

There is no question that the behavioral framework and adaptations of the attitudinal model have encouraged innovative quantitative methodologies and engendered significant knowledge about the link between jurisprudence and politics in the federal district courts. The tacit commitment to a shared set of assumptions and methods has engendered a rapid, "normal science" accumulation of knowledge (Riker 1982). It has directed our attention to appointment criteria codified in party platforms as the predictors of politicized dispute categories. Furthermore, it has encouraged inquiry not only into presidential appointment effects but into the effects of other extralegal preferences on policy outcomes. For example, we have learned that Carter appointees are almost six times more likely than Reagan appointees to support a woman's access to an abortion; that appointment effects on that issue are more pronounced in the North than the South, and that Carter's non-Catholic appointees are twice as supportive as his non-Catholic judges of such rights (Alumbaugh and Rowland 1990).

It is also indisputable, however, that in the life of any research paradigm the accumulation of *anomalous* findings and the missed research opportunities inherent in adherence to a single paradigm all combine to create the need for paradigmatic reform. The paths to such reform may converge from several sources. In the classic Kuhnsian sense, paradigmatic "revolutions" occur when, after a comfortable period of "normal science," persistent anomalies cannot be accommodated by the assumptions of the dominant paradigm (1970). Thus Newtonian physics was displaced by relativity because the Newtonian assumptions about time and space become anomalous. In the social sciences, paradigmatic change is usually engendered by the inability of dominant paradigms to accommodate important questions about the human subjects of social scientific research. The displacement of behaviorism by cognitivism in psychology in the 1960s came about not because behaviorists were faced with anomalous results but because their stimulus-response models assumed away important questions about the human cognition that precedes behavior and the importance of social context in cognition and behavior (Dewey 1929; Barone, Maddux, and Snyder forthcoming). By assuming away important questions, the behaviorists tended to ignore and denigrate the methods and results of other research.

Despite the seminal contributions of attitudinal models to our understanding of judicial behavior, adherence to the behavioral paradigm has diverted attention from important avenues and methods of inquiry. It has also encouraged us to denigrate or ignore anomalous findings from research programs guided by alternative frameworks. Therefore, as a precursor to a conceptual alternative set forth in chapter 7, we now set forth what we believe to be the basic flaws of attitudinal models in trial court settings.[1]

BEHAVIORAL APPROACHES

One is always reluctant to criticize an old friend, especially one whose guidance has proven as valuable as the behavioral paradigm. At a minimum, such a critique must be preceded by conciliatory caveats. In this case, two concessions are in order. First, we acknowledge the extremely important contributions of the psychometric and attitudinal models to our understanding of judicial behavior not only on the U.S. Supreme Court but at all levels of the federal judiciary. Indeed, one might argue that these models have been so successful in predicting judicial outcomes that they now appear as part of the "common knowledge." Their success has in effect precluded the expansion of scholarly inquiry to include new questions that cannot be accommodated by extant models.

Second, our main critique of judicial behavior deals with its capacity to explain trial judge decision making rather than the behavior of appellate judges. While the model we conceptualize in the next chapter has implications for appellate judges, its primary usefulness is for trial jurists as triers of fact. Our position in this regard is consistent with the recent contextual formulation by two of the attitudinal model's premier proponents. "Members of the Supreme Court further their policy goals because they lack electoral accountability or ambition for higher office, and they comprise a court of last resort that controls its own jurisdiction. All of these factors leave Supreme Court justices freer to implement their personal preferences than are their lower-court brethren" (Segal and Spaeth 1993, 69; see also 357–359).

While paying our due respects to the attitudinal model, and the behavioral paradigm into which it fits, we still contend that it is an inadequate framework for inquiry into the link between politics and policy judgments in the federal trial courts. First of all, since the 1960s, political scientists' utilization of the "attitudinal model" has borne little resemblance to the way psychologists have come to understand and define the concept of "attitudes." We will suggest that political scientists are using a behavioral conceptualization of attitudes that for at least three decades has been rejected by the parent discipline of psychology. Second, while attitudinal models may still be useful in understanding appellate court behavior, they are distinctly incompatible with fact-finding—the primary duty of federal and state trial judges. Specifically, we contend that the attitudinal model's axiomatic assumption that judges are motivated primarily by their personal policy preferences implies a fact-finding bias that cannot be reconciled with the norms of judicial behavior or, for that matter, the trial judge's oath of office. We shall subsequently argue that behavioral models, as with the traditional legal approach, divert research attention from the cognitive *process* by which judges rely on perception, memory, and inference to evaluate evidence and "find" facts. The result is a denigration not only of social scientific efforts to explain the cognitive judgment process but of qualitative legal analysis of judges' explanations of their judicial rulings.

Inadequate and Antiquated Conceptualization

The attitudinal model of judicial behavior is, by definition, a psychological model of human behavior in a judicial setting. As such, it applies the basic theoretical and empirical insights of the parent discipline to the special case of judicial decision making. Likewise, it invokes all the strengths and weaknesses of its psychological roots. Model proponents point with pride to its roots in logical positivism and, more concretely, the behavioral paradigm that evolved from Watson's early writings (1913) into psychology's dominant paradigm during the 1940s and 1950s (Barone, Maddux, and Snyder forthcoming). Certainly the judicial behaviorists of the 1940s (Pritchett 1948) and 1950s (Schubert 1965) demonstrated a commitment summarized by Somit and Tanenhaus's more general adaptation of behaviorism from basic psychology to applied political behavior: "data should be quantified and findings based on quantifiable data" (1967, quoted in Segal and Spaeth 1993, 76.) But it was Glendon Schubert, drawing on the work of Clyde Coombs, who first specified an attitudinal model of Supreme Court decision making with his publication of *The Judicial Mind* in 1965 (and *The Judicial Mind Revisited* in 1974). According to Schubert, justices' "votes" were a function of the relationship between the individual justice's ideological position on a given question (his "i" point) and the circumstances of the case stimulus before the justice (the "j" point). If the challenged behavior is inconsistent with the justice's ideological perspective, then the justice will vote to reject that behavior. Furthermore, because the justice's vote is ideologically driven, he or she will always vote to reject behaviors that fall outside the attitudinal parameters established for a given ideological dimension.

David Rohde and Harold Spaeth refined Schubert's model in two important ways (1976). First, they transformed the attitudinal model into an explicitly goal-oriented model by assuming that the goals that motivate justices are policy-based; and furthermore, that when they vote on specific cases, justices select the outcome that approximates most closely their preferred policy outcome (1976). Second, and most importantly for our purposes, they attempted to elevate the conceptual sophistication of the model by adopting explicitly a postbehavioral definition of "attitude" from Milton

Rokeach, a prominent social psychologist and leader in that discipline's rediscovery of the affective and cognitive processes that mediate behavior:

> a (1) relatively enduring, (2) organization of interrelated beliefs that *describe*, *evaluate* and advocate action with respect to an object or situation, (3) with each belief having *cognitive*, *affective*, and behavioral components [emphasis added]. (4) Each one of these beliefs is a predisposition that, when suitably activated, results in some preferential response for the attitude object or situation, or toward the maintenance or preservation of the attitude itself. (5) Since an attitude object must always be encountered within some situation about which we also have an attitude, a minimum condition for social behavior is the activation of at least two interacting attitudes, one concerning the attitude object and the other concerning the situation. (Rohde and Spaeth 1976, 72, quoting Rokeach 1968)

At first, the incorporation of Rokeach's conceptualization of its key variable into the attitudinal model made sense. The model was predicated on its rejection of legal fiction in favor of a "reality" that recognized the importance of extralegal psychological phenomena as determinants of individual differences and similarities in the judicial "vote." Thus, although Rokeach's definition was at least ten years old by 1976, it was important to incorporate into the attitudinal model of judicial behavior a conceptualization of attitude that reflected current thinking among social psychologists about the nexus of attitudes, description, evaluation, and behaviors in social settings. To do so was to capture nicely the nuances that had become a conceptual bridge for social psychologists between the declining behavioral paradigm, which tended to denigrate the cognitive *processes* that mediate the relationship between stimulus and vote, and the ascending cognitive paradigm that focused explicit attention on mediating cognitive processes, such as attribution (Heider 1958), which help humans make the kinds of social judgments judges must make every day.

In the field of social psychology the paradigmatic shift from behaviorism to cognitivism was fueled not by the failure of behaviorism to answer the questions it asked but by its inability to accommodate important questions about evaluation, perception, and a host of other aspects of information processing that define all forms of social judgment, including judicial judgment (Barrone, Maddux, and Snyder forthcoming). It is not surprising, therefore, that the transition from behaviorism to a cognitive perspective in psychology ignited a veritable explosion of inquiry into basic human information processing (Glass and Holyoak 1986) and engendered in social psychology a paradigmatic shift to "social cognition"—the description, explanation, and prediction of cognitive influences on human information processing and behaviors in social settings (Fiske and Taylor 1991). The result has been a parallel explosion of knowledge about social attributions, social inference, social judgments, and a host of other cognitive processes engaged in by human "judges" at all levels of decision making.

During the transition to the cognitive approach in psychology, complete reliance on the attitudinal model was largely abandoned because of mounting evidence that global attitudes are relatively weak predictors of individual behavioral differences. Attitudes have remained important not as proximate predictors of behaviors but as mediating influences on cognitive processes, such as memory and inference, that frequently precede behaviors in social settings (Fiske and Taylor 1991).

Given the obvious implications of psychology's cognitive perspective for judicial decision making, one could have anticipated an explosion of inquiry into judicial cognition that paralleled the parent discipline's more general inquiry into social cognition. Certainly the evolving emphasis among psychologists on "the creative capacity of the living thing to represent the environment, not merely respond to it" (Kelly 1955, 8) did nothing but reinforce the contention of the legal realists that judges create law in response to their own perceptions. And this anticipation is buttressed by the seminal contribution of social cognition to knowledge about how jurors use perception, long-term memory, inference, and other cognitive processes to subjectively transform complex case stimuli into manageable decision criteria (Kassin and Wrightsman 1988; Hastie, Penrod, and Pennington 1983). Unfortunately, however, the anticipated inclusion of cognitive processes into the attitudinal model never took hold in political science. Furthermore, we still ignore the cognitive and affective components of the attitudinal model's key concept in favor of the same narrow behavioral conceptualization that was responsible for the demise of the behavioral paradigm in psychology a quarter century ago. Nowhere is this failure more apparent than in the most recent explication of the attitudinal model by its premier proponents: "Though attitudes may be said to have cognitive, affective and behavioral components, our concern is with the votes of justices, and thus the behavioral component of attitudes. These attitudes and the values with which they associate should cause a behaviorally predisposed justice to support certain legal claims and to oppose others, while other justices behave in an opposite fashion" (Segal and Spaeth 1993, 69).

Putting a positive spin on the current political science approach, one can argue that our ability to identify justices' values, and the capacity of the attitudinal model to retroactively reproduce dimensions derived from justices' nonunanimous decisions renders questions about its conceptual foundations moot (Gibson 1991). This position is supported by the corollary argument that axiomatic theory should be judged not by the validity of its concepts or the accuracy of its assumptions but by its ability to predict behaviors (Popper 1963; Riker 1977). Certainly the notion that its conceptual flaws are outweighed by its empirical successes is implicit in Segal and Spaeth's eloquent defense of the capacity of the attitudinal model to reproduce voting patterns on the U.S. Supreme Court. In defending attitudinal models of Supreme Court justices' behavior, they point out appropriately that these jurists differ from other judges in ways that leave them relatively freer to pursue their personal policy goals than are lower court judges. Not only do justices lack electoral accountability, they generally have no ambition for higher office, and they sit on a court of last resort that controls its own jurisdiction.

We would add to Segal and Spaeth's contextual defense that the primary job of Supreme Court justices (as with appellate judges generally) is legal and constitutional interpretation. This contrasts directly with the primary task of trial courts, which is that of fact-finding. Some trial judges may indeed approximate the legal model, that is, "find the facts" and fit them to the appropriate legal standard. Others may, as asserted by Jerome Frank and other realists, begin with a legal "hunch" and unconsciously evaluate evidence in ways congruent with this hunch. But trial judges are primarily responsible for developing a factual basis for the application of laws interpreted by the appellate courts; their greatest powers derive from their discretion to "find" facts that are essentially immune from appellate scrutiny. We turn now to the implications of attitudinal models for fact-finding for the district courts.

Contextual Limitations

While the traditional attitudinal model may still have some utility as an explicator of appellate judge behavior, its usefulness for understanding the unique role and duties of the fact-finding trial judge leaves much to be desired. The main difficulty in applying the attitudinal model to trial judges is its fundamental assumption that these jurists are motivated primarily by their personal policy preferences. Attitudinal and psychometric models posit persuasively that each Supreme Court justice has a singular way of interpreting constitutional clauses, that these interpretations are applied consistently and predictably over time, and that they are understood in the context of each justice's particular belief system and preferences. These policy preferences are their preferred interpretations, that is, justices interpret the Constitution in such a way as to be consistent with their constitutional policy preferences. Thus, justices consistently vote to resolve constitutional disputes in favor of the party whose position is closest to their own ideological preference.

If the justice prefers a given policy position because he or she believes that position is an accurate reflection of what the Constitution does and should mean, then to say that a justice's constitutional policy decisions are motived by his policy preferences is hardly startling. Indeed, absent social science labels, such interpretations of judicial policy making are virtually indistinguishable from traditional legal analysis. If, on the other hand, one argues that justices are motivated by their policy preferences even when such preferences are contrary to what they believe to be the correct interpretation of the Constitution, then one is implicitly suggesting that they have violated the essence of their judicial oath. Therefore, unless one seriously wishes to contend that justices routinely ignore their oath, we must assume that justices' preferences are isomorphic with their ideological positions. Assuming isomorphism, more interesting than queries about whether preferences influence values are questions about the cognitive process by which policy preferences and ideological positions become isomorphic.

Whatever one may learn about appellate interpretations, to say that Supreme Court justices are motivated primarily by their constitutional policy preferences and that these preferences can be inferred from their "votes" is fundamentally different from contending that trial judges' fact-finding or evidence evaluation is motivated by their personal preferences. Taken at face value, the attitudinal model would have us accept axiomatically that the fact-finding and legal interpretation efforts of all 576 seated district judges, all of whom are committed by judicial oath to neutrality and objectivity, are driven primarily by their personal policy preferences rather than by the neutral admonitions of the judicial oath and by the norms of common-law jurisprudence. We readily acknowledge that the lines between interpretation and fact-finding are often blurred at the trial court level. For example, in our analysis of civil rights decisions, it was often clear that legal interpretation was relatively straightforward once evidence had been evaluated. And judges may be more likely to "find" these facts that are consistent with their preferred policy interpretations. Likewise, just as trial judges have more room to interpret statutes in some cases than others, so, too, is their fact-finding discretion greater in some instances than others. Still, the primary day-do-day focus of the trial judge is to establish facts and fit them to laws interpreted by appellate courts rather than to interpret ambiguous statutes and constitutional clauses. Indeed, fact-finding is not a discretionary part of the judicial role; it is, rather, what district judges do. Thus, while the attitudinal model may still have some utility in explaining the decision making of appellate judges, and some legal interpretation by trial judges, it is fundamentally lacking when it comes to understanding how a trial judge establishes facts and fits them to legal standards.

The seeds of doubt about the axiomatic assumption that judges are motivated by their personal preferences are nurtured by what trial judges tell us in their opinions, speeches, and off-the-bench writings. As indicated by our review of civil rights opinions, many codifications of decisions in this case category are explications primarily of the evidence and, secondarily, of why the found facts require the announced decision. Moreover, federal trial judges, including those with activist reputations, persistently and adamantly deny that their fact-finding or legal interpretations are motivated by their personal policy preferences (Johnson 1976). Indeed, even judges who acknowledge the influence of their experiences and attitudes on their judgment (Frank 1939) deny that they are *motivated* by extralegal preferences. While it may be naive to take every judge's protestations at face value, still, to reject out of hand their personal accounts is to argue implicitly that they are routinely deceitful or, at a minimum, duplicitous. Moreover, judges' denials seem less duplicitous when viewed in light of recent studies of judicial remediation (Cooper 1988; Rowland 1991).

The most informative of these remediation studies have been organized around Cooper's descriptive model that includes, inter alia, judges' assessments of liability, their formulation of remedies, and their refinement of these remedies (Cooper 1988). Guided by this descriptive framework, Cooper studied several remediation disputes, using interview and textual analysis to determine "what a judge saw at the time of the decision . . . and what forces constrained the judge's choices among options" (18). Given the discretion inherent in equitable remediation, adherents of attitudinal models would expect judges to take advantage of this discretion to impose their beliefs or preferences on the assessment, formulation, and refinement of remediation policies. But Cooper, who looked explicitly for external and internal influences on his subjects, found little evidence of this. Indeed, based on his qualitative analysis of the remediation process, he found that these trial judges adhered as best they could to a legalistic evaluation of facts and law and that they demonstrated little inclination to impose their own policy preferences on the disputes before them: "This study indicates that the judges in these cases were by and large more defensive in approach, more interested in resolving cases than in reforming the ills of American society" (328). In other words, when subjected to qualitative analysis that took seriously judges' and litigants' accounts of the judgment process, most of Cooper's judges behaved as we would expect judicial triers of fact to behave.

In sum, to say that a judge interpreting the Constitution is motivated by his consistent, belief-driven preferences is very different from saying that a trial judge's evaluation of evidence is motivated by these same preferences. One expects a jurist to judge the constitutionality of a search and seizure on the basis of his constitutional belief and to maintain the same constitutional threshold for what constitutes an unconstitutional search and seizure; one does not expect that same judge to evaluate the facts of a contested search on the basis of that belief. The axiomatic assumption that underlies psychometric or attitudinal models of trial judges' behavior is not only contrary to the norms of trial judging and the judicial oath, it is contrary to what judges tell us about their motives and contrary to qualitative evidence that district judges' remediation judgments are more legalistic than personal. Moreover, the findings of qualitative researchers reinforce our concerns about the attitudinal model's conceptual foundations and its applicability to triers of fact in the federal district courts. Certainly Cooper's accounts of judicial remediation underscore our concerns about the conceptual and contextual foundations of models derived from the behavioral paradigm and applied to the federal trial courts.[2]

Defenders of the behavioral paradigm might well retort that social scientific theories of judicial behavior (as with all axiomatic theories) must begin with certain unchallenged assumptions (Kuhn 1970), and that the value of an axiomatic theory is based not on the face validity of its assumptions and conceptualizations but on criterion validity—that is, its ability to explain and predict social phenomena (Popper 1963). For example, one's evaluation of rational-choice models of legislative behavior should be based on the model's ability to predict and explain congressional votes, not on the validity of the assumption that congressmen are rational maximizers of their reelection prospects (Mayhew 1966). And regardless of qualitative exceptions, attitudinal models do in fact "explain" some aspects of judicial behavior.[3] However, even when theories have some utility in predicting behavior, this does not mean that we should a priori retain them and refuse to consider others that might open the doors to new, important avenues of inquiry. We believe we have paid a high price for our blind adherence to the behavioral approach and our unwillingness to consider alternative models. In the following section we will argue that at least for trial judges, the deleterious costs of adherence to attitudinal and behavioral models outweigh the benefits.

THE COSTS OF COMMITMENT

We now examine several reasons for believing that the costs of adherence to preference-based, behavioral models are greater than their benefits. As with the case of psychology, the costs of axiomatic adherence derive less from the behavioral paradigm's inability to answer a narrow range of questions than from its inability to accommodate other, equally important questions.

The most serious cost of adherence to preference-based models is ironically analogous to the very limitations of mechanical jurisprudence that engendered the evolution of judicial behaviorism. Traditional adherents of the mechanical jurisprudence school generally ignored outside political variables because their existence was anathema to the belief that judges somehow "found" the law in some totally objective, neutral process quite devoid of the political. The model simply assumed away, as illegitimate, questions about the role of judges' personal values. But modern-day behavioral scholars have taken an equally obtuse position regarding political influences on judges. Because we have assumed axiomatically that discretionary outcomes are the product of *conscious motives* and that these motives can be inferred from the outcomes, adaptations of the attitudinal model render theoretically irrelevant any inquiry into the cognitive evidence-evaluation process that preceded the judge's "vote." Indeed, these models focus attention exclusively on aggregate "vote" outcomes rather than on the individual judgment processes that engendered these outcomes. As a consequence, we have come to ignore the critical cognitive process of judgment itself, that is, the evaluation of conflicting, complex, or ambiguous "facts." Such ignorance has prevented us from understanding more fully the critical link between politics and jurisprudence. Moreover, it has alienated us from the subjects of our research. Imagine beginning an interview with a federal district judge by asking: "Which policy preferences motivate you in your evaluation of evidence?"

A second problem with the preference-based models derives from their failure to take seriously the distinction between legal interpretation and fact-finding, and to recognize the primacy of the latter activity for trial judges. Ironically, this failure has diverted our attention from questions about the primary source of district judges' discretion and power. Thus, in trial courts where the perception and interpretation of ambiguous facts are often more important and controversial than the finding and interpretation of law, attitudinal models have actually prevented inquiry into the process of perceiving and interpreting these facts—that is, the process of judgment itself.

Related to our failure to emphasize the importance of fact-finding and our refusal to explore the whole process of judgment is the failure of modern behavioral researchers to take seriously judges' *legalistic* explanations of their decisions. Given the axiomatic constraints of the behavioral paradigm, this is not surprising. After all, if one assumes that political jurisprudence is the conscious product of political motives, then judges' legalistic explanations of the judgment process that preceded their decisions are, at best, irrelevant.[4] All evidence to the contrary, as derived from interviews, textual analysis of judges' opinions, and other qualitative sources tends to be ignored or denigrated as diversionary, self-serving, and duplicitous. But the attitudinal model's denigration of legal methods and sources produces an unnecessary, deleterious bifurcation between qualitative legal scholarship and quantitative social science research. This bifurcation is exemplified by the juxtaposition of political scientists' work on district judges' decisions with biographies of district judges by legal historians (Kemerer 1991). While both camps examine judicial policy making, their paradigmatic differences in methodology and basic assumptions have led inevitably to bifurcated research programs that barely acknowledge, much less complement, each other. As a result of this methodological and theoretical bifurcation, social, scientific, and other legal research programs pass like ships in the night. Until it is resolved, questions about the relationship between a legalistic process and politicized outcomes will continue to fall through the cracks.

We note one final cost of our relenting clinging to the attitudinal model of the behavioral paradigm. We have argued that the "attitudinal model" is a misnomer. Rokeach's conceptualization of attitudes was an explicit reaction to behavioral psychology's disdain for the cognitive and affective component of behavior. Yet, as Rogers Smith points out in his critique of the model's capacity to explain Supreme Court justices' behavior, the "attitudinal" model is concerned only with behavioral components of judicial votes. Thus, attitudinal models are, quite literally, attitudinal in name only. Moreover, as also noted earlier in the chapter, behavioralism and social psychological adaptations of its models have virtually disappeared from the social-psychological study of human behavior (Barone, Maddux, and Snyder forthcoming). Models that posit attitudes as the proximate causes of behavior are conspicuously rare. When attitudes are examined, they are usually conceptualized as information filters or intermediaries that influence the cognitive processes of perception, memory, and inference (Fiske and Taylor 1991).[5] In other words, attitudes remain conceptually relevant in their parent discipline primarily for the cognitive and affective properties treated as irrelevant by our adaptation of Rokeach's definition to judicial behavior. By clinging to models that are no longer relevant in their parent discipline, judicial behavioralists miss opportunities to incorporate empirical and theoretical developments regarding the affective and cognitive aspects of human judgment into their investigations of judicial decision making. Furthermore, we are not contributing to the evolution of general research on human judgment from the special perspective of judicial judgment.

SUMMARY AND CONCLUSIONS

Our criticisms of the behavioral paradigm and the models derived from it raise some obvious questions: Can we initiate an alternative and more robust model of trial judge decision making that accommodates quantitative evidence of the link between politics and jurisprudence? Can this new model allow this link to be the product of a legalistic judgment process rather than an artifact of judges' illegitimate personal motives? To respond affirmatively to these questions, we must introduce a model of individual judicial judgment whose paradigmatic foundations accommodate contemporary social-psychological conceptualizations of attitudes. Such a new model must not require inquiry into questions about unknown and unknowable individual motives; rather, it must focus on questions about the fact-finding process by which trial judges, constrained by legalistic procedures and norms, transform legal evidence into "politicized" judgments. The new model should encourage the utilization of both quantitative methods and qualitative methodologies that take seriously the legal system's constraints on judges' decision-making authority. The presentation of such a model is the goal of our final chapter, in which we first specify the unique organizational context of the federal district courts and then conceptualize trial judges' judgments in this organizational context as a special case of social judgments that can be explained by models adapted from social cognition and social judgment theory.

CHAPTER 7

Toward a Cognitive Approach for Understanding Judicial Judgment

This final chapter provides the theoretical context to expand our paradigm for studying trial judge decision making. We first conceptualize the context of judicial judgment in a way that captures both the discretion and the institutional constraints that structure the federal judiciary. We then propose a *cognitive* foundation for analyzing judicial judgments and for understanding political jurisprudence. After suggesting several ways in which this new approach could be applied to current phenomena, we finally outline nine benefits of a research program guided by a cognitive conceptualization of judicial judgment.

ORGANIZATIONAL CONTEXT

In our prior discussions of the organizational model's approach to judicial decision making, we noted positively that it does a good job of accounting for outside, environmental influences and also for the dynamic impact of the "judicial work group." On the other hand, the model tended to neglect the importance of individual judges' decision-making protocols and also the influence of the appellate courts on these trial judge protocols. We must then ask the question: Is it possible to conceptualize the context of federal trial courts in ways that acknowledge the importance of both the environmental and organizational contexts but also recognize the importance of constraints imposed by the formal and informal structure of the federal judiciary? Such conceptualizations are made difficult by the complexity of the federal judiciary and the balance of individual discretion within that system.

U.S. district courts defy easy organizational classifications. They are national institutions, and yet are situated in local settings and presided over by judges who typically have strong ties to the regional socioeconomic, political, and legal environments. When trial judges evaluate evidence and make choices about what law fits their "facts," they must explain—indeed justify—these evaluations to appellate judges who have the power to validate or invalidate the trial jurists' legal judgments. But these appellate bodies are dependent on—and deferential to—trial judges' evaluations of evidence; furthermore, they have little or no control over traditional organizational incentives such as employment, salary, promotions, or professional sanctions (Posner 1985). Thus the appellate and trial courts are involved in an information exchange in which the former, possessing virtually no capacity for imposing *personal* sanctions, review and supervise the legal interpretations of the latter on whom they are dependent for information about the controlling facts of the cases.

Given district judges' position in the judicial hierarchy, these horizontal and vertical dimensions of information exchange have important consequences for information processing and policy making in the federal trial courts. Ideally, information exchange would meet Norbert Weiner's standards for patterned relationships: "The first duty of the legislator or the judge is to make clear, unambiguous statements which not only experts, but the common man of the times will interpret in one way and one way only" (1961, 110). However, as anticipated by social and political jurisprudence, communication between trial and appellate judges usually fails to meet Weiner's ideal. This failure raises an important conceptual question not addressed by extant organizational models of the courts: How can one characterize the relationship between trial and appellate judges in a way that preserves the integrity of the judicial process but also allows for the persistent influence of outside political forces on judicial decision making?

The conceptual dilemma posed by the ambiguity of relationships in the federal judiciary is by no means unique. It is characteristic of a wide variety of information-based institutional structures, and is consistent with conceptual models in which principals are required by structural and functional imperatives to delegate discretion for implementation of rules and standards to professional agents on whom they depend for information, and over whom they have limited control. This relationship fits conceptually within the regulatory theory of agency (Mitnick 1980), a theory that has roots in legal theories of agency, and has been applied to litigation analogues in the regulatory and appellate processes (Moe 1985; Songer, Segal, and Cameron 1994). Therefore, we believe that it is necessary to incorporate many key aspects of agency theory into an improved model of trial judge decision making.

Agency concepts are applicable to any organizational setting where professional norms and the costs of perfect control make some disparity between principal preferences and agent behaviors inevitable. A standard topology of principal-agent relationships (Mitnick 1980) includes three levels of exchange—client, manager, and guardian—each of which has an analogue in the federal trial courts. At the *client* level are the consumers or recipients of the organizational products, that is, the litigants and their attorney-agents. Organizational product is directed by *managers* (i.e., the trial judges) and supervised by *guardians* (i.e., appellate judges), who shape organizational goals and "police" the organization's behavior with respect to these goals. The fiduciary norms of common-law jurisprudence and stare decisis define the trial manager's role as translator or implementor of policies specified by guardians or appellate principals. But the quality of principal-agent relationships depends on the principal-guardians' ability to specify manager-agent behaviors that satisfy principal preferences and police or monitor compliance with those preferences (Mitnick 1980).

Both specification and policing involve opportunity costs; for example, appellate courts can specify preferences most effectively by promulgating detailed opinions and reviewing carefully large numbers of decisions. However, time constraints and litigation pressures mean that most decisions cannot be set forth in the form of written opinions. Principals also face monitoring problems. The formal and informal norms of U.S. jurisprudence limit appellate monitoring to what McCubbins and Schwartz (1984) call "fire alarm" policing—that is, responding to perceived divergence—rather than "police-patrol" monitoring that is centralized and direct.

The difficulties of fire alarm policing are exacerbated by institutional *slippage* and individual *shirking*. Slippage, which refers to unintended information loss in the transfer between agent and principal, is the inevitable result of agent discretion. It is exaggerated in the judicial setting by a variety of factors: institutional arrangements that allow litigants to initiate trial courts' agendas; the inherent ambiguity of codified standards (Carter 1994); the evolution of new legal questions that obviate appellate specification of principles (Shapiro 1964); and, in the case of trial judges, the factual ambiguities characteristic of complex litigation.

A more serious threat to patterned relationships between trial agents and appellate or legislative principals is *shirking*, the intentional avoidance or circumvention by agents of principal preferences. Shirking is encouraged by a politicized, ideological appointment process that may create ambiguous or polarized principal specifications of decision criteria. It is exacerbated by institutionalized appellate deference to trial judges as "triers of fact" and by trial judges' duty to evaluate and interpret for appellate courts factual information presented by client litigators. This element of judicial interaction makes it very difficult for principals to distinguish shirking from slippage. Moreover, in the context of the federal judiciary and other political settings (Chubb 1985), the problem is multiplied by the presence of multiple principals—that is, conflicting or confusing circuit panels. When faced with conflicting principals, will judicial agents respond to the first principal encountered in the judgment process, the most cognitively salient, or the principal whose preferences most closely resemble their own?

In sum, although agency concepts initially may seem a somewhat radical departure from recent sociological characterizations of district courts and their environments (Heydebrand and Seron 1990), they capture nicely a district judge's views of the information-based organizational context of the federal judiciary (Kemerer 1991) as well as the seminal works on the strategic relationship between federal trial and appellate judges. Most notably, this structural formulation evokes the study of lower-court responses to Supreme Court directives by Walter Murphy (1964) and his contemporaries (Peltason 1955, 1961). Murphy notes, inter alia, that lower-court judges can evade (shirk) Supreme Court decisions in response to ambiguity or inadequate reasoning; slippage and shirking are exacerbated, according to Murphy, by the duty of trial judges to interpret the facts, and the relative insulation of trial agents from professional or personal sanctions. Peltason, of course, exemplifies the processes of slippage and shirking in his account of desegregation.

Finally, agency concepts accommodate well contemporary analysis of politicized adjudication in judicial and regulatory settings. For example, Terry Moe could well be speaking of the federal district courts when he describes the NLRB in the context of agency theory as a "simple dynamic system in which imperfectly informed participants adapt to one another's decisions over time, yielding an array of outcomes" (1985, 731).

To conceptualize the institutional context of the district courts from an agency perspective is to raise a host of questions about how judicial agents "judge" in this organizational context. What shapes agents' judgments in a common-law information network when legal guidelines, facts, and the congruence between the two are ambiguous and indeterminant? Can the game model of judicial behavior account for shirking and slippage? What is the psychological *process* by which a trial judge agent committed by oath to political neutrality contributes individually to the politicized polarization of judgments between presidential appointment cohorts? To address such questions we turn to a cognitive conceptualization of human judgment in agency settings.

PSYCHOLOGICAL CONTEXT

To understand aggregate patterns of political jurisprudence, we must understand the judgments of individual jurists. We begin by conceptualizing the federal courts as an information-processing network in which the relationship between trial judges and their appellate or legislative supervisors is that of an agent to a principal. In this conceptual world "slippage" is inevitable and difficult to distinguish from "shirking," and our attention is directed to the effects of imperfect, ambiguous information on the judge's evaluation of legal and evidentiary disputes. This conceptualization focuses our attention on the mental process by which individual judicial agents evaluate ambiguous legal and evidentiary clues within discretion parameters established by appellate judges. Therefore, to enhance our understanding of ideological jurisprudence and to guide analogous inquiry in the future, we adopt concepts from cognitive psychology, social cognition, and social judgment theory to build a cognitive theory of trial judges' judgments. However, before introducing our conceptual framework, we will briefly examine cognate work by scholars who have relaxed the assumptions of dogmatic rational choice models and applied these relaxed standards to the U.S. Supreme Court.

The precursors of a cognitive model of judicial judgment were popularized by students of cybernetic approaches to rational decision making (Simon 1957; March 1978). Grounded in the concepts of bounded rationality and procedural rationality, cybernetic models of decision making and cognitive theories of choice (Tversky and Kahneman 1974) share a common assumption, derived from basic research in cognitive psychology (Glass and Holyoak 1986). Those models assume axiomatically that human decision makers (even those who wear robes) share cognitive limitations that inhibit their ability to respond directly to stimuli whose complexity exceeds their computational capacity (Simon 1986), or whose ambiguity (Hogarth 1987) forces the judge to subjectively select manageable choice criteria and assign probable outcomes to alternative nonprobabilistic criteria. Thus, when the quantity or quality of information exceeds the human judge's cognitive capacity, complexity becomes the functional equivalent of ambiguity because both require the judge subjectively to recreate the choice problem by choosing manageable information from an information universe that is unmanageable. Under such circumstances the conscientious judge must "go about making his or her decisions in a way that is procedurally reasonable in the light of available knowledge and means of computation" (Simon 1986, 27).

If we accept as axiomatic the inherent ambiguity of much legal information and the limited cognitive capacity of trial judges, then a theory of district judges' judicial judgments must account for the processes by which judges subjectively represent complex decision problems. Such theories are exemplified in nonjudicial settings and by the architects of "prospect theory." Prospect theory models the cognitive choice process as a two-stage sequence in which the decision maker initially *frames* the problem—that is, defines it in the context of available information and subjective probability. Framing is controlled by the manner in which the choice problem is presented and by the norms, habits, and expectancies of the decision maker (Kahneman and Tversky 1979; Tversky and Kahneman 1981). Moreover, the subjective influences on framing extend to experts as well as novices (Krosnick 1990). For example, physicians are more likely to select a treatment protocol when it is framed in survival probabilities than when it is framed in perfectly analogous mortality probabilities (Johnson 1988). Framing is followed by the second stage in the process, *evaluation*—that is, the selection between alternative choices. Evaluation is choice based on rational calculation of personal prospects; however, choice is calculated on the basis of a subjective framing of choice criteria rather than on the basis of the criteria per se. Thus, whether imposed or cognitively constructed, the frame and the process of framing are as important as the decision and the process of decision making. Moreover, small subjective differences in framing can engender categorically different evaluations.

The cognitive process described by prospect theory and cybernetic models is consistent with patterns of polarized judicial judgments on the district courts. If the factual components are unambiguous and unambiguously legal cues are congruent with principal preferences, the problem is institutionally framed *for* the judge, who need only evaluate on the basis of these criteria; if not, the judge must frame the dispute by constructing a cognitive representation of the perceived problem and evaluate alternative outcomes on the basis of these subjective representations.

Cognitive-cybernetic theories have been creatively applied to the analysis of U.S. Supreme Court decisions (Hagle 1989; Segal 1986). These adaptations do an admirable job of incorporating the reality of cognitive and informational imperfection into the behavioral paradigm and attitudinal model. However, despite their explicit relaxation of assumptions about human "computational capacity" and about the quality and quantity of legal information, prospect theory and cognitive-cybernetic models of appellate judicial behavior continue to assume that judges' decisions are goal-oriented, driven by personal preferences. In fact, Hagle explicitly incorporated the primacy assumption of behavioral theory into his cognitive-cybernetic theory: "The first assumption is that political actors, including the justices, are goal oriented [Rohde and Spaeth 1976]. The goal the justices work toward is the attainment of their personal policy preferences (or maintenance) if their preferences are already the status quo" (1989, 8).

As noted in the previous chapter, the assumed primacy of personal preferences may make sense in an institutional context, such as the Supreme Court, where the justices' role is to adhere consistently to their preferred interpretation of the Constitution. After all, as Hagle points out, "The autonomy of the Supreme Court allows it a great deal of freedom to pursue personal policy goals of the justices" (1989, 9). However, this freedom does not extend to district judges, who are primarily fact finders and constrained by oath to follow the legal preferences enunciated by Supreme Court and appellate principals. Thus, although theories of appellate judicial behavior that incorporate the wisdom of bounded rationality, procedural rationality, framing, and evaluation represent significant advances in the conceptualization of appellate judicial behavior, these preference-based models do not adequately conceptualize the institutionally constrained judgments of *trial* judges. Particularly distressing is the persistent assumption—shared with their behavioral and rational-choice predecessors—that decisions are made in pursuit of personal goals or preferences on the basis of a decision calculus designed to maximize personal utility. To accept this assumption axiomatically is to create an unpalatable image of activist judges who, if they think they can get away with it, will consciously impose their policy preferences on their evaluations of disputed facts.

The failure of judicial cybernetic models to accommodate evidence of an electoral link to policy judgments without relying on assumptions that trial judges with no immediate personal stake in the outcomes are motivated by their policy preferences leads us to abandon the stricture of preference-based models in favor of those less dependent on motivational assumptions. For guidance we turn to the paradigmatic roots of social judgment and social cognition.

A SOCIAL COGNITIVE PARADIGM

As an alternative to legal, psychometric, and cybernetic models of judicial behavior, we proffer a conceptual model of judicial cognition. The model adopts from prospect theory the notion that decision making is a two-stage process in which decisions are preceded by framing, that is, the mental transformation of ambiguous evidence and law into proximate decision cues. It also shares with prospect theory the assumption that all humans, including judges, have computational limitations that constrain the quality and quantity of their judgment protocols. And it accepts the behavioral premise that judges' policy preferences can influence their judgments. However, our model of judicial cognition rejects the general assumption that human judgment is necessarily goal-oriented and the axiomatic assumption of attitudinal models and their derivatives that judicial judgment is motivated by the judge's personal policy preferences. A judicial cognition model must rather attend to the process by which preferences influence judgment in the context of principal-agent relationships between federal trial and appellate judges.

As with all attempts to construct axiomatic theories of human behavior, our framework for judicial judgment must begin by outlining its core assumptions, specifying the conditions under which it applies, and defining conceptually its key terms.

Assumptions and Conditions

For the case of trial judges we borrow from basic work in cognitive psychology (Glass and Holyoak 1986) and applied work in social cognition (Fiske and Taylor 1991) and assume that, as with all people, judges are "cognitive misers," that is, they are individuals with limited short-term memories and capacious long-term memories. As such, judges share the computational limitations of Simon's procedurally reasonable actors; however, they are also assumed to possess a capacious long-term memory that allows them to compensate for these short-term limitations in ways that can be predicted and observed.

Our second assumption is that trial judges respect and adhere to the formal and informal norms contained in the judicial oath that binds them to fairness and objectivity. As such, they *do not* resolve disputes in which they have an immediate personal economic or reputational stake, nor do they consciously ignore or misrepresent facts that are contrary to their personal preferences. They *do,* however, take seriously their commitment to an unbiased evaluation of evidence and interpretation of the law. (This is not to say we assume that judges' decisions are purely objective; rather, we believe that they attempt to follow the law and evaluate the facts *as they see them.*)

The conditions under which our axiomatic theory of judicial cognition applies derive directly from its assumptions. As agents within the federal judiciary, trial judges are often given ambiguous legal cues by the appellate courts, and they are frequently confronted with conflicting pieces of evidence. Yet their formal and informal job requirements are to reach categorical, unequivocal judgments based on such ambiguous and equivocal stimuli. The cognitive model must operate under all of these assumptions.

Conceptual Definitions

Given the centrality of judgment and ambiguity to our model, it is important that we now operationally define these terms. Ambiguity is an intermediate stage of "knowing" where uncertain knowledge is greater than ignorance, but not characterized by known decision-related probabilities. In the context of a trial court, information is ambiguous to the extent that it has an alleged causal relationship to the evidence, the law, or the judge's (or jury's) decision in a given case. However, the probability that the alleged causal relationship is valid is unknown. Whatever the context, when forced to make decisions on the basis of nonprobabilistic ambiguous information, decision makers must first estimate subjectively the probability that the information is validly related to decision alternatives.

The distinction between ambiguity—which Ellsburg calls "uncertainty about uncertainty" (1961)—and probabilistic uncertainty can be illustrated by the different tasks facing regulators who must decide whether to require seat belts and judges who must decide liability. The regulator knows from research and experience the probability that a seat belt requirement will save a certain percentage of lives; he does not know whether a given accident will include fatalities, but he knows the probability that the accident will or will not include fatalities if driver and passengers are wearing seat belts. The trial judge, on the other hand, has no comparable probabilistic knowledge to guide his decision when faced with evidence and adversarial legal interpretations that are unclear and conflicting, or characterized by unknown causal relationships to contested outcomes. For example, when faced with allegations that a plaintiff's illness was caused by silicone breast implants manufactured by the defendant, the judge confronts conflicting testimony about contested facts, disagreement among qualified medical experts about the etiology of the plaintiff's illness, and a host of other uncertainties. All of this must be resolved and transformed before the judge can specify decision criteria—much less reach a verdict. In fact, the formal and informal norms of legal reasoning require that triers of fact derive from testimony and evidence their own probabilities, then determine whether the subjective probabilities are probative beyond the applicable burden of proof.

If ambiguity is a condition characterized by decision makers' perception of information as nonprobabilistic, then judgment is the cognitive process by which human decision makers constrained by probabilistic decision criteria subjectively assign causal probabilities to ambiguous information and transform ambiguous information into probabilistic decision cues. For judges, probabilistic decision criteria would refer to such legal concepts as "beyond a reasonable doubt" or "preponderance of the evidence." When, for example, the judge finds expert witness A more credible than expert B, he is reducing ambiguity by assigning a higher probability to the validity of expert A's causal analysis than to B's. Thus, judgment precedes the "judicial vote," just as the framing stage precedes evaluation in prospect theory. Moreover, since decisions are responses not to objective facts and law but to facts and law that have been subjectively transformed into probabilistic decision cues, judgment is a process that must be understood before one can explain the decisions that follow.

To understand judicial judgments it is important to remember that judicial transformations are *social judgments* made on behalf of society by an individual with authority to do so. Judicial judgments are social judgments because, unlike decisions about careers or personal finances, the persons with primary responsibility for making the judgment have little more immediate stake in judgment outcomes than do other members of society. Indeed, the judgments are made on behalf of society. To the extent policy makers' and other "social" judges' decisions are judged, it is on the basis of social, not personal, goals. Given the substitution of social for personal goals, it is not surprising that the social-psychological study of social judgments from a perspective that does not assume personal motives or outcome-based utilities has evolved into an important subfield for the potential analysis of trial judge decision making.

Judicial Judgment as Social Judgment: The Lens Model

The study of social judgment (Hammond, McClelland, and Mumpower 1980) has built on the work of Brunswick (1952) and others (Heider 1958) and has incorporated the conceptual foundations of ecological psychology into theories of human judgment. Conceptualizing judgment as a cognitive response to ambiguous facts and/or decision criteria (Nisbett and Ross 1980; Hammond, McClellan, and Mumpower 1980; Fiske and Taylor 1991), Social Judgment Theory (SJT) conceives of choice as part of a learning process defined by the interaction between an individual and his or her environment. This process (which is analogous to the common law) enables the individual to reduce ambiguity by incorporating the environmental effects (e.g., principal feedback, social impact) of prior choices into the perception or framing of present choice (Hammond, McClelland, and Mumpower 1980).

Judges may occasionally avoid ambiguity by manipulating information in response to objective, learned framing criteria. For example, a trial judge's probing of witnesses or counsel may elicit incontrovertible, probative evidence. But when variables cannot be manipulated to fit learned decision criteria, judges must passively utilize their cognitive resources—that is, exercise their judgment—to arrive at a conclusion about a state of affairs clouded by causal ambiguity. Thus, human (social) judgment is a cognitive activity of last resort.

When the human judge has no immediate personal stake in the outcome but must respond on the basis of imperfect, nonprobabilistic knowledge in the environment, the response *process* becomes *social judgment:* the process by which humans of limited cognitive capacity mentally construct alternative responses to ambiguous stimuli in the decision-making environment when response criteria and social consequences can be estimated but not known (Hammond et al. 1977; Hammond, McClelland, and Mumpower 1980).

As ambiguity increases, reliance on "mental simulation" to assign probabilities and frame the judgment problem increases. This simulation process has long been a focal point of judgment psychology, and can be depicted for the judicial setting by an adaptation of the lens model of probabilistic functionalism—that is, the process by which the judge interacts with the dis-

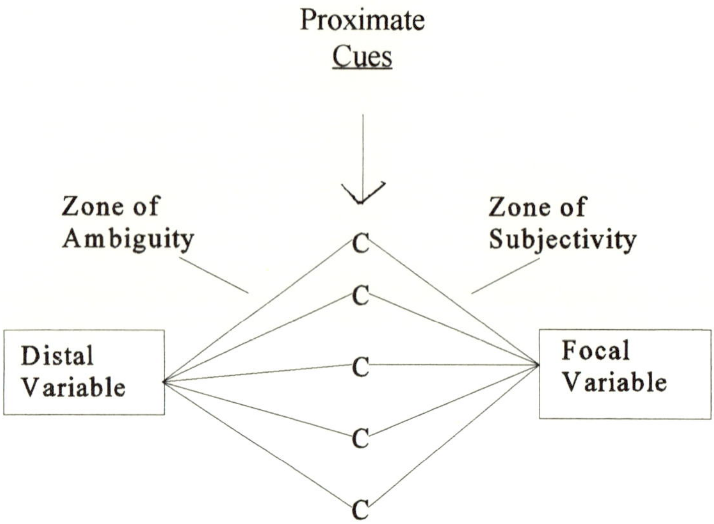

Figure 7-1. A lens model of judicial judgment (adapted from Brunswick 1952).

tal environment and reduces ambiguity by selecting, weighing, and ordering manageable proximate cues as surrogates for unmanageable distal stimuli (Brunswick 1952; Hammond 1966).

As the social judgment process is depicted in Figure 7-1, the judge is never confronted directly with the distal facts or the law defining a complex case. Never, for example, does the judge witness the dispute to be resolved; never is he privy to the intent of the legislators when he must interpret a statute. Rather, the judge is confronted with proximate cues (C), through which his cognitive system perceives the distal facts and law and reconstructs them mentally into a manageable *focal variable.* In Brunswick's words: "The distal cause in the environment scatters its effects and the organism recombines them" (1952, 37).

Between the proximate cues and the distal factual and legal stimuli is a *zone of ambiguity,* the depth and shape of which are a function of the quantity and quality of information defining a distal stimulus. In the legal setting the depth of this zone (for a given stimulus) is a function of the degree of the legal and factual ambiguity attached to that dispute. Faced with ambiguous stimuli, the judge must estimate the *ecological validity* of cues. When ambiguity is a function of complexity, judges of limited cognitive capacity must not only estimate the validity of cues, they must select and order a manageable number of cues from the unmanageable number available. In the legal setting the ecological validity of a given cue is a function of the (unknown) probability that it is a valid approximation of a given distal variable (e.g., the validity of physical evidence, the reliability of a witness). This estimated probability, in turn, establishes a functional, perceptual relationship between a proximate cue and a distal fact. The deeper the zone of ambiguity, the greater the degree of judgment required to estimate the ecological validity of cues and recombine the distal stimuli into a focal variable that is a combination of objective stimuli and the subjective recombination of proximate cues. This formulation is, of course, reminiscent of "cue" theories of Supreme Court case selection. If, over time, given cues prove to be ecologically valid, then justices learn to weight them heavily in analogous subsequent judgments (Tanenhaus et al. 1963).

For any judgment task delegated from principal to agent there also exists a *criterion variable*—that is, a preferred or acceptable judgment. Legal interpretation by trial judges assumes decision criteria by appellate courts. A decision criterion may be deterministic; however, for most judicial judgments it is ambiguous, and the judge can only estimate the congruence between his judgment and the judgment criterion. The *functional validity* of a given cue is a function of its association with validation of agents' judgments by principals. In the federal judiciary, the perceived functional validity of a given criterion variable is a function of its validation by appellate or, occasionally, legislative principals. Thus, validity estimates are shaped over time by feedback from appellate principals. To the extent principal feedback is explicit and redundant, the ambiguity of criterion variables is reduced, estimates of functional validity become reliable, and the judge can rely on known probabilistic criteria rather than mentally formulating his own functional probabilities.

Juxtaposed with the zone of ambiguity is a *zone of subjectivity*. The zone of subjectivity mirrors exactly the depth, shape, and functions of the zone of ambiguity because the subjective component of judgment is a function of the quantity and quality of ambiguity created by distal case stimuli. To the extent that the zone of ambiguity is deep, the organism must increase reliance on his or her cognitive representations to frame the judgment problem and assign probabilities to competing cues. Thus, just at the zone of subjectivity is a function of the zone of ambiguity defining a given dispute, the potential influence of the judge's individual cognitive system on his or her judgment is a function of the depth and shape of the zone of subjectivity.

Social judgment, as depicted by the lens model, offers potentially important conceptual contributions to understanding the exercise of judgment in trial courts because it diverts our attention from simplistic assumptions about the effect of extralegal motives on outcomes and focuses our attention on the more important framing process that preceded decision making—that is, it focuses our attention on judicial judgment rather than on the judicial "vote." Moreover, it recognizes that, as agents, trial judges must rely on their own cognitive systems to reconstruct unmanageable distal stimuli and estimate ecological and functional validity. But important theoretical questions remain. What determines differences among judges in their perceptions of ambiguous stimuli and, indirectly, their judgments? Most important, how can one account for the overwhelming evidence of aggregate appointment effects if individual judges are not motivated by appointment-based preferences? To accommodate this question we incorporate concepts from the study of social cognition into our cognitive framework.

Social Cognition: Perception, Memory, and Inference

As the dominant subfield of contemporary social psychology, social cognition is a cognitive approach to understanding human behavior in social settings. As such, it focuses empirical attention not on assumed linkages among social stimuli, attitudes, and behaviors but on the cognitive processes that account for individual differences—and similarities—in the perception, memory, and inferential interpretation of information. Of particular importance for our purposes is the fact that social cognition represents a virtual abandonment of simple, invalidated attitudinal models of behavior in favor of more complex models that characterize attitudes and other affective elements of human choice as influences on the evaluation of information rather than as crude indicators of motives that directly influence behavior. From a social cognition perspective, the quest to understand the link between value-based appointment and value-based decisions is a quest to understand how human judges rely on perception, memory, and interpretation of law and evidence to process ambiguous information and assign subjective probabilities that become the basis for the judicial vote. Therefore, understanding appointment-based differences in these processes is the key to understanding subsequent differences in decision making.

To the extent that perception, memory, and interpretation of ambiguous cues are subjective, one would expect variation among judges on all three dimensions. Likewise, because judges are responsive not only to objective stimuli but to subjective probabilities, one would expect individual differences in perception, memory, and interpretation of ambiguous cues to be predictive of individual differences in judicial "votes." More important, because judges *must* assign probabilities to subjective cues—that is, they can't say it's a toss-up, even if they want to—one need assume nothing about the judge's motives to accept the inevitability of subjective information processing. But the question remains: If differences in subjective reformulation of ambiguous evidence are not the product of different extralegal motives, what accounts for them? Thus, the challenge remains to explain how the extralegal values of trial judges who may or may not be motivated by these values influence their interpretation of ambiguous information.

To answer this question from the perspective of social cognition requires a conceptualization of how individuals forced by decision rules to make categorical decisions on the basis of ambiguous cues rely on their long-term memories to organize and prioritize these cues. Although alternative concepts are available within the social-cognition pantheon, we will rely on the schema concept to organize our theoretical exposition of the relationship between judges' cognitive processes, their framing of legal disputes, and their political experiences. Although "schema theory" remains somewhat controversial (Kuklinski, Luskin, and Bolland 1991), we rely on the schema concept as an analytic organizing tool, first, because it has established utility for the study of political (Conover 1984) and legal judgments (Kassin and Wrightsman 1988) in cognate settings and, second, because it accommodates nicely what judges say they do when faced with conflicting or confusing facts that must be reformulated as proximate decision cues.

As with our model of judicial cognition, schema-based explanations of human judgment begin with the assumption, validated by research in basic cognition, that all humans are cognitive misers. As cognitive misers, we rely on experience-based knowledge structures in our capacious long-term memories to compensate for the limitations of our short-term memories. For convenience these cognitive structures of stored episodic and impressionistic knowledge are referred to as *schemata* (Fiske and Taylor 1991). Whether they store knowledge about the person, other persons, or events, these structures contain category labels, specific descriptions of the stimulus domain, prototypical examples of that domain, and the causal connections within it (Fiske and Taylor 1991; Lau and Sears 1988). Thus, as defined conceptually by Fiske and Linville, a *schema* is a cognitive structure of organized prior knowledge, abstracted from experience with specific instances, that anchors the processing of new information and the retrieval of stored information (1980, 543).

Schemas may vary from general, abstract response repertoires (e.g., females) to "point-of-view" schemata (e.g., gender equality) embedded in abstract general schemata (Lodge and Hamill 1986; Conover and Feldman 1984). Whatever their scope, schemata "affect whether information is processed or ignored, how information is encoded and retrieved from memory, and how experiences and other phenomena are perceived and evaluated" (Carroll 1985, citing Taylor and Crocker 1981). When a schema's entry conditions are cued by complexity or ambiguity, schematic processing will begin. People will know what type of information to expect, and when that information is absent, they will frequently assume the default values available in long-term memory. Thus, schemata shape human inference by filtering estimates of missing or ambiguous information through judges' experience and existing knowledge (Conover and Feldman 1984). Schematic cognitive misers are most attentive to information that is compatible with available schemata in their long-term memories. They perceive and interpret information in ways that facilitate compatibility. And inferences drawn from information encoded in long-term memory are drawn not from the information per se but from the schematic perception and memory of that information. Because the selection, perception, memory, and interpretation of ambiguous information is a function of the compatibility of that information with available schemata, cognitive misers are faced with decision criteria that overwhelm their short-term memory. Thus complex social judgments are inevitably "selective" judgments (Conover and Feldman 1984).

To say that "selective" judgment is often inevitable is not to say that the schematic foundations of selectivity do not vary substantially among individual judges. Reliance on schematic processing may also vary among individuals; moreover, for a given subject matter, one may be more or less *schematic* depending on one's experience and cognitive structure for that subject (Lodge and Hamill 1986). These individual differences in schematic processing have predictable causes and consequences. The extent to which one is "schematic" for a given subject is caused by chronic differences in perceptual readiness or "information processing proclivities" (Lau 1986), which are a function of differences in the experiential schemata—valenced and unvalenced—that are stored in long-term memory (Fiske and Taylor 1991). Experienced fishermen are schematic about fishing (when told that a friend caught a bass on a top water lure, the experienced fisherman "sees" a vivid picture of gills, hooks, and exploding water that is not accessible to the nonfisherman). These differences in accessibility to available, experience-based cognitive constructs can cause differences in social judgments when people with different life experiences are exposed to the same set of ambiguous decision cues.

At first, experience-based individual differences in schematic perception, memory, and inference would seem to offer a firm theoretical foundation for understanding differences among individuals in their selective perception of conflicting evidence. It is not difficult to understand how a southern jurist who attended private schools and a fellow jurist who attended one-room schools would perceive the causes and consequences of corporal punishment differently. But the question remains: If judges are not motivated by the political values and policy preferences that secured their appointment, why do they so persistently evaluate facts and law in ways that are consistent with these values? Why, for example, would a Reagan appointee so consistently perceive an unemancipated minor as too immature to bypass parental notification if he were not motivated by his political opposition to abortion? The theoretical answer to this conundrum may be traced to the content of most political schemata. Schemata may be unvalanced, cognitive structures—that is, structures, such as an event schema for shopping, that do not require affect for activation (Fiske and Linville 1980). However, most political experience and, therefore, most political schemata are relatively high in affect (Conover and Feldman 1984), as are most of the disputes that engender platform-based ideological judicial judgments. Moreover, because most federal judges are politically involved before their appointment (Goldman 1985), they may be expected to have richer, more complex political schemata than the general public (Lodge and Hamill 1986). Therefore, although schematic information processing does not assume an affective link to behavior (Conover and Feldman 1984), a judicial cognition perspective would anticipate that judges, like other political elites recruited on the basis of affective political experience, would perceive, remember, and interpret evidentiary and legal cues through highly affective schematic lenses.

The theoretical expectation that politically experienced judges would process information by reference to their highly affective schemata does not explain the persistent ideological polarization between appointment cohorts. The fact that individual judges are recruited on the basis of affective political schemata does not offer a direct link to the effect of presidential appointment on ideological polarization. This link is established, however, by the politics of appointment and the importance of relevant social schemata as appointment criteria. When presidents and home-state recruiters establish ideological and policy-based appointment criteria, they select and reinforce *shared* ideological and policy schemata (Lodge and Hamill 1986). For example, when President Reagan pledged to appoint strict constructionists who opposed social regulation, this pledge implied a commitment to select highly schematic judges who shared relevant person, event, and role schemata and who would encode, retrieve, and interpret imperfect information by reference to those schemata. When, for example, a Reagan appointee is asked in the absence of clear appellate guidelines to decide whether a pregnant sixteen-year-old litigant is mature enough to have an abortion without telling her parents, no amount of testimony could be expected to overcome his casual schematic perception that pregnancy itself was an indicator of immaturity in unmarried teenagers. Thus, to the extent that the valanced schemata shared by one presidential cohort are contrary to the valanced schemata shared by another cohort, one would expect polarized differences in the perception, memory, and interpretation of ambiguous proximate cues, regardless of the individual cohort members' personal motives.

In sum, our cognitive conceptualization of trial judging treats the polarization of published judgments as the inevitable compensation of cognitive misers for ambiguous information and individual information-processing limitations. Polarization of district judges' policy decisions among presidential appointment cohorts is the product of individual appointment-based differences in perception, memory, and interpretation of evidence and law. Although some individuals are more "schematic" than others, and the same individual may be more schematic about some policy domains than others (Lodge and Hamill 1986), the domestic policy domains about which people are most likely to have developed policy-relevant, valanced schemata, such as racial and social concerns (Conover and Feldman 1984; Lodge and Hamill 1986), are the issues that have maximized politicized appointment and appointment-based polarization. Moreover, because most federal judges are politically active before their appointment (Goldman 1985), they may be expected to have richer, more complex policy schemata than the general public. Thus, to the extent that different appointing presidents select and reinforce different social schemata, schematic variation between appointment cohorts should be greater than variation within each cohort (Lodge and Hamill 1986; Goldman 1985), and one would expect polarization of perception, memory, and inferred stimuli, and, therefore, polarized social judgments regardless of the judge's extralegal motivations.

To say that schematic judges respond to ambiguity by reference to schemata selected and reinforced in the appointment process is not to say that all appointees of the same president are equally schematic or share identical cognitive systems or self-schema. Nor is it to say that shared schemata will be important in all, or even most, judgments. The cognitive perspective does, however, lead us to anticipate that a given presidential cohort's shared predilections will be relevant for social judgments that combine the requisite zone of ambiguity with legal and factual questions relevant to shared schematic identification with the presidential cohort. Thus, for social judgments that fit within schematic predilections, the politics of appointment will be linked to district judges' judgments by the schematic recombination of distal stimuli into proximate cues. This conceptualization obviates assumptions about judges' motivations by recognizing explicitly that cognitive misers—even those wearing robes—are required by ambiguity and their own cognitive limitations to estimate functional and ecological validity and to mentally recombine proximate cues by reference to the policy predilections that secured their appointment. Thus conceived, judges' decisions are responses not to the facts and law that defined the distal dispute but to the mental reformulation of that distal variable into focal variables that serves as the subjective stimulus that engenders their decision. The judicial "vote" is neither as interesting nor as important as the judgment process that formulated the voting cues.

Axiomatic Theories of Judicial Cognition

Having proposed the conceptual foundations of a paradigmatic shift to a social-cognitive framework for understanding trial judges' social judgments, we conclude by proposing tentatively an axiomatic theory of judicial cognition for trial-court settings and a research agenda designed to explore avenues of inquiry opened by this theory.

As with any axiomatic model of human behavior, we must begin with certain assumption(s) about human judges. For the case of trial judges we assume only that they, like the rest of us, are cognitive misers—that is, individuals with limited short-term memories and capacious long-term memories. This assumption is derived from basic work in cognitive psychology and applied research in social psychology (Glass and Holyoak 1986; Fiske and Taylor 1991). In the context of judicial cognition, trial judges' extrajudicial motives are treated as unknown and unknowable in the context of judicial norms and ethics.

The conditions under which the judicial cognition model would apply are implicit in the basic assumption of cognitive limitations. Our model would apply in trial courts when the complexity or ambiguity of information defining a despute render the judge's limited short-term memory inadequate and require him or her to reformulate that information by processing it in long-term memory. From our assumptions and specified conditions, and conceptualization of judicial decision making as a two-stage process, we derive the following general proposition: "Judicial misers" rely on their long-term memories when faced with judgment tasks that by definition require them to rely on long-term memory to frame disputes by transforming unmanageable information into manageable decision criteria.

From our specification of assumptions and context can be derived a set of general research questions suitable for specific formulation and exploration in future research. Because cognitive models are more concerned with judgment than with "votes," research questions will focus on the cognitive processes judges use to encode and retrieve facts and law from their long-term memories. Thus research will explore questions such as the following:

What are the subjective perceptions and selective memories that account for a trial judge's formulation of focal variable(s)?

What are the inferences and attributions that account for a trial judge's projections of motive, veracity, accuracy, and other qualities in litigants and witnesses?

To what extent can differences in perception, memory, and inference be explained by differences in political and personal experiences?

Application of the general judicial cognition questions to specific research topics is straightforward. If one were interested in perceptions of maturity in abortion bypass cases one would, for example, begin by estimating the zone of ambiguity for a given case or set of cases. For the judicial bypass example, the estimated zone would include explicit uncertainty about appellate principals' decision criteria and a high degree of interpretative uncertainty regarding behavioral indicators of maturity. Is the claimant's anxiety indicative of an immature adolescent; or is that anxiety indicative of a young woman whose maturity emboldened her to overcome her fears and exercise her legal rights?

After estimating the zones of factual and legal ambiguity, attention would turn to the cognitive process—the judgment protocols—by which the judge resolves uncertainty about legal and factual uncertainty. What attributions are made about the claimant's motives? What inferences are drawn from the fact that this is not her first problem pregnancy? What evidence does the judge attend to? What evidence is ignored? Are perception and recall of cited evidence selective? All of these questions are fundamental to understanding the judgment process by which the cognitive miser trying a judicial bypass claim reformulates distal facts and law into proximate decision criteria.

It is only after the researcher has identified key judgments that a meaningful search can be conducted for the foundations of these judgments in the judge's legal, political, and social schemata. Since these memory constructs cannot be observed directly, the search focuses on the interaction between experience and values that is both a cause and a consequence of the judge's valanced political and social schemata. For the example of the judicial bypass case, one would quite possibly be led by the judge's selection, specification, weighting, and ordering of cues to an exploration of the jurist's experience with a suicidal daughter.

Whatever the case specifics, researchers working from the judicial cognition perspective would infer from judgment protocols a hypothesized set of causal schemata and initiate a search for the valanced experiences that are both cause and consequence of those schemata. What the judicial cognitivist would *not* do is assume that either the judgment process or the decisions that follow were a product of the judge's conscious motivation to impose his or her personal preferences on the evaluation of evidence or the interpretation of legal standards handed down by appellate or legislative principals.

Even our brief outline of general and specific questions gleaned from the cognitive model of judicial judgment make it clear that the questions inherent in paradigms that focus on complex cognitive processes rather than assuming simplistic motivational explanations cannot be answered without the expenditure of substantial time and resources. However, we believe that these costs can be justified by at least nine benefits of a research program guided by a cognitive conceptualization of judicial judgment.

1. Our model views "judicial man" as a cognitive miser who must rely on cognitive shortcuts to process imperfect information, and thus our approach can accommodate quantitative evidence of extralegal polarization without implicitly impugning judicial competence or integrity. This accommodation reinforces the link between contemporary sociolegal research and its roots in legal realism and sociological jurisprudence (Llewellyn 1931). For example, when Jerome Frank argued over fifty years ago that trial judges were cognitively incapable of "objective" fact analysis, especially if evidence were ambiguous or contradictory, he explicitly recognized extralegal influences on judgment without assuming conscious extralegal motivations (Frank 1949).

2. By treating the complexity and ambiguity of information as key variables in judicial judgment, judicial cognition models will encourage qualitative refinement and quantitative measurement of these key concepts. Indeed, if we are to estimate ambiguity and address questions about judicial cognition in the context of information quality, it is imperative that ambiguity be refined conceptually, defined operationally, and measured quantitatively. Thus the switch to judicial cognition will serve as an impetus to refine and synthesize conceptual, qualitative, and quantitative research tools.

3. Judicial cognition should encourage a more general synthesis of qualitative and quantitative measurement. Such a synthesis should help behaviorists understand the qualitative links between politics and jurisprudence; and, because our model does not cast aspersions upon judges' motives, it should also encourage legal scholars to acknowledge quantitative evidence of extralegal effects and focus their analytic skills on the legal corollaries of these effects. Moreover, because cognitive structures do not necessarily require affect for activation (Fiske and Linville 1980), the methodological synthesis encouraged by cognitive approaches could be adapted to situations (e.g., complex civil litigation) where variation in judicial judgment may be engendered by unvalanced legal schemata (Conover and Feldman 1984) and where behavioral models are, by definition, of limited utility.

4. By treating the quality and quantity of information as important, a judicial cognition approach would encourage careful examination of case files. The content of incriminating documents, expert witnesses' affidavits, and a host of other information sources would be taken seriously not by idiographic researchers interested in a single case or single judge but by theory-

based scholars interested in judicial processing of ambiguous legal and factual cues. Because they are theory-driven, the aggregate result of such idiosyncratic examinations will be an accumulation of how and why judicial misers make manageable the unmanageable information that defines complex or amorphous disputes.

5. The cognitive perspective encourages a theory-driven revival of interest in judges' codified explanations of their judgment protocols. To the extent that scholars have been guided explicitly or implicitly by motivational models of judicial decision making, opinions were, at best, irrelevant. If one assumes that written judicial decisions are motivated primarily by extralegal reasons that cannot legitimately be acknowledged, it makes sense to ignore opinions as irrelevant. If, on the other hand, one assumes only that judges are cognitive misers who must rely on experience-based cognitive processes to mentally transform ambiguous information into viable decision criteria, judges' codified reports become extremely relevant (unless one assumes implicitly that judges' opinions are simply duplicitious or, at best, disingenuous).[1]

6. Because it focuses attention on the judgment process, the cognitive approach encourages new methodologies that enable one to observe, record, and analyze judgment protocols under strict controls for zones of ambiguity. Particularly encouraging is a nascent trend toward experimental designs using as subjects either retired trial judges or judicial participants in continuing judicial education programs mandated by many states. For example, a recent comparison of retired judges and mock jurors demonstrated that the two groups were equally susceptible to demeanor effects on their assessments of witness accuracy, but that the judges made their assessments more quickly and relied on fewer behavioral cues than did the mock jurors (Bayne 1991). Not only is Bayne's work a model of methodological innovation, it also suggests that, as with doctors (Johnson 1988), judge's procedural fact-finding expertise may not extend to substantive expertise.

7. A cognitive approach is robust enough to accommodate important concepts and approaches from the study of judicial behavior to the study of judicial judgment. This is true even though it shifts attention from preference-based behaviors to the cognitive processing of information. The most obvious adaptation from extant behavioral models is the concept of "judicial role" (Gibson 1983), which is, within the cognitive framework, a fairly specific role schema—that is, "the cognitive structure that organizes one's knowledge about . . . appropriate norms and behaviors" (Fiske and Taylor 1991). Less obvious but equally adaptable are "cue theory" (Tanenhaus et al. 1963; Armstrong and Johnson 1982) and fact-pattern analysis (Segal 1986) of Supreme Court justices' behaviors. Neither cue theory nor fact-pattern analysis requires assumptions of preference-based motivation; indeed, both share implicit assumptions that judges are cognitive misers who must take cognitive shortcuts when faced with complex or ambiguous cues.

8. A cognitive approach connects sociolegal research to important cognate developments in the study of legal, economic, and political choice (McGraw and Pinney 1990; Hogarth 1987). Most proximately, a cognitive approach will facilitate a comparison of judicial fact-finding with social-psychological studies of jury behavior. Given Bayne's nascent work and recent revelations regarding the limitations of "expert" judgment (Chi, Glaser, and Farr 1988) and the fact that judges are trained in law, not fact-finding, cognitive models of juror judgment (Kassin and Wrightsman 1988) may offer important insights into trial judges as triers of fact. Particularly intriguing is the potential fit of judicial judgment to "story" models of judicial judgment, which posit that jurors make sense of complex or ambiguous evidence by organizing ambiguous cues into case narratives that are consistent with and reinforced by their experience-based cognitive prepossessions (Hastie, Penrod, and Pennington 1983).

9. The call for a shift from a stimulus-response, preference-based model of judicial behavior to a cognitive, procedural model of judicial judgment is consistent with a more general paradigmatic shift in the study of decision choice. Indeed, it is analogous to Herbert Simon's general call for a shift to procedural models of human choice:

> We must construct a theory of the *processes* of decision. The theory must include . . . the processes that generate the actor's subjective representation of the decision problem, his or her frame. . . . The rational person of cognitive psychology goes about making his or her decisions in a way that is procedurally reasonable in light of available knowledge and means of computation. (1986, 27).

Although our model of judicial man and social judgment may eschew Simon's implicit assumptions about personal goal orientation, the basic theoretical implications of his exhortation for future research or judicial choice are straightforward. We cannot understand judicial choice without understanding the judgment process that precedes the judicial decision. Inquiry into the process by which humans, including those in black robes, compensate for informational and cognitive limitations will be tedious and complex. Modeling this process will require us to develop experimental as well as archival studies of judgment. However, if we are persistent, the potential payoffs arc great. We may learn that for trial judges, as for jurors, the distinction between *ratio decidende* and *ratio cogoscendi* is often a distinction without a difference. If so, we will have learned a great deal about the behavioral foundations of the link between politics and jurisprudence and the specific link between politicized judicial appointment and trial judge decision making.

Appendices

Appendix A. Case Categories

1. Habeas corpus—U.S.
2. Habeas corpus—state (includes all criminal pleas from state courts)
3. Motions made immediately before, during, and after trial
4. Conviction or nonconviction for a criminal offense; also includes forfeiture of property in a criminal case
5. Alien petitions
6. Indian rights and law
7. Right-to-vote and apportionment cases; also candidates' petitions to get on a ballot
8. Racial minority discrimination; also includes petitions by minority union members against union or company
9. Fourteenth Amendment cases and U.S. Civil Rights Act cases—but excluding cases brought by women and racial minorities
10. Freedom of expression (First Amendment cases)
11. Freedom of religion—both establishment and free-exercise
12. Union versus company
13. Union members versus union (or employees versus union)
14. Employee versus employer
15. Commercial regulation (antitrust, agriculture, independent regulatory agencies, and federalism issues)
16. Environmental protection (also includes pure food and drug, consumer protection cases)
17. Local and state economic regulation cases
18. Rent control, excessive profit, price control
19. Women's rights
20. Labor cases in which secretary of Labor or the NLRB is suing the employer (also includes all Fair Labor Standards Act cases)
21. Labor cases in which the secretary of Labor or the NLRB is suing a union or employees
22. Rights of the handicapped
23. Reverse discrimination cases for gender (support for petitioner is "conservative")

24. Reverse discrimination cases for gender (support for petitioner is "conservative")
25. Right to privacy (includes cases on abortion, homosexuality, contraception, violations of the Privacy Act, body cavity searches, and random drug searches other than ordinary Fourth Amendment issues)
26. Age discrimination suits

Appendix B. Liberal Decisions in Order of Magnitude of Partisan Voting Differences for Nineteen Types of Cases, 1933–1977

Type of Case	Overall	Democrats	Republicans	Partisan Difference	Odds Ratio
1. Local economic regulation	67%	75%	57%	18%	2.28
2. Race discrimination	51	57	42	15	1.90
3. Fourteenth Amendment[a]	42	48	34	14	1.81
4. Criminal conviction	38	43	20	13	1.75
5. U.S. habeas corpus pleas	27	29	20	9	1.63
6. Freedom of religion	52	56	46	10	1.52
7. Freedom of expression	52	57	47	10	1.48
8. U.S. commercial regulation	68	71	64	7	1.39
9. Criminal court motions	27	30	24	6	1.35
10. State habeas corpus pleas	23	25	20	5	1.32
11. Alien petitions	40	42	35	7	1.31
12. Union vs. company	47	50	45	5	1.20
13. Employee vs. employer	38	40	35	5	1.20
14. Union member vs. union	55	57	53	4	1.14
15. Environmental protection	61	62	59	3	1.14
16. Indian rights and law	49	51	49	2	1.10
17. Fair Labor Standards Act	57	57	55	2	1.08
18. Rent control, excess profit	61	61	59	2	1.05
19. Voting rights cases	48	46	50	−4	0.86

[a] The women's rights cases are included in this category rather than listed as a separate case type, since our data on the women's rights category includes only the years after 1973.

Source: Robert A. Carp and C. K. Rowland, *Policymaking and Politics in the Federal District Courts* (Knoxville: University of Tennessee Press, 1983), 38.

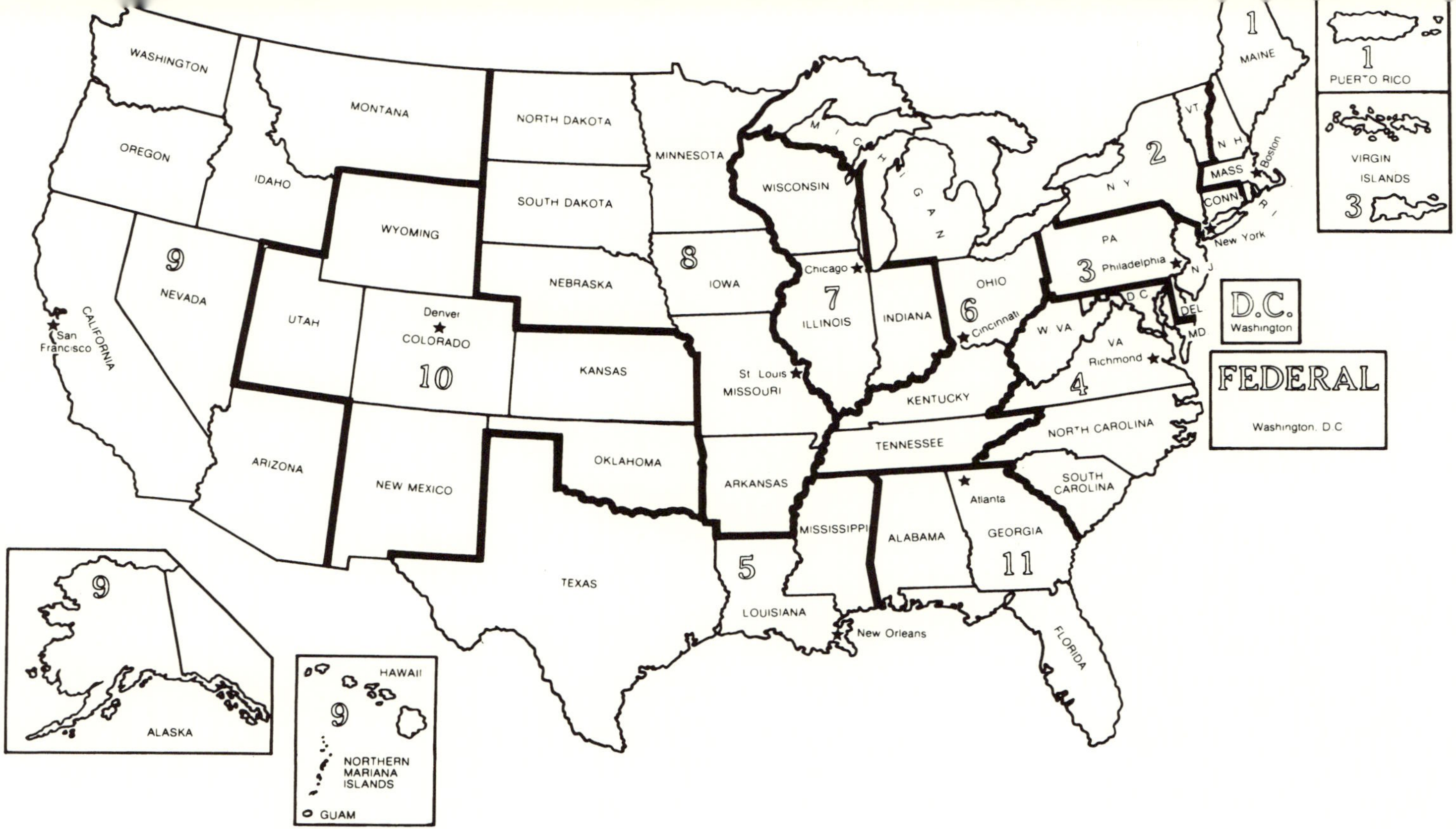

Appendix C. The thirteen federal judicial circuits (reprinted from the Federal Supplement *with the permission of West Publishing Company).*

Notes

1. U.S. Trial Judge Decision Making

1. Interview with Judge Henry H. Graven in Greene, Iowa, on November 1, 1968.

2. *Webster's Third International Dictionary* (Springfield, Mass.: G. and C. Merriam, 1978).

3. For a good, recent discussion of this same theme from a more sociological perspective, see Wolf V. Heydebrand and Carroll Seron, *Rationalizing Justice: The Political Economy of Federal District Courts* (Albany: State University of New York Press, 1990).

4. For a good discussion of this phenomenon, see Jethro Lieberman, *The Litigious Society* (New York: Basic Books, 1981).

5. For an excellent discussion of the causes and consequences of this phenomenon, see Richard Posner, *The Federal Courts* (Cambridge, Mass.: Harvard University Press, 1985), pt. 2.

6. For a good discussion of the problem of obtaining an accurate and *meaningful* figure for rates of appeals, see ibid., chap. 3.

7. Interview with Judge Constance Baker Motley in Lawrence, Kansas, on October 13, 1986.

8. Donald L. Horowitz, *The Courts and Social Policy* (Washington, D.C.: Brookings Institution, 1977); Malcolm M. Feeley, "The Significance of Prison Condition Cases: Budgets and Regions," *Law and Society Review* 23 (1989): 273–282; but see Stephen L. Wasby, "Arrogation of Power or Responsibility: Judicial Imperialism Revisited," *Judicature* 65 (1981): 208–221.

9. For example, see Richard J. Richardson and Kenneth Vines, *The Politics of Federal Courts* (Boston: Little, Brown, 1970).

10. The first quantitative work in the realm of U.S. district courts was Kenneth M. Dolbeare, "The Federal District Courts and Urban Public Policy: An Exploratory Study (1960–1967)," in *Frontiers of Judicial Research*, ed. Joel Grossman and Joseph Tanenhaus (New York: Wiley, 1969).

11. C. K. Rowland, Robert A. Carp, and Bridget Todd, unpublished, ongoing research.

12. For example, see James L. Gibson, "From Simplicity to Complexity: The Development of Theory in the Study of Judicial Behavior," *Political Behavior* 5 (1983): 7–49.

13. For example, see Donald R. Songer, "Nonpublication in the United States District Courts: Official Criteria Versus Inferences from Appellate Review," *Journal*

of Politics 50 (1988): 206–219; and Peter Siegelman and John J. Donohue III, "Studying the Iceberg from Its Tip: A Comparison of Published and Unpublished Employment Discrimination Cases," *Law and Society Review* 24 (1990): 1133–1170. For an analysis of this same phenomenon for the U.S. Courts of Appeals, see Donald R. Songer, "Criteria for Publication of Opinions in the U.S. Courts of Appeals: Formal Rules Versus Empirical Reality," *Judicature* 73 (1990): 307–314.

14. Bridget Todd, "The Relative Effects of Legal Environment and Appointing President on District Judges' Unpublished Decisions" (paper presented at the annual meeting of the Southwest Political Science Association; Little Rock, Ark., 1989); and other unpublished, ongoing research.

2. *The Influence of the Appointing President and Political Party Affiliation on District Judge Voting Behavior*

1. The cross-product ratio, frequently called the odds ratio, is a measure of the relationship between two dichotomous variables. Specifically, it is a measure of the relative odds of respondents from each independent variable category. In measuring the relationship between party identification and liberal-conservative propensities, the odds ratio is the ratio between the odds that a Democratic judge's opinion will be liberal (conservative) and the odds that a Republican jurist's opinion will be liberal (conservative).

The odds ratio is computed for two-by-two tables by the formula:

(Alpha) = (N11/N12) divided by (N12/N22)

Thus, for Table 2-1 the computation would be:

(Alpha) = (11,950/13,101) divided by (7,466/11,588) = 0.91/0.64 = 1.42

The odds of a Democrat's opinion being liberal (0.91) are different from the odds of a Republican's opinion being liberal (0.64). The ratio between these odds (1.42) is therefore a measure of the relative odds of Democratic and Republican opinions being liberal.

Interpretation of the odds ratio is straightforward. If political party has no effect on liberal propensity, the odds would be the same for both groups of judges, and the odds ratio would be 1.0, indicating independence or no relationship. Departures from 1.0 in either direction indicate association. Values between zero and 1.0 suggest a negative relationship, while values from 1.0 to infinity indicate a positive association, that is, a relationship that supports the hypothesized association. Thus, an odds ratio of 2.0 would mean that respondents from the designated category of the independent variable are twice as likely to respond in the predicted direction on the dependent variable as are respondents from the other category. In Table 2-1 the odds of a Democratic jurist rendering a liberal decision are 1.42 times greater than the odds of a GOP counterpart.

In addition to its straightforward interpretation, the odds ratio has two other properties that make it particularly useful and appropriate for measuring the relative Democratic and Republican liberal propensities. First, unlike most nominal measures, its value is not a function of sample size or of marginal distributions. Second, the log odds of the odds ratio are perfectly symmetrical. Values range from negative to positive infinitely, with zero indicating no relationship between the independent and dependent variables.

For a helpful discussion of the propensities and application of the odds ratio measure, see H. T. Reynolds, *Analysis of Nominal Data* (Beverly Hills, Calif.: Sage, 1977), 20–29.

2. For similar conclusions that have been reached in more recent years, see Vincent Blasi, ed., *The Burger Court: The Counter-Revolution That Wasn't* (New Haven, Conn.: Yale University Press, 1983); Bernard Schwartz, *The Ascent of Pragmatism: The Burger Court in Action* (Reading, Mass.: Addison-Wesley, 1990).

3. On matters such as the *Miranda* rule, search and seizure, and the right to counsel, many Burger court decisions fall clearly in the conservative column. For example, see *Harris v. New York*, 401 U.S. 222 (1971); *Kirby v. Illinois*, 406 U.S. 682 (1972); *Oregon v. Hass*, 420 U.S. 714 (1975); *Wainwright v. Sykes*, 434 U.S. 880 (1977); *Zurcher v. Stanford Daily*, 436 U.S. 547 (1978); *Rhode Island v. Innis*, 446 U.S. 291 (1980); *New York v. Quarles*, 467 U.S. 649 (1984); *United States v. Leon*, 468 U.S. 902 (1984); *Moran v. Burbine*, 475 U.S. 412 (1986); and *California v. Ciraolo*, 476 U.S. 207 (1986).

4. In matters dealing with obscenity, the standards of the Burger Court were clearly more restrictive than those of the Warren Court era. For example, see *United States v. Reidel*, 402 U.S. 351 (1971); *United States v. Thirty-Seven Photographs*, 402 U.S. 363 (1971); *Miller v. California*, 413 U.S. 15 (1973); *Paris Adult Theater I v. Slayton*, 413 U.S. 49 (1973); *Hamling v. United States*, 418 U.S. 87 (1974); *Young v. American Mini Theatres, Inc.*, 327 U.S. 50 (1976); and *Ward v. Illinois*, 431 U.S. 767 (1977).

5. *United States v. Washington*, 431 U.S. 181 (1977); *United States v. Wong*, 431 U.S. 174 (1977).

6. For example, see *Roe v. Wade*, 410 U.S. 113 (1973); *Doe v. Bolton*, 410 U.S. 179 (1973); *Akron v. Akron Center for Reproductive Health*, 462 U.S. 416 (1983); *Thornburgh v. American College of Obstetricians and Gynecologists*, 476 U.S. 747 (1986); *Reed v. Reed*, 404 U.S. 71 (1971); *Frontiero v. Richardson*, 411 U.S. 677 (1973); *Regents of University of California v. Bakke*, 438 U.S. 265 (1978); *Swann v. Charlotte-Mecklenburg Board of Education*, 402 U.S. 1 (1971); and *Keyes v. School District*, 413 U.S. 189 (1973).

7. For example, see Ronald Stidham and Robert A. Carp, "Trial Courts' Responses to Supreme Court Policy Changes: Three Case Studies," *Law and Policy Quarterly* 4 (1982): 215–235; and Ronald Stidham and Robert A. Carp, "U.S. Trial Court Reactions to Changes in Civil Rights and Civil Liberties Policies," *Southeastern Political Review* 10 (1984): 3–27.

8. For criminal justice issues the trend is more difficult to discern. Between 1969 and 1975, 28 percent of trial judge decisions were liberal on criminal justice matters, but this figure actually *increased* during the next time frame to 33 percent. Then a modest conservative trend set in when the figure declined to 32 percent between 1980 and 1985.

9. See the discussion of this in Jeffrey A. Segal and Harold J. Spaeth, "Decisional Trends on the Warren and Burger Courts: Results from the Supreme Court Data Base Project," *Judicature* 73 (1989): 103–107.

10. For example, see Ronald Stidham and Robert A. Carp, "Judges, Presidents, and Policy Choices: Exploring the Linkage," *Social Science Quarterly* 68 (1987): 395–404.

11. For criminal justice cases Democrats and Republicans on the bench continued to move in similar directions, albeit with the Democrats consistently remaining more liberal. For the three time frames in question, Democratic support for the criminal justice petitioner went from 33 percent to 36 to 35. GOP jurists began at 22 percent, then went up to 30 percent, and then dropped back to 27 percent. If there is any evidence of Democratic "rear guard" action against the conservative tide, there is a modest hint of it in the 1981 through 1985 time frame, that is, during this more recent period when Republicans became mildly more conservative on criminal justice matters, Democrats on the bench did not back away from their fairly liberal stance held during the late 1970s.

12. Between 1953 and 1969 the coefficient of variation (which measures the relative entropy or homogeneity of aggregates with different means) was 3.55. This indicates a good deal of fluctuation during these years. Viewing each year as a separate unit, the mean difference between Republican and Democratic judges was 1.1 percent and the standard deviation was 4.2.

13. For example, see Maurice Kelman, "The Forked Path of Dissent," *Supreme Court Review* (1985): 227–298; Laura Ray, "The Justices Write Separately: Uses of the Concurrence by the Rehnquist Court," *University of California at Davis Law Review* 23 (1990): 777–833; David M. O'Brien, *Storm Center: The Supreme Court in American Politics*, 2d ed. (New York: Norton, 1990), chap. 5; and Nancy Maveety, "The Judicial Strategy of the Concurring Opinion: A Preliminary Discussion, with Special Attention to Justices O'Connor and Scalia" (paper presented at the annual meeting of the American Political Science Association, Washington, D.C., August 29–September 1, 1991).

14. Justice William Rehnquist in *Metromedia, Inc. v. San Diego* 453 U.S. 569–570.

15. For example, see Robert A. Carp and C. K. Rowland, *Policymaking and Politics in the Federal District Courts* (Knoxville, University of Tennessee Press, 1983), chap. 3; and Ronald Stidham and Robert A. Carp, "Judges, Presidents, and Policy Choices: Exploring the Linkage," *Social Science Quarterly* 68 (1987): 395–403.

16. Gerald Ford's presidency is something of an exception, given the number of constraints placed upon his selection of his judicial nominees. See Carp and Rowland, *Policymaking and Politics*, 69.

17. Viewing each year as a separate unit, the mean difference between Republican and Democratic judges was 11.72 percent and the standard deviation of the partisan difference was 3.78. (For the period between 1953 and 1969 the mean difference between the two groups of judges had been 1.1 percent, and the standard deviation was 4.2.)

18. For the category of criminal justice during the period 1969 through 1986, the coefficient of variation was 0.61; the mean difference was 8.39; and the standard deviation was 5.1. For the category of labor and economic regulation, the coefficient

of variation was 0.58; the mean difference was 11.24, and the standard deviation was 6.56. For the category of civil rights and liberties, the coefficient of variation was 0.31; the mean difference was 14.86; and the standard deviation was 4.57.

19. Interview with Judge Constance Motley in Lawrence, Kansas, on October 13, 1986.

20. There is some good, albeit sometimes indirect, evidence for this that runs throughout J. Woodford Howard, Jr., *Courts of Appeals in the Federal Judicial System: A Study of the Second, Fifth, and District of Columbia Circuits* (Princeton, N.J.: Princeton University Press, 1981).

21. For extensive and up-to-date data and discussion of this general phenomenon, see Robert S. Erikson and Kent L. Tedin, *American Public Opinion: Its Origins, Content, and Impact*, 5th ed. (Boston: Allyn & Bacon, 1995).

22. Also, studies reveal that many environmental cases are brought by local groups with very low levels of legal efficacy against state and local governments with significantly greater resources. Many of these suits reflect frustration with the political arena but have little legal merit, and judges are forced (by the values of the legal subculture) to rule against the plaintiff regardless of the judge's possible sympathy for the cause of environmentalism. See, for example, Lee Epstein and C. K. Rowland, "Debunking the Myth of Interest Group Invincibility," *American Political Science Review* 85 (1991): 205–221.

23. The beginning of this trend is often associated with the Supreme Court's decision of *Younger v. Harris* in 1971 (401 U.S. 37). More specifically, these cases are typical of the Burger Court desire to restrict federal court involvement with state criminal proceedings: *Harris v. New York*, 401 U.S. 222 (1991); *U.S. v. Calandra*, 414 U.S. 338 (1974); and *Stone v. Powell*, 427 U.S. 465 (1976). See also Nathan Lewin, "Avoiding the Supreme Court," *New York Times Magazine*, October 17, 1976, 31.

24. For an excellent discussion of presidential politics and the decision making of the NLRB, see Terry M. Moe, "Control and Feedback in Economic Regulation: The Case of the NLRB," 79 *American Political Science Review* 79 (1985): 1094–1116.

25. For example, see Carp and Rowland, *Policymaking and Politics*, chap. 3.

26. It is appropriate to say a word here about the voting patterns of presidents' opposite-party appointees. In previous research we found that such appointees decided cases differently than presidents' same-party jurists (Carp and Rowland 1983, 77–81). Furthermore, we learned that the direction and magnitude of these differences varied from state to state. For example, President Nixon's California Democrats were exceptionally liberal, while his opposite-party appointees in other states approximated more closely the norm of his GOP judges (Rowland, Carp, and Stidham 1984).

In this particular study (for the Carter and Reagan judges), differences between same- and opposite-party appointees have virtually disappeared. The variances we did find appeared tiny and random. We suggest three related factors that might account for this phenomenon (all of which are elaborated on more fully in chapter 4). The first and most fundamental explanation is that (with the exception of Reagan's final two years in office) both Presidents Carter and Reagan had supportive partisan majorities on the Senate Judiciary Committee as well as committee chairs who were ideologically compatible. This concentration of partisan and ideological support in the confirmation process left little or no incentive to engage in partisan or ideological compromises over opposite-party appointees; basically the presidents got the kind of ideological cohort they wanted regardless of judges' party identification.

Second, as we shall document in chapter 4, the commitment to ideologically correct judicial appointments escalated substantially during these two presidencies. Neither of these chief executives was willing to relax ideological appointment criteria for in-party or out-party candidates. Moreover, this escalation was accompanied by institutionalized reviews of judicial candidates' political and judicial philosophies, thus making it unlikely that an out-party "renegade" would slip through the ideological screen. Thus, both the commitment to ideological appointment criteria and the institutionalization of executive review committees to implement that commitment help explain the recent absence of systematic opposite-party effects.

A third explanation derives from the parallel demise of opposite-party "courtesy" in the appointment process. As discussed in chapter 4, the role of opposite-party senators in recruitment and confirmation was virtually nil by the end of the Reagan administration. The extent to which this demise of courtesy began during the Carter administration is the subject of debate. What is not debatable is that by 1986, opposite-party senators were not a viable source for the nomination of opposite-party candidates.

27. Under ideal circumstances it would be best to compare the liberalism indices of presidential appointees for an identical time frame because that would hold constant matters such as the mix of cases and definitions of "liberalism" and "conservatism." When, in fact, we have done this, the results tend to be much the same. For instance, Table 2-8 reveals that the liberalism scores for all cases for the appointees of Presidents Nixon, Ford, Carter, and Reagan are, respectively, 39, 44, 53, and 36. When these same cohorts are examined for an identical time frame (the years 1981 to 1987), the scores are 40, 42, 53, and 36. Thus, there are some variations according to time, but we contend that they are not significant enough to alter the content of our basic substantive generalizations.

28. For example, see the empirical data and discussion in Erikson and Tedin, *American Public Opinion*, especially chap. 6, "Ideology, Partisanship, and Political Opinions."

29. To some degree the lack of a large disparity in voting patterns on environmental cases between the Carter and Reagan cohorts may be a function of the case category itself. This broad category takes in a very wide range of issues—from local "save-our-train-depot" cases to large class action suits against the federal government or industry. Some involve relatively low economic costs (e.g., regulation of wild horses in the national wilderness areas), while others deal with subjects of immense cost potential (e.g., the cleanup of toxic wastes). The hodgepodge of issues in this environmental category may thus mask presidential cohort differences that might appear if our category were more precisely tailored. For example, for environmental issues that involve great financial cost to industry, Reagan judges may be significantly more conservative than Carter jurists, while for environmental issues that are more symbolic in nature the differences between the two cohorts are negligible.

30. Although our complete data set goes only up to 1987, we do have some limited data on the Bush judges. This is because we have done a selective sample of the

more recent decisions published in the *Supplement* and looked only for those written by Bush judges. By doing this we have been able to obtain a small but still reasonably reliable sample that will permit us to make some preliminary observations about the Bush cohort.

Regarding an *n* of this small size, we would note that when our book *Policymaking and Politics* was first published, the *n* for the Gerald Ford cohort was only 197 cases; his liberalism score was 44. At the present time we have some 1,724 cases decided by the Fort cohort—but the liberalism index remains precisely at 44 percent.

31. The figure of 33 percent is for Bush cohort decision since 1989, but this limited sampling does not include any decisions of other judges during this recent time period. Thus there is no control for an identical time period. This may "inflate" somewhat the conclusion that the Bush cohort is the most conservative on record. It is possible that all judges on the bench in this new conservative judicial era have moved to the right of center in recent years. Thus Reagan judge decisions since 1989 may well have been as conservative as those of the Bush cohort. We will not know for certain until the data set is completely brought up to date.

32. For a more elaborate discussion of this model, see Ronald Stidham, Robert A. Carp, and C. K. Rowland, "Patterns of Presidential Influence on the Federal District Courts: An Analysis of the Appointment Process," *Presidential Studies Quarterly* 14 (1984): 548–560.

33. "Bush Should Fill Vacant Judgeships," *Beaumont Enterprise*, February 11, 1990, B12.

34. "State Judge Nominated to Serve on Federal Bench," *Houston Chronicle*, July 11, 1989, A7.

35. For example, in order to obtain Senator Eastland's blessing for appointing the black and liberal Thurgood Marshall to a federal judgeship, Kennedy was obliged to nominate Eastland's former college chum William Cox to a judicial post. Cox was not only outspokenly hostile to the cause of civil rights but often from the bench referred to black litigants as "niggers" and "chimpanzees." For example, see Joseph C. Goulden, *The Benchwarmers* (New York: Weybright and Talley, 1974), 63–64.

36. Still, it is true that the degree to which they respect the existing paradigm depends on the nature of the case. As we have previously argued, in instances where the judge is called upon to make largely a factual determination with little prospect of appellate court reversal (e.g., a charge of racial discrimination, or a routine criminal court motion), new judges might be very quick to make their presence felt. However, with cases involving legal interpretation, newly appointed jurists are significantly more obliged to respect the existing judicial order as established by the appellate courts.

3. *The Influence of Geographic Factors on Judicial Voting Patterns*

1. For further discussion of this general theme in American history, see Charles A. Beard, *An Economic Interpretation of the Constitution of the United States* (New York: Macmillan, 1913); and Arthur N. Holcomb, *The Political Parties of To-day* (New York: Harper, 1924).

2. For example, see Frederick J. Turner, *The Significance of Sections in American History* (New York: Holt, 1932); and Merrill Jensen, ed., *Regionalism in America* (Madison: University of Wisconsin Press, 1952).

3. For examples of traditional literature on this subject, see Angus Campbell et al., *The American Voter* (New York: Wiley, 1960); Everett Carll Ladd Jr. and Charles D. Hadley, *Transformations of the American Political System*, 2d ed. (New York: Norton. 1978); V. O. Key Jr., *Politics, Parties, and Pressure Groups*, 5th ed. (New York: Crowell, 1964); V. O. Key Jr., *Public Opinion and American Democracy* (New York: Knopf, 1967); and Samuel A. Stouffer, *Communism, Conformity, and Civil Liberties* (New York: Doubleday, 1955). For more recent examples of this phenomenon, see Samuel Patterson and Gregory Caldeira, "Getting Out the Vote: Participation in Gubernatorial Elections," *American Political Science Review* 77 (1983): 675–689; Robert S. Erikson, John P. McIver, and Gerald C. Wright Jr., "State Political Culture and Public Opinion," *American Political Science Review* 81 (1987): 797–813; and Robert S. Erikson, Norman R. Luttbeg, and Kent L. Tedin, *American Public Opinion: Its Origins, Content, and Impact*, 4th ed. (New York: Macmillan, 1991), esp. chap. 7.

4. For examples of traditional literature on this subject, see Barbara Hinckley, *Stability and Change in Congress* (New York: Harper & Row, 1978); Randall B. Ripley, *Congress: Process and Policy*, 2d ed. (New York: Norton, 1978); Key, *Politics, Parties, and Pressure Groups*, esp. chaps. 9 and 24; and J. H. Fenton, "Liberal-Conservative Divisions by Sections of the United States," *Annals* 344 (1962): 122–127. For more contemporary examples of this phenomenon, see John R. Wright, "PACS, Contributions, and Roll Calls: An Organizational Perspective," *American Political Science Review* 79 (1985): 400–415.

5. For example, see Jack W. Peltason, *Fifty-Eight Lonely Men: Southern Federal Judges and School Desegregation* (Urbana: University of Illinois Press, 1961); Kenneth Vines, "Federal District Judges and Race Relations Cases in the South," *Journal of Politics* 26 (1964): 337–357; and Michael W. Giles and Thomas Walker, "Judicial Policy Making and Southern School Segregation," *Journal of Politics* 37 (1975): 917–937.

6. For example, see Steve Alumbaugh and C. K. Rowland, "The Links Between Platform-Based Appointment Criteria and Trial Judges' Abortion Judgments," *Judicature* 74 (1990): 153–162.

7. Lettie M. Wenner and Lee E. Dutter, "Contextual Influences on Judicial Decision Making," *Western Political Quarterly* 41 (1988): 115–134.

8. For an excellent recent discussion of this phenomenon for Supreme Court cases, see Lawrence Baum, "Measuring Policy Change in the U.S. Supreme Court," *American Political Science Review* 82 (1988): 905–912.

9. In determining which states are "southern," we decided to follow Stuart Nagel's practice of including those states that constituted the Confederacy and also those whose predominant cultural socioeconomic character has been southern: Ala., Ark., Del., Fla., Ga., Ky., La., Md., Miss., Mo., N.C., Okla., S.C., Tenn., Tex., Va., and W.Va. The northern states consisted of the other thirty-three (see, Nagel, *The Legal Process from a Behavioral Perspective* [Homewood, Ill.: Dorsey Press, 1969], 240). The states in our "eastern" (really northeastern) category are those in the First, Sec-

ond, and Third Circuits: Maine, Mass., N.H., R.I., Conn., N.Y., Vt., Del., N.J., and Pa. The western states consisted of the other forty.

10. For example, see Erikson, Luttbeg, and Tedin, *American Public Opinion*, chap. 7, pt. 5; and Alumbaugh and Rowland, "The Links Between Platform-Based Appointment Criteria and Trial Judges' Abortion Judgments."

11. Erikson et al., *American Public Opinion*, chap. 7, pt. 5.

12. See the citations contained in Sheldon Goldman, "Voting Behavior on the United States Courts of Appeals, 1961–64," *American Political Science Review* 60 (1966): 375 n. 6; and Sheldon Goldman, "Conflict on the U.S. Courts of Appeals 1965–1971: A Quantitative Analysis," *University of Cincinnati Law Review* 42 (1973): 636 n. 3. See also, for example, Jeffrey B. Morris, "The Second Most Important Court: The United States Courts of Appeals for the District of Columbia Circuit" (Ph.D. diss., Columbia University, 1972); J. Woodford Howard Jr., "Litigation Flow in Three United States Courts of Appeals," *Law and Society Review* 8 (1973): 33–53; Burton M. Atkins, "Opinion Assignments on the United States Court of Appeals: The Question of Issue Specialization," *Western Political Quarterly* 27 (1974): 409–428; Burton M. Atkins and William Zavoina, "Judicial Leadership on the Court of Appeals: A Probability Analysis of Panel Assignments in Race Relations Cases on the Fifth Circuit," *American Journal of Political Science* 18 (1974): 701–711; Charles M. Lamb, "Warren Burger and the Insanity Defense: Judicial Philosophy and Voting Behavior on a U.S. Court of Appeals," *American University Law Review* 24 (1974): 91–128; Sheldon Goldman, "Voting Behavior on the United States Courts of Appeals Revisited," *American Political Science Review* 69 (1975): 491–506; Christopher E. Smith, "Polarization and Change in the Federal Courts: *En Banc* Decisions in the U.S. Courts of Appeals," *Judicature* 74 (1990): 133–138; William E. Kovacic, "The Reagan Judiciary and Environmental Policy: The Impact of Appointments to the Federal Courts of Appeals," *Boston College Environmental Affairs Law Review* 18 (1991): 669–713; and William E. Kovacic, "Reagan's Judicial Appointees and Antitrust in the 1990s," *Fordham Law Review* 60 (1991): 49–124.

13. For more specific information on these interviews and other citations, see Carp and Rowland, *Policymaking and Politics*, 87 n. 11.

14. For a summary of the literature that reveals the close ties that appellate court judges have to their respective regions, see Carp and Rowland, *Policymaking and Politics*, 88 n. 15.

15. Until this point we have used the odds ratio to measure the association of variables. However, since this ratio is appropriate only for two-by-two relationships, we shall also rely on a new measure of association—eta—when the odds ratio requirements are not met.

For purposes of interpretation, eta is analogous to the more familiar correlation coefficient—that is, it measures the strength of the relationship between one or more independent variables and a single dependent variable. The square of eta may be interpreted as the amount of variance in the dependent variable "explained" by differences in the independent variable. Unlike the correlation coefficient, however, eta does not assume negative values. Thus, eta ranges from zero (no relationship) to 1 (perfect statistical association).

For an expanded discussion of eta and its utility in this context, see John H.

Mueller, Karl F. Schuessler, and Herbert L. Costner, *Statistical Reasoning in Sociology*, 2d ed. (Boston: Houghton Mifflin, 1970), 325–333. See also Herbert Costner, "Criteria for Measures of Association," *American Sociological Review* 30 (1965): 341–351. Given the bivariate dependent variable, it is interesting to note that parametric and nonparametric ANOVA produced essentially identical results. When measuring differences between parties, we report eta rather than the odds ratio to facilitate comparisons between space and party effects when more than two spatial units are being compared.

16. For a more extensive literature review of this subject, see Carp and Rowland, *Policymaking and Politics*, 118–120.

17. For direct and implicit evidence of this, see Nathan Hakman, "The Supreme Court's Political Environment: The Processing of Noncommercial Litigation," in *Frontiers of Judicial Research*, ed. Joel Grossman and Joseph Tanenhaus (New York: Wiley, 1969), 199–254. See also Robert A. Carp, "An Analysis of Censorship Pressures on Iowa High School Social Studies Teachers" (master's thesis, University of Iowa, 1967).

18. Much of the early literature is covered J. A. F. Stoner, "Comparison of Individual and Group Decisions Involving Risk" (master's thesis, Massachusetts Institute of Technology, School of Industrial Management, 1961). More recent literature that is relevant to our judicial theory here is found in M. A. Wallach and N. Kogan, "The Roles of Information, Discussion, and Consensus in Group Risk Taking," *Journal of Experimental Social Psychology* 1 (1965): 1–19; M. A. Wallach, N. Kogan, and D. J. Bem, "Diffusion of Responsibility and Level of Risk Taking in Groups," *Journal of Abnormal and Social Psychology* 68 (1964): 263–274; M. A. Wallach, N. Kogan, and D. J. Bem, "Group Influence on Individual Risk Taking," *Journal of Abnormal and Social Psychology* 65 (1962): 75–86; D. C. Marquis, "Individual Responsibility and Group Decisions Involving Risk," *Industrial Management Review* 3 (1962): 8–23; D. J. Bem, M. A. Wallach, and N. Kogan, "Group Decision Making Under Risk of Aversive Consequences," *Journal of Personality and Social Psychology* 1 (1965): 453–460; Allen I. Teger and Dean G. Pruitt, "Components of Group Risk Taking," *Journal of Experimental Social Psychology* 3 (1967): 189–205. For a broader discussion of small-group and related phenomena, see Richard J. Ofshe, ed., *Interpersonal Behavior in Small Groups* (Englewood Cliffs, N.J.: Prentice-Hall, 1973); Paul L. Wuebben, Bruce C. Straits, and Gary I. Schulman, *The Experiment as a Social Occasion* (Berkeley, Calif.: Glendessary, 1974); Bruce J. Biddle and Edwin J. Thomas, eds., *Role Theory: Concepts and Research* (New York: Wiley, 1966).

19. It must be acknowledged, of course, that judicial independence vis-à-vis the community can be in either a liberal or a conservative direction. If a large urban center were quite liberal, then "risky behavior" might be conservative policy making by judges and vice versa. (Surely this is becoming more the case as the Reagan-Bush judicial cohorts have been bringing their influence to bear in the large cities as well as in the rest of the country.) Or, one may hypothesize—as we do here—that "risky behavior" is making policy that is *significantly more liberal* than a community's already-liberal values.

20. By this statement we do not mean to suggest that it is impossible to render

innovative and/or *conservative* decisions. It is just that during the past several decades the vast majority of highly unpopular district court decisions have been of a "liberal" nature, for example, determining that the public burning of the American flag is a protected form of freedom of expression; ordering a state university to grant recognition to a campus gay organization; the freeing of an obviously guilty criminal on a legal technicality.

21. In *Policymaking and Politics* we represented the urban-rural character of the district courts by using the number of judges assigned to the court when a given case was decided rather than the population figures of the cities wherein the district courts were located. This technique has been used successfully by other researchers (see Richardson and Vines, *The Politics of Federal Courts* 100–105; and Walter G. Markham, "Draft Offenders in the Federal Courts: A Search for the Social Correlates of Justice" [Ph. D. diss., University of Pennsylvania, 1971], 94–95), and we have elaborated on this justification in *Policymaking and Politics*, 130–132.

In discussing the size of the district court we continue to use four general categories of districts arranged according to the following number of judges assigned to them: one, two, three to six, and seven or more. While there is nothing "magical" about these categories, the evidence gleaned from our interviews of court personnel and from the empirical data itself suggests that they are meaningful ordinal stages representing progressive sizes and types of American communities. Examples of single-judge rural courts throughout all or most of the time span of our study would include the Central District of Illinois, the Eastern District of Kentucky, and the Eastern District of Oklahoma. (When we suggest that single-judge districts are rural, we not mean that the entire district is agricultural and/or devoid of towns or small cities. Rather, such districts tend to be devoid of cities with populations in excess of 100,000 residents.)

Courts in small-sized urban areas, generally consisting of at least 100,000 inhabitants, included two-judge cities such as Grand Rapids, Michigan; Beaumont, Texas; and Rochester, New York. Larger American cities with three-to-six jurists included such urban centers as Birmingham, Alabama; Denver, Colorado; and Wilmington, Delaware. Finally, in the category of very large metropolitan areas with seven or more judges were New York City, Chicago, and Los Angeles.

22. In fact the relationship in our previous study of all cases (from 1933 to 1978) had also been curvilinear. It is just that the jump in liberalism occurred at the break point between one- and two-judge cities while in the more recent study the break occurs between two-judge and three- to six-judge cities. Given the growth in American cities during the past decade, with the corresponding increase in the number of district judges assigned to the courts, it is likely that we are measuring the same phenomenon.

4. *The Politics of Home-State Recruitment*

1. The states are Arkansas, California, Colorado, Connecticut, Florida, Hawaii, Illinois, Louisiana, Massachusetts, Michigan, Minnesota, Mississippi, North Carolina, Oregon, Pennsylvania, and Texas. These states were selected primarily because

they represent a cross-section of geography, demographics, partisan representation, and selection systems. A secondary consideration was the availability and cooperation of informed respondents who did not require anonymity.

5. *Appointment Effects on Unpublished Decisions*

1. These two jurisdictions were selected for several reasons. First, each is large enough to include on its dockets a wide variety of civil disputes. Second, although all urban jurisdictions are somewhat unique, these court points are reasonably representative of the diversity that defines urban America. Third, each of these jurisdictions had a balance of Nixon, Carter, and Reagan appointees. Finally, from a practical perspective, the courts and court personnel were accessible to the authors and their research assistants.

6. *A Critique of Behavioral Models of Trial Judging*

1. For an excellent constructive critique of Segal and Spaeth see *Law and Courts Newsletter*, 1994. However, these criticisms are reactions to the book, which is devoted to the behavior of Supreme Court justices.

2. Even if one concedes that judges perceive their judicial role as that of "lawmaker" it is difficult to generalize the attitudinal model's motivational assumptions to all district judges. When one focuses specifically on district judges, accumulated evidence makes it clear that only a small minority identify themselves as lawmakers. For example, only 14 percent of Kitchin's respondents were classified as "lawmakers" (1978). If one assumes that all trial jurists are strongly inclined to impose their policy preferences on their jurisprudence, Kitchen's findings can be interpreted as evidence that 14 percent of the judges perceive few role-oriented barriers to such impositions. If, on the other hand, one does not accept axiomatically the primacy of preferences, then Kitchin's findings suggest that the assumption is valid only 14 percent of the time. In other words, many trial judges appear to be motivated primarily by their role orientation—that is, their "secondary" perceptions of what a judge should do—and not by their personal preferences.

3. If these conservative criteria for evaluating paradigms were taken literally, we would still be committed to phlogiston theories of fire. Indeed, to say that if something burns it must contain phlogiston is somewhat analogous to saying that if a trial judge reaches a decision consistent with his or her policy preferences it must be motivated by preferences.

4. The honest, indignant reaction of judicial interviewees to the notion that fact-finding might be motivated by their personal policy preferences was an important impetus for our critique of the attitudinal model.

5. It is interesting to note, moreover, that in the study of mass and elite political behavior such models have first been largely replaced by rational-choice models of preference-based behaviors and more recently supplemented by cogni-

tive models of human information processing (Lodge and Hamill 1986; Lau and Sears 1988).

7. Toward a Cognitive Approach for Understanding Judicial Judgment

1. To say that content analysis of judges' opined protocols is an important implication of judicial cognition is not to say that opinions are not selective, subjective framings of fact and law. In the final analysis, that is why they are called opinions. But the shadow of appellate scrutiny and the norms of legal culture also limit judges' discretion to selectively report facts and law. And it is also true that, given our conceptualization of judgment, these subjective representations (and the reasoning behind them) are appropriate sources for understanding judicial resolution of ambiguity. Indeed, because ambiguity, like judgment, is a subjective state perceived by the judge, it is reasonable to estimate a dispute's zone of ambiguity by reference to the judge's codified references to ambiguous facts or law that required the exercise of judicial judgment. One could, for example, define ambiguity operationally in the context of judges' published opinions—i.e., their own reports of scanty, unreliable or conflicting information, and their reported confidence about the estimates and expectations of the litigants—and impose rigorous content analysis on the measurement of those indicators.

Bibliography

Alumbaugh, Steve, and C. K. Rowland. 1990. "The Links Between Platform-Based Appointment Criteria and Trial Judges' Abortion Judgments." *Judicature* 74:153–162.

Armstrong, Virginia, and Charles Johnson. 1982. "Certiorari Decision Making by the Warren and Burger Courts: Is Cue Theory Time Bound?" *Polity* 15:141–150.

Atkins, Burton M. 1974. "Opinion Assignments on the United States Court of Appeals: The Question of Issue Specialization." *Western Political Quarterly* 27:409–428.

Atkins, Burton M., and William Zavoina. 1974. "Judicial Leadership on the Court of Appeals: A Probability Analysis of Panel Assignments in Race Relations Cases on the Fifth Circuit." *American Journal of Political Science* 18:701–711.

Barone, David, James Maddox, and C. R. Snyder. Forthcoming. *Social Cognitive Psychology: History and Current Domains.* New York: Plenum.

Baum, Lawrence. 1988. "Measuring Policy Change in the U.S. Supreme Court." *American Political Science Review* 82:905–912.

Bayne, William. 1991. "Judicial Susceptibility to Demeanor Cues." Unpublished manuscript, University of Kansas.

Beard, Charles A. 1913. *An Economic Interpretation of the Constitution of the United States*. New York: Macmillan.

Bem, D. J., M. A. Wallach, and N. Kogan. 1965. "Group Decision Making Under Risk of Aversive Consequences." *Journal of Personality and Social Psychology* 1:453–460.

Biddle, Bruce J., and Edwin J. Thomas, eds. 1966. *Role Theory: Concepts and Research.* New York: Wiley.

Blasi, Vincent, ed. 1983. *The Burger Court: The Counter-Revolution That Wasn't.* New Haven, Conn.: Yale University Press.

Brunswick, Egan. 1952. "The Conceptual Framework of Psychology." In *International Encyclopedia of Unified Science.* Chicago: University of Chicago Press.

Bush, George. 1988. "Candidates State Positions on Federal Judicial Selection." *Judicature* 72:77–78.

Campbell, Angus, Philip E. Converse, Warren E. Miller, and Donald E. Stokes. 1960. *The American Voter*. New York: Wiley.

Carp, Robert A. 1967. "An Analysis of Censorship Pressures on Iowa High School Social Studies Teachers." Master's thesis, University of Iowa.

Carp, Robert A., and C. K. Rowland. 1983. *Policymaking and Politics in the Federal District Courts*. Knoxville: University of Tennessee Press.

Carp, Robert A., and Russell Wheeler. 1972. "Sink or Swim: The Socialization of a Federal District Judge." *Journal of Public Law* 21:359–393.

Carroll, Susan. 1985. "Gender Schemata and Mass Policies." Paper presented at Midwest Political Science Association Meetings. Chicago.

Carter, Lief. 1994. *Reason in Law*. 4th ed. New York: HarperCollins.

Chase, Harold W. 1972. *Federal Judges: The Appointing Process*. Minneapolis: University of Minnesota Press.

Chi, M. T., R. Glaser, and M. T. Farr, eds. 1988. *The Nature of Expertise*. Hillsdale, N.J.: Erlbaum.

Church, Thomas, 1978. *Justice Delayed: The Pace of Litigation in Urban Trial Courts*. Williamsburg, Va.: Center for State Courts.

Conover, Pamela. 1984. "The Influence of Group Identification on Political Perception and Evaluation. *Journal of Politics* 46:760–785.

Conover, Pamela, and Stanley Feldman. 1984. "How People Organize the Political World: A Schematic Model." *American Journal of Political Science* 28:95–126.

Cook, Beverly B. 1973. "Sentencing Behavior of Federal Judges: Draft Cases, 1972." *Cincinnati Law Review* 42:597–633.

Cooper, Phillip. 1988. *Hard Judicial Choices*. New York: Oxford University Press.

Costner, Herbert. 1965. "Criteria for Measures of Association." *American Sociological Review* 30:341–351.

Danelski, David J. 1972. "Toward Explanation of Judicial Behavior." *University of Cincinnati Law Review* 42:659–667.

Dewey, John. 1929. *The Quest for Certainty: A Study of the Relation of Knowledge and Action*. New York: Capricorn Books.

Dolbeare, Kenneth M. 1969. "The Federal District Courts and Urban Public Policy: An Exploratory Study (1960–1967)." In *Frontiers of Judicial Research*, edited by Joel Grossman and Joseph Tanenhaus. New York: Wiley.

Donohue, John, and Peter Siegelman. 1989. "The Changing Nature of Employment Discrimination Litigation." *Stanford Law Review* 43:983–1033.

Ducat, Craig R., and Robert L. Dudley. 1989. "Federal District Judges and Presidential Power." *Journal of Politics* 51:98–118.

Dudley, Robert L. 1989. "Lower Court Decision-Making in Pornography Cases: Do We Know It When We See It?" Paper presented at the annual meeting of the Midwest Political Science Association, Chicago.

Eisenberg, Theodore. 1989. "Litigation Models and Trial Outcomes in Civil Rights and Prisoner Cases." *Georgetown Law Journal* 77:1567–1602.

Eisenberg, Theodore, and Stewart J. Schwab. 1989. "What Shapes Perceptions of the Federal Court System?" *University of Chicago Law Review* 56:501–543.

Eisenstein, James. 1973. *Politics and the Legal Process*. New York: Harper & Row.

Eisenstein, James, and Herbert Jacob. 1977. *Felony Justice: An Organizational Analysis of Criminal Courts*. Boston: Little, Brown.

Ellsburg, Daniel. 1961. "Risk, Ambiguity, and the Savage Axioms." *Quarterly Journal of Economics*. 75:643–669.

Epstein, Lee, and C. K. Rowland. 1991. "Debunking the Myth of Interest Group Invincibility." *American Political Science Review* 85:205–221.

Erikson, Robert S., Norman R. Luttbeg, and Kent L. Tedin. 1991. *American Public Opinion: Its Origins, Content, and Impact*. 4th ed. New York: Macmillan.

Erikson, Robert S., John P. McIver, and Gerald C. Wright Jr. 1987. "State Political Culture and Public Opinion." *American Political Science Review* 81:797–815.

Erikson, Robert S., and Kent L. Tedin. 1995. *American Public Opinion: Its Origins, Content, and Impact.* 5th ed. Boston: Allyn & Bacon.

Feeley, Malcolm M. 1989. "The Significance of Prison Condition Cases: Budgets and Regions." *Law and Society Review* 23:273–282.

Fenton, J. H. 1962. "Liberal-Conservative Divisions by Sections of the United States." *Annals* 344:122–127.

Fiske, Susan, and Patricia Linville. 1980. "What Does the Schema Concept Really Buy Us?" *Personality and Social Psychology Bulletin* 6:543–557.

Fiske, Susan, and Shelly Taylor. 1991. *Social Cognition*. 2d ed. New York: McGraw-Hill.

Flanders, Steven (Project Manager). 1977. *Case Management and Court Management in United States District Courts*. Washington, D.C.: U.S. Government Printing Office.

Fowler, W. Gary. 1983. "A Comparison of Initial Recommendation Procedures: Judicial Selection Under Reagan and Carter." *Yale Law and Policy Review* 1:299–356.

Frank, Jerome. 1949. *Law and the Modern Mind.* 6th ed. New York: Tudor Publishing.

Galanter, Marc. 1988. "Beyond the Litigation Crisis." In *New Directions in Liability Law,* edited by William Olson. New York: Academy of Political Science.

Gibson, James. 1983. "From Simplicity to Complexity: The Development of Theory in the Study of Judicial Behavior." *Political Behavior* 5:7–49.

_____. 1991. "Decision Making in Appellate Courts." In *The American Courts: A Critical Assessment,* edited by John Gates and Charles Johnson. Washington, D.C.: Congressional Quarterly Press.

Giles, Michael W., and Thomas Walker. 1975. "Judicial Policy Making and Southern School Segregation." *Journal of Politics* 37:917–937.

Glass, A. L., and K. J. Holyoak. 1986. *Cognition*. 2nd ed. New York: Random House.

Glazer, Nathan. 1978. "Should Courts Administer Social Services?" *Public Interest* 50:64–80.

Goldman, Sheldon. 1966. "Voting Behavior on the United States Courts of Appeals, 1961–64." *American Political Science Review* 60:370–385.

_____. 1973. "Conflict on the U.S. Courts of Appeals 1965–1971: A Quantitative Analysis." *University of Cincinnati Law Review* 42:635–658.

_____. 1975. "Voting Behavior on the United States Courts of Appeals, Revisited." *American Political Science Review* 69:491–506.

_____. 1985. "Reorganizing the Judiciary: The First Term Appointments." *Judicature* 68:315–325.

_____. 1989. "Reagan's Judicial Legacy: Completing the Puzzle and Summing Up." *Judicature* 72:318–330.

_____. 1991. "The Bush Imprint on the Judiciary: Carrying on a Tradition." *Judicature* 74:294–306.

_____. 1993. "Bush's Judicial Legacy: The Final Imprint." *Judicature* 76:282–297.

Goulden, Joseph C. 1974. *The Benchwarmers*. New York: Weybright & Talley.

Hagle, Timothy. 1989. "A Cognitive-Cybernetic Theory of United States Supreme

Court Decision Making." Paper presented at Southern Political Science Association Meetings. Memphis.

Hakman, Nathan. 1969. "The Supreme Court's Political Environment: The Processing of Noncommercial Litigation." In *Frontiers of Judicial Research,* edited by Joel Grossman and Joseph Tanenhaus. New York: Wiley.

Hammond, Kenneth, ed. 1966. *The Psychology of Egon Brunswick.* New York: Holt, Rinehart & Winston.

Hammond, Kenneth, Gary McClelland, and Jeryl Mumpower. 1980. *Human Judgment and Decision Making: Theories, Methods and Procedures.* New York: Praeger.

Hammond, Kenneth, James Rohrbaugh, Jeryl Mumpower, and L. S. Adelman. 1977. "Social Judgment Theory: Applications in Policy Formation." In *Human Judgment and Decision Processes in Applied Settings,* edited by M. F. Kaplan and S. Schwartz. New York: Academic Press.

Hastie, Reid, Steven D. Penrod, and Nancy Pennington. 1983. *Inside the Jury.* Cambridge, Mass.: Harvard University Press.

Heider, Fritz. 1958. *The Psychology of Interpersonal Relations.* New York: Wiley.

Heydebrand, Wolf V., and Carroll Seron. 1990. *Rationalizing Justice: The Political Economy of Federal District Courts.* Albany: State University of New York Press.

Hibbing, John R., and John R. Alford. 1990. "Constituency Population and Representation in the U.S. Senate." *Legislative Studies Quarterly* 25:581–598.

Hinckley, Barbara. 1978. *Stability and Change in Congress.* New York: Harper & Row.

Hogarth, Robin. 1987. *Judgment and Choice.* New York: Wiley.

Holcomb, Arthur N. 1924. *The Political Parties of To-day.* New York: Harper.

Horowitz, Donald L. 1977. *The Courts and Social Policy.* Washington, D.C.: Brookings Institution.

Howard, J. Woodford, Jr. 1973. "Litigation Flow in Three United States Courts of Appeals." *Law and Society Review* 8:33–53.

_____. 1981. *Courts of Appeals in the Federal Judicial System: A Study of the Second, Fifth and District of Columbia Circuits.* Princeton, N.J.: Princeton University Press.

Jackson, Donald Dale. 1974. *Judges.* New York: Atheneum.

Jacob, Herbert. 1983. "Trial Courts in the United States: The Travails of Explanation." *Law and Society Review* 17:407–423.

Jensen, Merrill, ed. 1952. *Regionalism in America.* Madison: University of Wisconsin Press.

Johnson, Charles. 1987. "Law, Politics and Judicial Decision Making: Lower Federal Court Uses of Supreme Court Decisions." *Law and Society Review* 21:325–342.

Johnson, Charles, and Bradley C. Canon. 1984. *Judicial Policies: Implementation and Impact.* Washington, D.C.: Congressional Quarterly Press.

Johnson, E. J. 1988. "Expertise and Decision Under Uncertainty: Performance and Process." In *The Nature of Expertise,* edited by M. T. Chi, R. Glaser, and M. J. Farr. Hillsdale, N.J.: Erlbaum.

Johnson, Frank. 1976. "The Constitution and the Federal District Judge." *Texas Law Review* 54:903–916.

Kahneman, Daniel, and Amos Tversky. 1979. "Prospect Theory: An Analysis of Decision Under Risk." *Econometrica* 47:283–301.

Kassin, Saul, and Lawrence Wrightsman. 1988. *The American Jury on Trail.* Washington, D.C.: Hemisphere Publishing.

Kelly, G. A. 1955. *The Psychology of Interpersonal Constructs.* New York: Norton.

Kelman, Maurice. 1985. "The Forked Path of Dissent." *Supreme Court Review* 1985: 227–298.

Kemerer, Frank R. 1991. *William Wayne Justice: A Judicial Biography*. Austin: University of Texas Press.

Key, V. O., Jr. 1964. *Politics, Parties, and Pressure Groups*. 5th ed. New York: Crowell.

_____. 1967. *Public Opinion and American Democracy*. New York: Knopf.

Kitchin, William. 1978. *Federal District Judges*. Baltimore, Md.: Collage Press.

Kogan, M. A., and D. J. Bem. 1964. "Diffusion of Responsibility and Level of Risk Taking." *Journal of Abnormal and Social Psychology* 68:263–274.

Kovacic, William E. 1991a. "Reagan's Judicial Appointees and Antitrust in the 1990s." *Fordham Law Review* 60:49–124.

_____. 1991b. "The Reagan Judiciary and Environmental Policy: The Impact of Appointments to the Federal Courts of Appeals." *Boston College Environmental Affairs Law Review* 18:669–713.

Kritzer, Herbert. 1978. "Political Correlates of the Behavior of Federal District Judges: A Best Case Analysis." *Journal of Politics* 40:25–58.

_____. 1993. *Let's Make a Deal: Understanding the Negotiation Process in Ordinary Litigation*. Madison: University of Wisconsin Press.

Krosnick, Jon. 1990. "Expertise and Political Psychology." *Social Cognition* 8:1–8.

Kuhn, Thomas. 1970. *The Structure of Scientific Revolutions*. 2d ed. Chicago: University of Chicago Press.

Kuklinski, James, Robert Luskin, and John Bolland. 1991. "Where Is the Schema? Going Beyond the 'S' Word in Political Psychology." *American Political Science Review* 85:1341–1356.

Ladd, Everett Carl, Jr., and Charles D. Hadley. 1978. *Transformations of the American Political System*. 2d ed. New York: Norton.

Lamb, Charles M. 1974. "Warren Burger and the Insanity Defense: Judicial Philosophy and Voting Behavior on a U.S. Court of Appeals." *American University Law Review* 24:91–128.

Lamb, Charles M., and Stephen C. Halpern, eds. 1991. *The Burger Court: Political and Judicial Profiles*. Urbana and Chicago: University of Illinois Press.

Lau, Richard R. 1986. "Political Schemata, Candidate Evaluations, and Voting Behavior." In *Political Cognition,* edited by R. Lau and D. Sears. Hillsdale, N.J.: Erlbaum.

Lau, Richard, and David Sears. 1988. "An Introduction to Political Cognition." In *Political Cognition,* edited by Richard Lau and David Sears. Hillsdale, N.J.: Erlbaum.

Lewin, Nathan. 1976. "Avoiding the Supreme Court." *New York Times Magazine*. October 17:31.

Lieberman, Jethro. 1981. *The Litigious Society*. New York: Basic Books.

Llewellyn, Karl. 1931. "Some Realism About Realism." *Harvard Law Review* 44:1222–1264.

Lodge, Milton, and Ruth Hamill. 1986. "A Partisan Schema for Political Information Processing." *American Political Science Review* 80:505–519.

McCubbins, Matthew, and Thomas Schwartz. 1984. "Congressional Oversight Overlooked: Police Patrols vs Fire Alarms." *American Journal of Political Science* 28:165–179.

McFeeley, Neil. 1987. *Appointment of Judges: The Johnson Presidency*. Austin: University of Texas Press.

McGraw, Kathleen, and Neil Pinney. 1990. "The Effects of General and Domain-Specific Expertise on Political Memory and Judgment." *Social Cognition* 8:9–30.

March, James. 1978. "Bounded Rationality, Ambiguity, and the Engineering of Choice." *Bell Journal of Economics* 9:587–608.

Markham, Walter G. 1971. "Draft Offenders in the Federal Courts: A Search for the Social Correlates of Justice." Ph.D diss., University of Pennsylvania.

Marquis, D. C. 1962. "Individual Responsibility and Group Decisions Involving Risk." *Industrial Management Review* 3:8–23.

Mason, Alpheus Thomas. 1974. "The Burger Court in Historical Perspective." *Political Science Quarterly* 89:27–45.

Mason, Alpheus Thomas, and William M. Beaney. 1978. *American Constitutional Law*. 6th ed. Englewood Cliffs, N.J.: Prentice-Hall.

Maveety, Nancy. 1991. "The Judicial Strategy of the Concurring Opinion: A Preliminary Discussion, with Special Attention to Justices O'Connor and Scalia." Paper presented at the annual meeting of the American Political Science Association, August 29–September 1, Washington, D.C.

Mayhew, David. 1966. *Party Loyalty Among Congressmen*. Cambridge, Mass.: Harvard University Press.

Mitnick, Barry. 1980. *The Political Economy of Regulation*. New York: Columbia University Press.

Moe, Terry. 1985. "Control and Feedback in Economic Regulation: The Case of the NLRB." *American Political Science Review* 79:1094–1116.

Morris, Jeffrey B. 1972. "The Second Most Important Court: The United States Court of Appeals for the District of Columbia Circuit." Ph.D diss., Columbia University.

Mueller, John H., Karl F. Schuessler, and Herbert L. Costner. 1970. *Statistical Reasoning in Sociology*. 2d ed. Boston: Houghton Mifflin.

Murphy, Walter. 1959. "Lower Court Checks on Supreme Court Power." *American Political Science Review* 53:1017–1031.

______. 1964. *Elements of Judicial Strategy*. Chicago: University of Chicago Press.

Murphy, Walter F., and C. Herman Pritchett. 1979. *Courts, Judges, and Politics: An Introduction to the Judicial Process*. 3d ed. New York: Random House.

Nagel, Stuart. 1969. *The Legal Process from a Behavioral Perspective*. Homewood, Ill.: Dorsey Press.

Navasky, Victor. 1971. *Kennedy Justice*. New York: Atheneum.

Neff, Alan. 1981. "Breaking with Tradition: A Study of the U.S. District Judge Nominating Commissions." *Judicature* 64:256–278.

Nisbett, R. E., and Laurence Ross. 1980. *Human Inference: Strategies and Shortcomings of Social Judgments*. Englewood Cliffs, N.J.: Prentice-Hall.

O'Brien, David M. 1990. *Storm Center: The Supreme Court in American Politics*. 2d ed. New York: Norton.

Ofshe, Richard J., ed. 1973. *Interpersonal Behavior in Small Groups*. Englewood Cliffs, N.J.: Prentice-Hall.

Olson, Susan M. 1992. "Studying Federal District Courts Through Published Cases: A Research Note." *Justice System Journal* 15:782–800.

Packer, Herbert L. 1968. *The Limits of Criminal Sanction.* Stanford, Calif.: Stanford University Press.

Partridge, Anthony, and William B. Eldridge. 1974. *The Second Circuit Sentencing Study: A Report to the Judges of the Second Circuit.* Washington, D.C.: Federal Judicial Center.

Pear, Robert. 1986. "U.S. Starts Culling Ineligibles from Disability Benefit Rolls." *New York Times,* May 14.

Peltason, Jack W. 1955. *Federal Courts in the Political Process.* New York: Random House.

_____. 1961. *Fifty-Eight Lonely Men: Southern Federal Judges and School Desegregation.* Urbana: University of Illinois Press.

Popper, Karl. 1963. *Conjectures and Refutations: The Growth of Scientific Knowledge.* London: Routledge and Paul.

Posner, Richard. 1985. *The Federal Courts.* Cambridge, Mass.: Harvard University Press.

Priest, George, and B. Klien. 1984. "The Selection of Disputes for Litigation." *Journal of Legal Studies* 13:1–35.

Pritchett, C. Herman. 1948. *The Roosevelt Court: A Study in Judicial Politics and Values, 1937–1947.* New York: Macmillan.

Ray, Laura. 1990. "The Justices Write Separately: Uses of the Concurrence by the Rehnquist Court." *University of California at Davis Law Review* 23:777–833.

Resnick, Judith. 1982. "Managerial Judges." *Harvard Law Review* 96:376–397.

Reynolds, H. T. 1977. *Analysis of Nominal Data.* Beverly Hills, Calif.: Sage.

Richardson, Richard J., and Kenneth Vines. 1970. *The Politics of Federal Courts.* Boston: Little, Brown.

Riker, William. 1977. "The Future of a Science of Politics." *American Behavioral Scientist* 21:11–38.

_____. 1982. "The Two Party System and Duverger's Law: An Essay on the History of Political Science." *American Political Science Review* 76:753–766.

Ripley, Randall B. 1978. *Congress: Process and Policy.* 2d ed. New York: Norton.

Robinson, Glen O., and Ernest Gellhorn. 1974. *The Administrative Process.* St. Paul, Minn.: West.

Rohde, David, and Harold Spaeth. 1976. *Supreme Court Decision Making.* San Francisco: W. H. Freeman.

Rokeach, Milton. 1968. *Beliefs, Attitudes and Values.* San Francisco: Josey-Bass.

Rowland, C. K. 1991. "The Federal District Courts." In *The American Courts: A Critical Assessment,* edited by John Gates and Charles Johnson. Washington, D.C.: Congressional Quarterly Press.

Rowland, C. K., and Robert A. Carp. 1983a. "Presidential Effects on Federal District Court Policy Decisions: Economic Liberalism, 1960–77." *Social Science Quarterly* 64:386–392.

_____. 1983b. "The Relative Effects of Maturation, Time Period, and Appointing President on District Judge's Policy Choices: A Cohort Analysis." *Political Behavior* 5:109–133.

Rowland, C. K., Robert A. Carp, and Donald R. Songer. 1985. "The Effect of Presidential Appointment, Group Identification and Fact-Law Ambiguity on Lower Federal Judges' Policy Judgments." Paper presented at the annual meeting of the American Political Science Association, New Orleans.

Rowland, C. K., Robert A. Carp, and Ronald A. Stidham. 1984. "Judges' Policy Choices and the Value Basis of Judicial Appointments: A Comparison of Support for Criminal Defendants Among Nixon, Johnson, and Kennedy Appointees to the Federal District Courts." *Journal of Politics* 46:886–902.

Rowland, C. K., and Bridget Todd. 1991. "Where You Stand Depends on Who Sits: Platform Promises and Judicial Gatekeeping in the Federal District Courts." *Journal of Politics* 53:175–185.

Rubin, Eva. 1987. *Abortion, Politics and the Courts*. New York: Greenwood Press.

Schmidhauser, John. 1961. "Judicial Behavior and the Sectional Crisis of 1837–1860." *Journal of Politics* 23:615–640.

Schubert, Glendon. 1965. *The Judicial Mind: Attitudes and Ideologies of Supreme Court Justices, 1946–1963.* Evanston, Ill.: Northwestern University Press.

———. 1974. *The Judicial Mind Revisited: Psychometric Analysis of Supreme Court Ideology.* New York: Oxford University Press.

Schwartz, Bernard. 1990. *The Ascent of Pragmatism: The Burger Court in Action.* Reading, Mass.: Addison-Wesley.

Segal, Jeffery A. 1986. "Supreme Court Justices as Human Decision Makers: An Individual Level Analysis of Search and Seizure Cases, 1962–1981. *American Political Science Review* 78:891–900.

Segal, Jeffrey A., and Harold J. Spaeth. 1989. "Decisional Trends on the Warren and Burger Courts: Results from the Supreme Court Data Base Project." *Judicature* 73:103–107.

———. 1993. *The Supreme Court and the Attitudinal Model.* New York: Cambridge University Press.

Shapiro, Martin. 1964. *Law and Politics in the Supreme Court: New Approaches to Political Jurisprudence.* London: Free Press.

Siegelman, Peter, and John J. Donohue III. 1990. "Studying the Iceberg from Its Tip: A Comparison of Published and Unpublished Employment Discrimination Cases." *Law and Society Review* 24:1133–1170.

Simon, Herbert. 1957. *Models of Man.* New York: Wiley.

———. 1986. "Rationality in Psychology and Economics." In *Rational Choice: The Contrast Between Economics and Psychology,* edited by Robin Hogarth and M. W. Reder. Chicago: University of Chicago Press.

Slotnick, Elliot E. 1979. "The U.S. Circuit Nominating Commission." *Law and Politics Quarterly* 1:465–496.

———. 1980a. "Reforms in Judicial Selection: Will They Affect the Senate's Role?" *Judicature* 63:60–73.

———. 1980b. "Reforms in Judicial Selection: Will They Affect the Senate's Role? Part II." *Judicature* 64:115–131.

———. 1984. "Judicial Selection Systems and Nomination Outcomes: Does the Process Make a Difference?" *American Politics Quarterly* 12:225–240.

———. 1988. "Federal Judicial Recruitment and Selection Research: A Review Essay." *Judicature* 71:317–324.

Smith, Christopher E. 1990. "Polarization and Change in the Federal Courts: *En Banc* Decisions and the U.S. Courts of Appeals." *Judicature* 74:133–138.

Smith, Rogers. 1994. Communication. *Newsletter, Law and Courts Section of American Political Science Association.*

Songer, Donald R. 1988. "Nonpublication in the United States District Courts: Official Criteria Versus Inferences from Appellate Review." *Journal of Politics* 50:206–219.

_____. 1990. "Criteria for Publication of Opinions in the U.S. Courts of Appeals: Formal Rules Versus Empirical Reality." *Judicature* 73:307–314.

Songer, Donald R., Jeffrey A. Segal, and Charles M. Cameron. 1994. "The Hierarchy of Justice: Testing a Principal-Agent Model of Supreme Court–Circuit Court Interactions." *American Journal of Political Science* 38:673–696.

Stidham, Ronald, and Robert A. Carp. 1982. "Trial Courts' Responses to Supreme Court Policy Changes: Three Case Studies." *Law and Policy Quarterly* 4:215–235.

_____. 1984. "U.S. Trial Court Reactions to Changes in Civil Rights and Civil Liberties Policies." *Southeastern Political Review* 10:3–27.

_____. 1987. "Judges, Presidents, and Policy Choices: Exploring the Linkage." *Social Science Quarterly* 68:395–404.

Stidham, Ronald, Robert A. Carp, and C. K. Rowland. 1984. "Patterns of Presidential Influence on the Federal District Courts: An Analysis of the Appointment Process." *Presidential Studies Quarterly* 14:548–560.

Stoner, J. A. F. 1961. "Comparison of Individual and Group Decisions Involving Risk." M.A. thesis, Massachusetts Institute of Technology, School of Industrial Management.

Stouffer, Samuel A. 1955. *Communism, Conformity, and Civil Liberties.* New York: Doubleday.

Taggart, W. A. 1989. "Redefining the Power of the Federal Judiciary: The Impact of Court-Ordered Prison Reform on State Expenditures for Corrections." *Law and Society Review* 23:241–272.

Tanenhaus, Joseph, Marvin Schick, Matthew Muraskin, and Daniel Rosen. 1963. "The Supreme Courts' Certiorari Jurisdiction: Cue Theory." In *Judicial Decision Making,* edited by Glendon Schubert. New York: Free Press.

Taylor, Shelby, and Jennifer Crocker. 1981. "Schematic Bases of Social Information Processing." In *Social Cognition: The Ontario Symposium,* edited by E. T. Higgins, C. P. Herman, and M. P. Fanna. Hillsdale, N.J.: Laurence Erlbaum.

Teger, Allen I., and Dean G. Pruitt. 1967. "Components of Group Risk Taking." *Journal of Experimental Social Psychology* 3:189–205.

Todd, Bridget. 1985. "A Comparison of President Carter's Traditional and Non-Traditional Nominees to the Federal District Courts: What Difference Does the Difference Make?" Master's thesis, University of Kansas.

_____. 1989. "The Relative Effects of Legal Environment and Appointing President on District Judges' Unpublished Decisions." Paper presented at the annual meeting of the Southwest Political Science Association, Little Rock, Ark.

Turner, Frederick J. 1932. *The Significance of Sections in American History*. New York: Holt.

Tversky, Amos, and Daniel Kahneman. 1974. "Judgment Under Uncertainty: Heuristics and Biases." *Science* 185:1124–1131.

______. 1981. "The Framing of Decisions and the Psychology of Choice." *Science* 211:453–458.

______. 1983. "Extensional vs. Intuitive Reasoning: The Conjunction Fallacy in Probability Judgment." *Psychological Review* 90:293–315.

Vestal, Allan D. 1966a. "Reported Opinions of the Federal District Courts: Analysis and Suggestions." *Iowa Law Review* 52:379–405.

______. 1966b. "A Survey of Federal District Court Opinions: West Publishing Company Reports." *Southwestern Law Journal* 20:63–96.

______. 1970–1971. "Publishing District Court Opinions in the 1970s." *Loyola Law Review* 17:673–681.

Vines, Kenneth. 1964. "Federal District Judges and Race Relations Cases in the South." *Journal of Politics* 26:337–357.

Walker, Thomas, and Deborah Barrow. 1985. "Diversification of the Federal Bench: Policy and Process Ramifications." *Journal of Politics* 47:596–617.

Walker, Thomas G., Lee Epstein, and William J. Dixon. 1988. "On the Mysterious Demise of Consensual Norms in the United States Supreme Court." *Journal of Politics* 50:261–289.

Wallach, M. A., and N. Kogan. 1965. "The Roles of Information, Discussion, and Consensus in Group Risk Taking." *Journal of Experimental Social Psychology* 1:1–19.

Wallach, M. A., N. Kogan, and D. J. Bem. 1962. "Group Influence on Individual Risk Taking." *Journal of Abnormal and Social Psychology* 65:75–86.

______. 1964. "Diffusion of Responsibility and Level of Risk Taking in Groups." *Journal of Abnormal and Social Psychology* 68:263–274.

Wasby, Stephen L. 1981. "Arrogation of Power or Responsibility: Judicial Imperialism Revisited." *Judicature* 65:208–221.

Watson, James. 1913. "Psychology as the Behaviorist Sees It." *Psychological Review* 20:158–177.

Weiner, Norbert. 1961. *Cybernetics*. Cambridge, Mass.: MIT Press.

Wenner, Lettie M. 1982. *The Environmental Decade in Court*. Bloomington: Indiana University Press.

Wenner, Lettie M., and Lee E. Dutter. 1988. "Contextual Influences on Judicial Decision Making." *Western Political Quarterly* 41:115–134.

Wright, John R. 1985. "PACs, Contributions, and Roll Calls: An Organizational Perspective." *American Political Science Review* 79:400–415.

Wuebben, Paul L., Bruce C. Straits, and Gary I. Schulman. 1974. *The Experiment as a Social Occasion*. Berkeley, Calif.: Glendessary.

INTERVIEWS

Telephone interview with Frank Conway, chairperson of Massachusetts Federal Selection Commission, May 5, 1986.

Interview with Kim Elliot, administrative assistant to Senator Lowell Wicker (R.CN), Washington, D.C., May 13, 1986.

Interview with Susan Fryar, administrative assistant to Senator Jessie Helms (R.NC), Washington, D.C., May 21, 1986.

Telephone interview with Ira Glass, staff member, Senator Pete Wilson (R.CA), Washington, D.C., February 13, 1986.

Interview with Craig Higgins, administrative assistant to Senator Mark Hatfield (R.OR), Washington, D.C., February 13, 1986.

Telephone interview with Wells Madden, chairman of Recruitment Committee for Senator Phil Gramm (R.TX), Washington, D.C., February 20, 1986.

Interview with Stephen Markman, Office of Legal Policy, Washington, D.C., February 12, 1987.

Interview with Steve Metalitz, chief nominations counsel for Senate Judiciary Committee, Washington, D.C., April 14, 1987.

Interview with Paul Michel, administrative assistant to Senator Arlen Specter (R.PA), Washington, D.C., March 14, 1986.

Interview with Steve Moore, administrative assistant to Senator David Durenberger (R.MN), Washington, D.C., July 7, 1986.

Interview with Judge Constance Baker Motley, Lawrence, Kans., October 13. 1986.

Interview with Brian Nakamura, administrative assistant to Senator Daniel Inoye (D.HI), Washington, D.C., April 17, 1986.

Telephone interview with J. Reed, administrative assistant to Congressman John P. Hammerschmid, Washington, D.C., May 12, 1986.

Interview with Frank A. Sanchez, administrative assistant to Senator Lloyd Bentsen (D.TX), Washington, D.C., February 27, 1986.

Interview with Duke Short, administrative assistant to Senator Strom Thurmond (R.SC), Washington, D.C., March 11, 1986.

Interview with Jack Sinclair, administrative assistant to Congressman William Broomfield, Washington, D.C., April 4, 1986.

Telephone interview with Linda Slade, administrative assistant to Senator Thad Cochran (R.MS), Washington, D.C., March 17, 1986.

Interview with Wayne Smith, administrative assistant to Congressman Steve Moore, Washington, D.C., April 17, 1986.

Interview with Greg Welcher, administrative assistant to Senator William Armstrong (R.CO), Washington, D.C., February 14, 1986.

Interview with Laurie Westal, administrative assistant to Senator Herbert Simon (D.IL), Washington, D.C., February 18, 1986.

Interview with Sharon Yard, administrative assistant to Congressman Paul Michel, Washington, D.C., April 1, 1986.

Index